MONUMENTAL JAVA

THE BORO BUDOOR

(Cephas Sr.)

MONUMENTAL JAVA

J.F. SCHELTEMA, M.A.

WITH ILLUSTRATIONS, AND VIGNETTES AFTER DRAWINGS OF JAVANESE CHANDI ORNAMENT BY THE AUTHOR

ISBN : 978-93-5324-503-0 (HB)

First Published, 1912

Published, 2020

Published by

Facsimile Publisher
12 Pragati Market
Ashok Vihar, Ph-2
Delhi-110052
E-mail: books@facsimilepublisher.com

Printed at: G. Print Process, Delhi.

Monumental Java

Author: J. F. Scheltema, M.a.

TO

MY DEAR COUSIN AND FRIEND

PROFESSOR AUGUST ALLEBÉ

DIRECTOR EMERITUS OF THE NETHERLANDS STATE ACADEMY

OF THE FINE ARTS AT AMSTERDAM

IF this book needs an apology, it is one to myself for taking the public at large into the confidence of cherished recollections. The writing was a diversion from studies in a quite different direction and letting my pen go, while living again the happy hours I spent, between arduous duties, with the beautiful monuments of Java's past, I did nothing but seek my own pleasure. Should it turn out that my personal impressions, given in black and white, please others too—so much the better. In any case they must be taken for what they are: a beguilement of lone moments of leisure.

Whoever find them readable, they will not satisfy, I hope, a certain class of critics; those, I mean, who extend the paltry rule of mutual admiration, *nul n'aura de l'esprit que nous et nos amis*, to any field they claim their own and "of whom to be dispraised were no small praise." Desirous, I must confess, to stimulate their flattering disapproval, I hasten to admit in advance my many shortcomings, a full list of which they will doubtless oblige me with in due process of censorious comment. My work sets up no pretence to completeness: there is no full enumeration of all the Hindu and Buddhist temples known by their remains; there are no measurements, no technical details, no statistics—a great recommendation to my mind, as Dutch East Indian statistics go. I am not guilty of an ambitious attempt to enrich the world with an exhaustive treatise on ancient Javanese architecture and sculpture—far be it from me to harbour such an audacious design! I disclaim even the presumption to aspire at being classed as a useful companion on a visit to the island; I deny most emphatically that I intend to swell the disquieting number of tourists' vade-mecums already up for sale, clamouring for recognition, and, *horribile dictu*, scores more coming! Be they sufficient or insufficient, qualitatively speaking, I am not going to increase their quantity.

So much for what this book is not. What it is, I could not help making it, choosing from the material stored in my memory; reliving, as fancy dictated in long northern winter evenings, the sunny spells between 1874 and 1903 when I might call Java my home; resuming my walks in the charming island pleasance of the East, fain to leave the congested main roads and disport myself along by-paths and unfrequented lanes where solace and repose await the weary wanderer. The undertaking, somewhat too confidently indicated by the title, tempted to excursions off the beaten historical, geographical and archaeological tracks, which perhaps will contribute to a better understanding of the monuments described in their proper setting, their relations to natural scenery and native civilisation, but certainly do not tend to conformity with the regulation style of compositions of the kind. Invoking the aid of Ganesa, the sagacious guide, countenancer of poor mortals in creative throes—for, thank Heaven! the fever of production is indissolubly one with the anguish that heightens its delights,—I never hesitated in letting the idea of self-gratification prevail, even when the question of illustration arose after the plan had ripened of inviting indulgent readers to partake. In this respect too I struggled free from anxious deliberation: *Wer gar zu viel bedenkt, wird wenig leisten.* And, Ganesa aiding, the following kaleidoscopic view of the land I love so well, was the result of my delicious travail.

Looking for the flowers in the ill-kept garden of Java, the delinquencies of the gardeners could not be ignored and here I touch the unpleasant side of the recreation I sought, especially disagreeable when proposing to strangers that they should share; but a picture needs shade as well as light to become intelligible. And to paint true to life the picture of Dutch East Indian passivity (activity only in vandalism!) regarding treasures of art inconvertible into cash, shade ought to be preponderant and light relegated to the subordinate place of a little star glimmering dimly in the darkness, a little star of hope for the future. Disinclined, however, to spoil my pleasure by dwelling on the tenebrous general aspect of governmental archaeology in the past, I have no more than mentioned such disgraceful incidents as the Mendoot squabbles, and omitted, *e.g.*, all reference to such ludicrously heated controversies as that about the *kala-makara* versus the *garuda-naga* ornament, exhaustive of the energy which the officially learned might have employed to so much greater advantage by rescuing the venerable temples they fought over, from decay and willful demolition.

The neglect of the ancient monuments of Java has been nothing short of scandalous, the evil effects of the habitual languid detachment of the colonial authorities from the business they are supposed to look after, being, in their case, intensified by acts of dilapidation which even a Government centuries back on the road of enlightenment would have checked,[1] not to speak of downright plunder and theft. The more honour deserve men like Junghuhn among the dead and Rouffaer among the still living, who lifted their voice against the intolerable negligence which hastened the ruin of some of the finest existing specimens of Hindu and Buddhist architecture. At last, in 1901, an Archaeological Commission was appointed, whose labours were directed by Dr. J. L. A. Brandes, their head and

[1] See, *e.g.*, the edict, issued more than thirteen centuries ago by the Emperor Majorian, as quoted by Gibbon: Antiquarum aedium dissipatur speciosa constructio; et ut aliquid reparetur, magna diruuntur. Hinc iam occasio nascitur, etc.

soul. After his regretted death in 1905, he was succeeded by Dr. N. J. Krom, who has no easy task in fanning the spark, struck by his predecessor from the hard flint of official *laisser-aller* into a steady, bright flame of real, continuous solicitude for the country's antiquities.

Antiquities, except when sold, do not bring money to the exchequer, and the Dutch Government's most holy colonial traditions are diametrically opposed to expenses without promise of immediate pecuniary profit. If sympathies in matters alien to that prime purpose are miraculously aroused, such interest, revealing itself at the very best by fits and starts to serve ambitious schemes, soon flags and dies. Especially in Dutch East Indian enthusiasm for enterprises financially uncommendable, the adage holds good that *tout lasse, tout casse, tout passe.* The efforts of the Archaeological Commission can be traced only at the respectful distance of at least a couple of years, the drowsy dignity of red-tapeism putting as long a space as possible between the vulgar gaze of the unofficially curious and the official accounts of things accomplished, meetly compiled, arranged, amended, corrected, revised, purged, padded and bolstered up by the editing experts of successively the circumlocution offices at Batavia, Buitenzorg and the Hague. The reports, published in this manner, whatever they represent as having been done, lay no stress, of course, upon what has been left undone, upon the architectural marvels unprovided for, still suffered to crumble away, to be stripped and demolished, the valuable statuary and ornaments to be carried off piecemeal by unscrupulous collectors, the lower priced stones they left, sculptured or not, by the builders of private dwellings and factories, of Government bridges, dams and embankments.

The illustrations, inserted to explain, imperfect though it be, the charm of the temple ruins I treated of, are reproductions of photographs, taken for the Dutch East Indian Archaeological Service, I obtained from Messrs. Charls and van Es at Weltevreden, by courtesy of Dr. N. J. Krom, and of photographs taken for the Centrum Company at Batavia, and by Mr. C. Nieuwenhuis and the late Cephas Sr. at Jogjakarta. The work of restoration can be appreciated from the photo-prints of the *chandi* Pawon and, with respect to the *chandis* Mendoot and Boro Budoor, from those facing pp. 215 and 280; they are the numbers 24 and 40 on the list of the illustrations, and I owe them to Major T. van Erp, also through the intermediary of Dr. Krom. My indebtedness for the text so far as it does not rest on personal observation and information obtained in the localities referred to, is a very large one to many authors on many subjects separately specified in the notes. Concerning the historical parts, I beg leave to state that my readings on controversial points have been determined by a careful sifting of the most acceptable theories advanced, at the risk of critics of the stamp alluded to, proving my preferred records absolutely inadmissible. If so, I having pulled the long bow *à l'instar* of the annalists and chroniclers of ancient Java, and consequently being shown up for indicating the way in which things did not happen and could not have happened, instead of sticking to the historical truth agreed upon until one of the hall-marked omniscient makes a name for himself by inducing the others to agree upon something else, my sin falls back on the shoulders of the *savants* prone to lead their admirers astray by their occasional imitation of the eminent historian at whose inborn disrespect for facts Professor Freeman used to poke fun. I am afraid that the system of transliteration I adopted, will also meet with scant recognition in the same quarter, but finding none that, strictly carried through, adjusts itself equally well to the exigencies both of Javanese and Malay names and expressions, I shall adhere to this one until taught better.

This must suffice for a preface if, indeed, it does not exceed the measure allowed by my readers' patience. Knowing Java, they will, however, excuse my fervour in introducing reminiscences of beauty breathing scenes which, once enjoyed, linger like delights in memory

. . . . the memory of a dream,
Which now is sad because it hath been sweet.

Not knowing Java yet, they will forgive later, when they have visited the matchless old shrines, images of her past and symbolic of her hopes for blessings hidden in the womb of time, when they have tried to read the riddle of her children's destiny in the Boro Budoor

> *. . . . . . seated in an island strong,*
> *Abounding all with delices most rare.*

J. F. S.

EDINBURGH.

CONTENTS

CHAPTER VIII

CHAPTER IX

CHAPTER X

ILLUSTRATIONS

CHAPTER I

THE COUNTRY, THE PEOPLE AND THEIR WORK

It is the crowning virtue of all great Art that, however little is left of it by the injuries of time, that little will be lovely. JOHN RUSKIN, *Mornings in Florence* (*Santa Croce*).

JAVA'S ancient monuments are eloquent evidence of that innate consciousness of something beyond earthly existence which moves men to propitiate the principle of life by sacrifice in temples as gloriously divine as mortal hand can raise. Fear, however, especially where Buddhism moulded their thought by contemplation intent upon absorption of self, entered little into the religion of the children of this pearl of islands. Nature, beautiful, almighty nature, guided them and their work; even the terror inspired by the cosmic energy throbbing under their feet, by frequent volcanic upheavals dealing destruction and death, flowered into promise of new joy, thanks to the consummate art of their builders and sculptors, whose master minds, conceiving grandly, devising boldly and finishing with elaborate ornament, emphasised most cunningly the lofty yet lovely majesty of their natural surroundings. They made them images of the Supreme Being in his different aspects and symbolised attributes, free from the abject dread which dominated his worship by other earthlings of his fashioning in other climes, whose notion of All-Power was more one of Vengeance than of All-Sufficiency. They lived and meditated and wrought, impressing their mentality upon the material world given for their use; and so they created marvels of beauty, developed an architecture which belongs pre-eminently to their luxuriant soil under the clear blue of their sky, in the brilliant light of their sun.

Truly high art ever shows a natural fitness, as we can observe in our gothic cathedrals, in the classic remains of Hellas, including those of Magna Graecia, the temples of Poseidonia, Egesta and Acragas, the theatres of Syracuse and Tauromenium, gates opened to the splendour of heaven and earth by the undying virtue of mortal endeavour. Other countries, other revelations of the divine essence in human effort, but not even the shrines of India as I came to know them, born of a common origin with Javanese religious structures in almost similar conditions of climate, physical needs, moral aspirations, can equal their stately grandeur balanced by exquisite elegance, calm yet passionate, always in keeping with the dignified repose of landscapes which at any moment may have their charms dissolved in earthquakes, fire and ashes. Angkor-

Vat, turned from the service of four-faced Brahma to Buddhist self-negation, stands perhaps nearest in the happy effect produced, if not in outline. And what is the secret of that quiet, subtle magic exercised by the builders of Java? Nothing but a matter of technical skill, of such a control over the practical details of their craft as, for instance, made them scorn metal bindings, while using mortar only to a very limited extent? Or was it their faith, leavening design and execution, attaching the master's seal to general plan and minutest ornamental scroll? In this connection it seems worthy of remark that architect and sculptor, though independent in their labours (with the exception of one or two edifices of a late date), achieved invariably, in the distribution of surfaces and decoration, both as to front and side elevations, complete unity of expression of the fundamental idea.

Geographically, the ancient monuments of Java may be divided into three main groups: a western one, rather scanty and confined to a comparatively small area; a central one, rich both in Sivaïte and Buddhist temples of the highest excellence; an eastern one, including Madura and Bali, illustrative of the island's Hindu art in its decadence. Taking it roughly, the order is also chronologically from West to East, and to a certain extent we can trace the history of the remarkable people who improved so nobly upon the ideas they received from India, in the ruins they left to our wondering gaze. There has been a good deal of controversy respecting the date up to which the inhabitants of Java developed themselves on lines of aboriginal thought before the advent of the Hindus or, more correctly speaking, before Hindu influences became prevalent. In fact, there is hardly any question regarding the history of the island and its civilisation before the white conquerors carried everything before them, which has not given rise to controversy, and many important points are still very far from being settled—perhaps they never will be. In the face of such disagreement it behoves us to go warily and what follows hereafter rests but on arguments *pro* and *contra* deemed most plausible and founded principally on the accounts of the *babads* or Javanese chronicles,[1] always liable to correction when new discoveries with new wordy battles in their wake bring new light—if they do! Rude attempts at rock carving near Karang Bolong, Sukabumi, and Chitapen, Cheribon, are ascribed by some to artists of the pre-Hindu period. Professor J. H. C. Kern's reading of inscriptions on four monoliths in Batavia, glorifications of a certain king Purnavarman, proves that the first Hindus of whom we have knowledge in Java, were Vaishnavas. Then comes a blank of several centuries while they made their way to Central and East Java where, however, when the

[1] Strictly speaking, says Dr. BRANDES in his notes to his translation of the *Pararaton*, or the Book of the Kings of Tumapel and Mojopahit (p. 178), there is only one *babad tanah jawi*, which received its final redaction about 1700. The other *babads*, though they may contain recapitulations of the general history of Java, treat of local affairs or of certain selected periods, as the *babads* Surakarta, Diponegoro, Mangkunegoro, Paku Alaman, etc.

veil is partly lifted, the Saivas predominate, almost swamping the rival sect. Fa Hien, the Chinese pilgrim who visited the island in 412 or 413, having suffered shipwreck on its coast, speaks of Brahmanism being *in floribus* and making converts, but complains of Buddhism as still of small account among the natives.

The strangers arrived in increasing numbers on the hospitable shores of the good and generous *negri jawa*, whose kindly reception of those adventurers is marvellously well represented on two of the sculptured slabs of the Boro Budoor, a tale of rescue from the dangers of the sea, a picture of the past and a prophetic vision of the welcome extended in later days also to Muhammadans and Christians—to be how repaid! The Hindus acquitted their debt of gratitude by building and carving with an energy, to quote James Fergusson, and to an extent nowhere surpassed in their native lands, dignifying their new home with imperishable records of their art and civilisation. . . . The Venggi inscriptions of the Diëng and the Kadu leave no doubt that the oldest manifestations of Hinduïsm in Central and West Java were intimately related and that the first strong infusion of the imported creed must have operated until 850 Saka (A.D. 928). In 654 Saka (A.D. 732), according to an inscription found at Changgal, Kadu, the ruler of the land bore a Sanskrit name and sacrificed to Siva, erecting a *linga*.[1] An inscription of 700

[1] Emblem of Siva's fructifying virility.

Saka (A.D. 778), found at Kalasan, Jogjakarta, is Buddhistic and confirms the evidence of many other records carved in stone and copper, of the oldest Javanese literature, last but not least of the temple ruins, all concurring in this that the two religions flourished side by side, the adoration of the Brahman triad, led by Siva, acquiring a tinge of the beatitude derived from emancipation through annihilation of self; Buddhism, in its younger *maha-yana* form, becoming strongly impregnated with Sivaïsm, to the point even of endowing the Adi-Buddha in his five more tangible personifications with spouses and sons. Between two currents of faith, each imbued with the male and female principle in a country where the problem of sex will not be hid, it depended often upon a trifle what kind of emblematic shape the sculptor was going to give to his block of stone, whether he would carve a *linga* or a *yoni*,[1] a Dhyani Buddha, a Bodhisatva, a Tara or one of her Hindu peers.

Subsequent waves of immigration, the Muhammadan invasion, the Christian conquests, did little to nourish the artistic flame; on the contrary, they damped artistic ardour. Hereanent our historical data are somewhat more precise. The Islām takes its way to Sumatra in the wake of trade; conversions *en masse* seem to have first occurred in Pasei and Acheh, while merchants of Arabian and

[1] Emblem of the fecundity of Siva's *sakti* or female complement, Parvati or Uma, Doorga, Kali or whatever other name she goes by according to the nature of her manifestations.

Persian nationality prepared its advent also in other regions of the north and later of the west coast. Marco Polo speaks of a Muhammadan principality in the North at the end of the thirteenth century; Ibn Batutah of several more in 1345; Acheh is fully islāmised under Sooltan Ali Moghayat Shah, 1507–1522; about the same time Menangkabau, ruled by maharajahs proud of their descent in the right line from Alexander the Great, Iskander Dzu'l Karnein, reaches its apogee as a formidable Moslim state and remains the stronghold of Malayan true believers until the fanaticism of the *padris*, stirred by the Wahabite movement, ends, in 1837, in the submission of the last Prince of Pagar Rujoong to the Dutch Government, which annexes his already much diminished empire. About 1400 the Islām had been introduced into Java, Zabej, as the Arabs called it, probably via Malacca and Sumatra, more especially Palembang. The oldest effort recorded was that of a certain Haji Poorwa in Pajajaran, but it appears not to have met with great success. Gresik in East Java, a port of call frequented by many oriental skippers, offered a better field for the religious zeal of Arab sailing-masters, supercargoes and tradesmen, every one of them a missionary too. Maulana Malik Ibrahim secured the largest following and was succeeded in his apostolic work by Raden Paku, who settled at Giri, not far from Gresik, whence his title of Susuhunan Giri, and by Raden Rahmat, who married a daughter of Angka Wijaya, King of Mojopahit, and founded a Muhammadan school at Ngampel, Surabaya. Their teachings resulted soon in the conversion of the population of the northeast coast of the island, where Demak, Drajat, Tuban, Kalinjamat and a few smaller vassal states of Mojopahit made themselves independent under Moslim princes or *walis*, who at last combined for a holy war against Hindu supremacy. They wiped Mojopahit in her idolatrous wickedness from the face of the earth and the leadership went to Demak, from which Pajang derived its political ascendency to merge later in Mataram. While the Islām spread from Giri in East and Central Java, even to Mataram and, crossing the water, to Madura, by the exertions of saintly men who "knew the future," an Arab sheik, arriving at Cheribon, directly from foreign parts, at some time between 1445 and 1490, Noor ad-Din Ibrahim bin Maulana Israïl, better known as Sunan Gunoong Jati, undertook the conversion of West Java. And of Cheribon in her relation to the Pasoondan may be repeated what a Javanese historian said of Demak, where the Evil One was outwitted by the building of a *mesdjid*, a Muhammadan house of prayer, the oldest in the island: two human virtues remained; so many as embraced the true religion went after them.

The two remaining virtues got hard pressed when Christian strangers came to explore and exploit: Portuguese, English and Dutch, the latter dominant up to this day. Viewed from the standpoint of the dominated, their god was a god of plunder; their emblem, to suit the symbolism of the Hindu Pantheon, was a *maryam*, a heavy piece of ordnance; their *vahana*, the animal representative of their most characteristic qualities, was the tiger, *machan* still being synonymous with *orang wolanda* (Hollander) in confidential, figurative speech. How Skanda, the deity of war, incited and Kuwera, the corpulent bestower of riches, directed their warriors and negotiators after the appearance of Cornelis Houtman's ships in the Bay of Bantam, need not detain us. That story of the past, with a hint at the possible future, is told in the legend of the legitimately wedded but for the time cruelly separated *maryams* of which one, very appropriately, awaits the fulfilment of a prophecy at the capital of the intruders, and the other where they first put foot on land, both being objects of veneration and granters of desires, especially kind to barren women who come, in a spirit of humiliation, to pray for the blessing of motherhood. A visit to Batavia is not complete without a pilgrimage to the Pinang gate, once an approach to the East India Company's castle, now in its supernatural cleanness, with its hideously black funeral urns and statues of Mars and Mercury or whoever they may be, giving access to the old town, the first public monument which attracted the attention of young Verdant Green in the age of sailing vessels after he had paid his due to the customs at the *boom*. Not far from that Pinang gate, symbolic of a colonial system under which short weight flourished with forced labour and trade carried on at the edge of the sword, lies the man-cannon, Kiahi Satomo, whose pommel presents a hand, closed so as to make the gesture of contempt, *la fica*, which Vanni Fucci of Pistoja permitted himself when interrogated in the abode of despair by the poet, *quem genuit parvi Florentia mater amoris*, and which accounts for the peculiar forms sacrifice assumes at this altar. His favourite spouse, discovered floating on the sea near old Bantam, an extraordinary thing to do for such a big heavy piece of metal, was given a temporary home on the spot where finally she lay down to rest from her travels: a certain Haji Bool built her a bambu house after the eruption of Krakatoa in 1883, her presence having saved Karang Antu from the fate of Anyer and Cheringin. Waiting for the great consummation, when her reunion with her lord at Batavia will announce the hour of the oppressors' defeat and their expulsion from Java, she is not less honoured than he. Dressed in a white cloth, which covers the circular inscription in Arabic characters on breech and cascabel, while the priming hole is decorated in square ornament, with five solid rings to facilitate conveyance if she prefers being carried to moving by her own exertion as of yore, anointed and salved with *boreh*,[1] the spouse, expecting the summons in the fragrance of incense and flowers,

[1] Generic name for ointments and salves, used specifically for a preparation of turmeric and coco-nut oil, which is smeared over the body on gala occasions and applied to objects held in veneration.

kananga and *champaka*, is often surrounded by fervent devotees, muttering their *dzikr* on their prayer-mats, grateful for bounty received or hopeful of future delivery from bondage. Husband and wife will meet and then a third cannon, far away in Central Java, in the *aloon aloon* [1] before the *kraton* [1] of the Susuhunan of Surakarta, inhabited by a ghost, dispenser of dreams, the *sapu jagad*, will vindicate that name, "broom of the world", by sweeping all infidels into the sea. Though the scoffing unbeliever counts this a dream of dreams, to the confiding children of the land it is a disclosure of things hidden in the womb of time, not the less true because Kiahi Satomo has an older mate, Niahi Satomi, the wife of his youth, the robed in red of the Susuhunan's artillery park, which glories in many *maryams* renowned in myth and history, among them another married couple, Koomba-rawa and Koomba-rawi, who shielded the ancient Sooltans of Pajang, being the official defenders of their palace. But Kiahi Satomo's heart is in Bantam, at Karang Antu, as Niahi Satomi has reason to suspect since she, the more legitimate and more advanced in age, cannot keep him at her side. It avails nothing that the Susuhunan's retainers chain the reluctant head of the family to the Bangsal Pangrawit, the imperial audience-chamber constructed after a heavenly model in gold; always

[1] An *aloon aloon* is an open square before the dwelling of a native chief; the *kratons* or palaces with their dependencies of the semi-independent princes in Central Java have two *aloon aloons*, one to the north and one to the south, on which no grass is allowed to grow.

and always he flies back to Batavia, anxious to be ready where the beloved *bini muda* (lit. young wife) has trysted him for sweet dalliance, from which victory will be born and release.

While predictions of the kind may be laughed at, the native belief in them and the foundations on which that belief rests, are no laughable matter by any means. Stories of mythical beings like Kiahi Satomo and Niahi Satomi, transformed into pieces of ordnance connected with the legendary lore of Trunajaya on one side and Moslim fanaticism personified in the cannon of Karang Antu on the other, prove that the native mind is still strongly imbued with pre-Muhammadan and even pre-Hindu ideas and modes of thought. Its imagination is fed by the fortunes (and misfortunes!) of an island which may be compared in the heterogeneous factors of its culture with Sicily, where Greek colonists built their temples in the high places of aboriginal idolatry; and the Saracens constructed their qubbehs overtopping the churches and cloisters into which the Christians had transformed the cellae and colonnades consecrated to Zeus, Hera, Poseidon, Aphrodite, Pallas Athene, Artemis, the Dioscuri; and the Normans added their arched doorways and massive masonry to perplex posterity entirely. In Java the Hindu element, with a strong Buddhist admixture, predominates; it prevails wholly in ancient architectural activity, not to speak of Soondanese and Javanese folklore and literature, while later Christian influence is negligible if not negative. Everywhere in the island we find under the Muhammadan coating the old conceptions of life from which the Loro Jonggrang group and the Boro Budoor sprang: scratch the *orang slam* and the Saiva or Buddhist will immediately appear. As the Padang Highlands, which preserve the traditions of Menangkabau, still ring with the fame of the Buddhist King Adityawarman, and scrupulously Moslim Palembang still cherishes the memory of Buddhist San-bo-tsaï, while South Sumatra clings to Hindu customs and habits for all its submission to Islām, so Java reveres whatever has been handed down from her pantheistic *tempo dahulu* (time of yore), however attached to the law of the Prophet. Sivaïsm and Buddhism were deeply rooted in the island; if the political power of its old creeds was broken in 1767 with the taking of Balambangan, Hinduïsm nevertheless lingering among the Tenggerese and in Bali, their spirit goes on leavening the new doctrine and we meet with their symbolism at every turn. Not to mention Central Java, where especially in Surakarta and Jogjakarta their tenacious sway strikes the most casual observer, the great staircase of the Muhammadan sanctum at Giri is adorned with a huge *naga*, the worshipful raincloud descending in the likeness of a serpent, despite the Qorānic injunction to abstain from the representation of animate creation. The pillars of reception-halls and audience-chambers in the houses of the high and mighty, East and West, bear a remarkable resemblance to the *linga*, witness, *e.g.*, the *kedaton*[1] built by the Sooltan Sepooh Martawijaya of Cheribon, a Moslim prince who ought to have evinced the strongest repugnance to Siva's prime attribute.

Under the circumstances we need not wonder that the Islām did so little to stimulate art in Java. Christianity did still less, rather clogged it in its application to native industries, which suffered from the country being flooded with stuff as cheap as possible in every respect, but sold at the highest possible prices to benefit manufacturers in Europe. This is not the place to expatiate on this subject nor to discuss present efforts (in which alas! personal ambitions play first fiddle and jeopardise results) to revive what lies at the point of death after centuries of culpable discouragement, the professional secrets and peculiar devices of native arts and crafts, requiring hereditary skill and the delicate touch of experienced fingers to attain former perfection, being now already half forgotten or altogether lost. Concerning the ancient monuments of Java, it is to the British Interregnum, to Sir Thomas Stamford Raffles that we owe the first measures for their preservation and the first systematic survey of specimens of Hindu workmanship as beautiful as any in the world, more in particular of the Prambanan temples, and also of the Boro Budoor, by common consent the masterpiece of Buddhist architecture. Marshalling his assistants in the archaeo-

[1] *Kedaton* has the same meaning as *kraton*, but is generally used for that part of a princely residence occupied by the owner himself with his wives, concubines and children, as distinct from the quarters of his retinue.

logical field, especially Cornelius and Wardenaar (whose fruitful explorations and excavations deserved fuller acknowledgment than they received from him), a diligent student besides of the history and literature of the island, doing for Java in that respect what Marsden had done for Sumatra, he inspired Dr. Leyden, Colonel Mackenzie and his rival John Crawfurd among his contemporaries, and of younger generations now equally gone, Wilsen, Leemans, Brumund, Friederich, Junghuhn, Cohen Stuart, Holle,—*j'en passe et des meilleurs*! The value of their labours must be recognised and it is the fault of the Dutch Government's apathetic attitude that with such forces at its disposal, so little has been achieved. Each of them, with few exceptions, worked independently of the other and blazed his own personal path in the wilderness of Dutch East Indian antiquities. There was, as Fergusson complained, no system, no leading spirit to give unity to the whole. Disconnected, sometimes misdirected investigation did not result in more than an accumulation of fragmentary material for possible future use, *rudis indigestaque moles.* And meanwhile the glorious remains of a lost civilisation went more and more to ruin. They were drawn upon for purposes of public and private building; statues and ornament disappeared, not only in consequence of the unchecked, persistent nibbling of the tooth of time, and it seemed almost so much gained if Doorga or Ganesa reappeared occasionally in the function of domestic goddess or god to some Resident or

Assistant Resident who demonstrated his devotion to ancient art and care for the preservation of its masterpieces by a periodical process of whitewashing or tarring. Worse than that: dilettantism began to tamper with the finest temples and the miserable bungling of mischievous, quasi-scientific enthusiasts reached its climax in the sorry spectacle prepared for the visitors of the last international exhibition in Paris (1900). There was to be seen in the Dutch East Indian section, a mean, ridiculous imitation of one of the Buddhist jewels of Central Java, a caricature of the *chandi*[1] Sari, the exterior in nondescript confectioner's style, daubed dirty white, the interior made hideous by a purple awning, abomination heaped on abomination. And that piteous botch, in fact an unconscious avowal of Dutch colonial shortcomings, did service as a sample of *la magnificence d'une religion prodigue en ornaments, en feuillages et en voluptés*!

After an era of dabbling by pseudo-Winckelmanns and Schliemanns, spicing their pretences with mutual admiration, the Government decided finally to appoint a permanent Archaeological Commission. Things, indeed, had come to such a pass that there was danger in delay: the island is becoming more and more accessible to globe-trotters of all nationalities, not a few of whom publish their

[1] *Chandi* means in its correct, restricted sense: "the stones between and under which in olden times the ashes of a burnt corpse were put," or "a mausoleum built over the ashes of one departed" (ROORDA and GERICKE); by extension, in native speech, any monument of the Hindu period. The *chandi* Sari is supposed to have been a *vihara* or Buddhist monastery.

impressions, and if erring authority wields a vigorous Press Law to silence criticism at home, against foreign criticism it has no weapon of the kind, however touchy it may be. So it began to move and the Archaeological Commission (short for Commission for Archaeological Research in Java and Madura), though without a single trained archaeologist among its members, displayed at once a good deal of activity under its first President, Dr. J. L. A. Brandes, exploring in East Java, restoring the *chandi* Toompang, attending to the Mendoot and Boro Budoor in Central Java, in order that, acting upon King Pururava's injunction, at last understood and accepted, after a fashion, by Batavia and the Hague, no monument shall be lost which has been wrought in the right spirit. It can be imagined that subordinate officials, eager to follow their superiors' lead, now revel daily in numberless finds, reported not only from districts, near and remote, in the star island, but from the exterior possessions, from Soombawa, from Jambi in Sumatra, from Kutei in East, from Sanggau and Sakadan in West Borneo, etc. etc. Like the encouraging of native art applied to weaving, wood-carving, the manufacture of pottery, of household utensils of copper and bronze, and so on, the ferreting out of sculptural and architectural ties with the past is quite the latest craze, a stepping-stone to preferment or at least a means of ingratiation with those who set the pace. There would be no harm in this if obsequious ambition did not burgeon here and there into an excess of zeal which makes one tremble, pregnant as it proves to be with dangers well defined by Ruskin: Of all destructive manias that of restoration is the frightfullest and foolishest.

Curiosity being excited, there is the impulse to satisfy vulgar demands, to cater to coarse appetites when admitting every one who knocks at the door of the treasure-house however unworthy. Trippers from the trading centres on the coast swarm round as their fancies guide; tourists from distant climes scour the land, either single spies or driven in noisy battalions of "conducted parties". Travel in Java is already assuming the character of holiday excursions pressed upon the public in bombastic handbills and posters of transportation companies. Revenue being the principal objective of Dutch colonial solicitude, the opportunity they create is gladly seized to levy gate-money from visitors to the *chandi* Mendoot.[1] And since the Philistines, who do not appreciate the beauties of a building they cannot comprehend, expect something in exchange for their contribution to the upkeep, visible tokens of their really having been there, we shall soon hear of photographers established in the temple to perpetuate the memory of spoony couples, giggling and offensive, magnesium flashed at the feet of the Most Venerable, or of the Boro Budoor in a blaze of Bengal fire to please mediocrity, which wants barbarous stimulants. And apart from such

[1] A tax of f.50 (ten pence), the payment of which secures also admission to the *chandis* Pawon and Boro Budoor.

concessions to the exigencies of inane modern travel, how distressing the plain tokens of neglect and spoliation! As Psyche began to mourn Love after she had come to grasp his excellence, so the discerning one, advancing to the apprehension of eternal truth there enshrined in beauty, a call to heaven in stone, laments less what is gone of material substance by the ravages of time, than what is taken from the spiritual essence by willful mutilation; by methods of repair embodied in iron scrapers to remove moss and weeds, incidentally spoiling the delicate lines of reliefs and decoration; by filling gaps with any rubbish lying about, mending and patching *à la grosse morbleu*; by additions for the convenience of sightseers, like the unsightly staircase askew near one of the original, dilapidated approaches. It is devoutly to be hoped that the overhauling now in progress will, at least, remove such incongruities and avoid new horrors of so-called restoration.[1]

Dr. Brandes, whose learning and good sense led the Archaeological Commission in a track of sound activity, died, unfortunately, in 1905. Though the theft of antiquities has been discontinued on paper, impudent souvenir hunting is still winked at by authorities fawning on distinguished guests. Untitled and unofficial collectors will have some trouble perhaps, at any rate incur a good deal more expense than formerly, in filling their private art galleries,

[1] Thanks to Major T. van Erp of the Engineers, who conducted the work of restoration, this pious wish has been granted.

but for officials of the type of Nicolaus Engelhard[1] no difficulties seem to exist and even the Boro Budoor was very recently despoiled to please a royal personage. So much for Java; as to the exterior possessions, the Minahassa was plundered, even more recently, for the benefit of foreign explorers of name and fame. Since the respective Government edicts[2] multiplied, fixing responsibility at random, cases of strange disappearance multiplied too, on the principle, it seems, of making hay while the sun shines; the pen-driving departments, issuing circulars on everything, for everything, against everything, about everything, effect absolutely nothing unless their insistence be taken, often rightly by him who reads between the lines, for a covert invitation to do precisely the contrary, considering friendships, family relations, party obligations, etc. etc., of powers and dominions. The force of regulations and rescripts in the Dutch East Indies is notoriously short-lived in the best of circumstances, and we have it on the authority of Hans Sachs, *Je mehr Hürten, je übler Hut.* The very scrupulous and wise, moreover, drag off whatever is loose or can be detached, separating details of ornament, reliefs and statues from their surroundings, which are

[1] Governor of Java's northeast coast from 1801 to 1808, in whose garden at Samarang "several very beautiful subjects in stone were arranged, brought in from different parts of the country." RAFFLES, *History of Java*, vol. ii., p. 55.

[2] Paraphrases of a fossil statute, periodically paraded and then returned to its pigeon-hole, like a relic carried round in procession on the day of the particular saint it belongs to and then shut away in its repository for the rest of the year. Of what avail are enactments and ordinances persistently ignored and never enforced?

indispensable to their proper understanding, to hide and forget them in cellars and lofts of museums until, the stars being favourable, accidentally rediscovered after years and years, and ticketed and huddled together with other ticketed objects in long, dreary rows of forbidding, bewildering aspect. That is, *if* they are rescued and classified and ticketed *tant bien que mal*: the colonial section in the Museum of Antiquities at Leyden, a byword among the lovers of Dutch East Indian architecture, shows clearly the obstruction caused by hopeless negligence in the past and lack of backbone in the present zeal, energy, ardour, nay, frenzy of investigation. Everything in Dutch colonial affairs goes by fits and starts with long blanks of indifference between. To give but one instance: the *Corpus Inscriptionum Javanarum*, planned with flourish of trumpets in 1843, still awaits the preliminaries of a beginning of execution. Concerning the fever of restoration which has broken out, one feels inclined, in support of Ruskin's opinion quoted above, to sound the note of warning engraved on the signet ring of Prosper Mérimée, Inspector of the Historical Monuments of France almost a century ago: μέμνασ' ἀπιστεῖν, lest the last state become worse than the first, and excess of zeal deface what time and the hand of man, even the Department of Public Works itself, quarrying its material for bridges, dams, embankments and the shapeless Government buildings of which it possesses the monopoly, have left standing. Without, however, insisting on the dark aspect of the situation, let us trust that a sense of shame, if not of duty, will sustain the interest in the old monuments of Java now in vogue, and may then the faddish, pompous display, turned into channels of quiet, responsible, persistent endeavour, herald a brighter day!

CHAPTER II

WEST JAVA

Quedaron mudos los cuerpos,
Solas las almas se hablan,
Que en las luces de los ojos
Iban y venian las almas.[1]
Romancero Morisco (Celin de Escariche).

The Batu Tulis, lit. "the inscribed stone", near Bogor, commemorates the feats of a certain prince, Parabu Raja Purana, otherwise Ratu Dewata, and calls him the founder of Pakuan, ruler, *maharajah ratu aji*, of Pakuan Pajajaran. That kingdom is the centre of everything tradition has transmitted regarding the Hindus in West Java. Its origin, according to native belief, goes back to a settlement of princely adventurers from Tumapel in East Java, and when Mojopahit flourished after the fall of that mighty empire, it rose to equal eminence at the other end of the island, only to be destroyed by the same agency, the growing power of Islām. The

[1] The bodies remained silent,
Only the souls did commune,
For in the light of the eyes
Came and departed the souls.

subjection of the mountain tribes of the Priangan by the settlers from the East proceeded in the beginning but slowly and the children of the land, even after they had yielded to the inevitable, must have retained a share in the management of their affairs, for Soondanese *pantoons*[1] mention separately, as two factors of government, the *ratu*, king of Pakuan, and the *menak*, nobility of Pajajaran. However this may be, from about 1100 until the beginning of the sixteenth century, Pajajaran was a political unity that counted. She could send an army of a hundred thousand warriors into the field. Her kings disposed at will of large territories, gained by conquest; one of them conferred upon his brother Kalayalang the dominion of Jayakarta, in later years better known under the name of Yacatra, and on his brother Barudin the dominion of Bantam, principalities destined to play an important part in the overthrow of the sovereign state. Nothing, save the meagre accounts of the *babads* and the scanty remains to be referred to at the end of this chapter, reminds now of Pajajaran, except the Badooy in South Bantam, who constitute

[1] The oldest, perhaps the only original form of native poetry, happily compared, by Professor R. BRANDSTETTER, with the Italian *stornelli*. In contradistinction to the *sha'ir*, the charm of the *pantoon* lies, or should lie, in its being improvised. It consists of four lines, of which the third rimes with the first and the fourth with the second; the first two contain some statement generally but loosely connected with the meaning of the last couplet, except, to quote Dr. J. J. DE HOLLANDER, that they determine the correspondence of sound. Here is one in translation:

> Whence come the leeches?
> From the watered ricefield they go straight to the river.
> Whence comes love?
> From the eyes it goes straight to the heart.

a community apart, entirely isolated from the rest of the population and whose peculiar customs and religious observances so far as known, make it probable that they are the descendants of fugitives before the Muhammadan inroad.

When Noor ad-Din Ibrahim bin Maulana Israïl had established in Cheribon not only his religion but also his political power, he began, under the name and title of Sunan Gunoong Jati, to propagate the faith by force of arms in the whole of West Java. First he cast his eyes on Bantam, then a mighty realm, the possession or at least the control of which, leaving spiritual motives alone, would materially benefit Moslim trade by securing a free passage through the Straits of Soonda whenever trouble with the Portuguese made the Straits of Malacca unsafe. The Sivaïte Prince of Bantam, trying to preserve his independence by fostering the commercial rivalry between his Muhammadan and Christian friends, received the latter with open arms and besought their assistance against Cheribon and Demak, but Maulana Hasan ad-Din, a son of Sunan Gunoong Jati, defeated him none the less and introduced the Islām among his people both in Bantam proper and in the Lampongs. Another son of Sunan Gunoong Jati founded the Muhammadan principality of Soonda Kalapa, notwithstanding the fortifications erected there by the Portuguese, at the instance of their Bantamese ally, to stem the tide of Muhammadan conquest. After subjugating the vassal state, Maulana Hasan ad-Din attacked, about

1526, the troops of Pajajaran under the King's son Sili Wangi, and routed them, taking the capital and proselytising by the sword wherever he went, following the example set by Raden Patah of Demak in East Java. It is probable that Bantam, once islāmised and consequently turning against the Portuguese, took the side of Cheribon in these wars. At any rate, we find Bantam and Cheribon together acknowledging the suzerainty of Demak, like the more eastern principalities of the north coast, and when that central Muhammadan state of Java lost the hegemony in consequence of its breaking up after the death of Pangeran Tranggana, and at last the Sooltan of Pajang,[1] into which it dissolved, had to humble himself with his allies, the Adipati of Surabaya and the Sunan of Giri, before the Senapati of Mataram, his former regent in that territory, this valiant and clever potentate claimed the lordship over the island. These were the beginnings of a glorious new Mataram, perhaps identical with Mendang Kamulan.

Cheribon, which had conquered Bantam and Pajajaran, lost gradually her strength, became tributary to Mataram in 1625 and wholly dependent in 1632. She declined still more after the death of Panambahan Girilaya, who divided his succession between his sons Pangeran Martawijaya (later Sooltan Sepooh) and Pangeran Kartawijaya (later Sooltan Anom), on condition of their providing for

[1] The title of Sooltan was assumed, probably for the first time in the history of Java, by the ruler of Pajang when, in 1568, he added Jipang to his domains.

a third son, Pangeran Wangsakarta of Godong (later Panambahan). Embroiled in the rebellion of Trunajaya against the authority of Mataram and captured, Martawijaya and Kartawijaya were kept as hostages at its capital, Karta. Released through the intervention of Sooltan Tirtayasa of Bantam, more commonly known as Abu'l-Fatah, they returned home only to get again mixed up in hostilities against Mataram and the Dutch East India Company, which overran Cheribon with its soldiers and improved the opportunity by regulating the affairs of Girilaya's three sons to its own best advantage. The foundation of Batavia on the site of old Yacatra, taken by Jan Pietersz Coen, May 30, 1619, had meant, among other things, an always keener competition in trade with Bantam or, rather, the "establishment of a free rendezvous", *i.e.* free of bickerings with native princes and princelings, for the fleets of the Company on their long voyage to the Moluccos. Bantam having outstripped Cheribon by the importance she derived from English and Dutch shipping, resented the blow which threatened to relegate her to a second or third place, and this resulted in frequent conflicts with the intruders, though the boundary line of their settlement and their mutual relationship had been carefully defined in the treaty of 1659. On the other side in occasional difficulties with Mataram, the Company, acting on the *divide et impera* principle, encouraged the rivalry between the middle and western empires, which both strove for supremacy in the Priangan.

How the Company accomplished its purpose and triumphed, needs here no detailed examination. Its objects and the considerations which moved it, are wittily discussed in a Javanese mock-epic, the *Serat Baron Sakendher*, a satire on the rise of Dutch power at Batavia, the foundation of Moor Yang Koong (Jan Pietersz Coen). If that pattern of regents *outre mer*, the first Dutch Governor-General in Java, whose motto was "never despair", whose grip like the grip of the tiger, has invited comparison with Ganesa (firstborn of Siva and Parvati) for wisdom and cautious statecraft, with Skanda (also sprung from the Mahadeva's loins but without the Devi's collaboration) for resolution and mettle, here we find him as the son of Baron Sookmool, Baron Sakendher's brother, and Tanaruga,[1] daughter of the Pajajaranese Princess Retna Sakar Mandhapa, and the poet makes the personification of the Company say to his twelve hopefuls, the earliest Tuạn Tuan Edeleer, or honourable members of the Governor-General's Council: Good measures you will enforce, without quarrelling amongst yourselves, and, even if it were larceny, the moment you have decided upon it by common consent, I give my permission,—a speech delightfully in keeping with the tactics of his father, whose artillery prevailed,

[1] This lady was a prisoner of the Pangeran of Jakarta (Yacatra) from whom Baron Sookmool, charmed by her beauty when he arrived in Java to trade for his father, the wealthy merchant Kawit Paru, bought her for three big guns, whose history, in the legendary lore of the island, is inextricably mixed up with the *mariage à trois* of Kiahi Satomo (for the nonce taking domicile at Cheribon), Niahi Satomi and the *maryam* of Karang Antu referred to in the preceding chapter.

not with iron cannon-balls, but with golden grape-shot of ducats and doubloons.

The ruins of the Fort Speelwijck and the minaret of Pangeran Muhammad's *mesdjid* at Old Bantam are very illustrative of the insinuating way in which the pioneers of the Company planted their factories; once admitted on the strength of their promises, they gained a firm footing by military superiority, driving hard bargains and ousting the Islām from what it had come to regard as its own. Near by is the neglected, overgrown Dutch cemetery, where many of those pioneers were laid to rest, far from home, family and friends, killed in the Company's battles or by strenuous obedience to exacting orders, bartering their health in a murderous climate for a handful of silver, wasting body and soul to swell the Company's dividends. A tangle of weeds and briars closes over their remains; thick moss, covering their broken gravestones, effaces their forgotten names; even the mausoleums dedicated to the memory of the leaders among them, commanders and commercial agents-in-chief, are crumbling away, harbouring hungry guests which leave safe lairs in the forests, when deer and wild pigs become scarce, to raid at night the village sheepfolds, while snakes may dart forth from the cracks and fissures at any moment and mosquitoes swarm round in myriads, the worst plague of all to him who seeks communion with the dead in that jungle. The burial-ground of the Sooltans of Bantam, gathered round Hasan ad-Din, the first preacher of the true faith in this region, is in better condition. Though Shafei, to whose *madsheb* or school the Moslemin of the Dutch East Indies belong, disapproved of elaborate tombs and prescribed that sepulchral cavities, after the deposition of the bodies, should be filled up and made level with the ground, memorial tokens to mark the graves of Muhammadan saints, famous princes and heroes, often venerated as *kramats*, are a familiar sight in Java; they consist generally of pieces of wood or stone, *tengger*, standing upright at both ends, at the head and at the feet, differently shaped for men and for women. Many such are found where Pangeran Muhammad raised his *mesdjid* with the minaret detached like the campanile of some mediaeval Italian church. Tombs all round, tombs of Sooltans, their brothers and sons and cousins, their great councillors and generals, a Bantamese Aliscamps with Hasan ad-Din occupying the place of honour under a canopy, prayer-mats and prayer-books lying around, a benign breeze stirring the muslin hangings and filling the air with the fragrance of the *kambojas*.[1] Whoever wants to know of the excellent deeds of the Sooltans of Bantam, their acts of devotion in peace and their prowess in war, can receive information from Pangeran Muhammad Ali in *kampong* Kanari, one of their descendants, keeper of the archives of the *mesdjid* and the surrounding garden of the departed. He will tell furthermore of the well near the north

[1] *Plumeria acutifolia Poir.*, fam. *Apocynaceae*, planted extensively in cemeteries; its flowers, for this reason called *boonga kuboor* (grave-flowers), have a very pleasant odour and are used to scent clothes, etc.

wall of the new building, which is fed from the well Zemzem at Mecca and, thanks to the child Ishmaïl, beneath whose feet its water bubbled forth, possesses the property of curing disease. It is also connected with the miraculous source at Luar Batang, whose water possesses the property of detecting perverters of the truth: the man who tries there to slake his thirst with a falsehood on his conscience, from a downright lie to a terminological inexactitude, or even a little fib for the sake of domestic tranquillity, will not be able to swallow a drop, his throat refusing liquid comfort until expiation of guilt; and so the devotees who flock to the shrine of the saint of Hadramaut at Pasar Ikan, Batavia, leave that source prudently alone—one may have sinned unwittingly or under strong provocation. Such holy places are thickly strewn and the last habitation of Hasan ad-Din is one of the holiest, being overshadowed by the venerable minaret of Pangeran Muhammad's *mesdjid*, which signified to Bantam what the *mesdjid* of Ngampel did to the eastern and the *mesdjid* of Demak to the middle states of Moslim Java. The intact preservation of the latter as the oldest existing edifice erected[1] for Muhammadan worship in the island, is of high importance *superstitionis causa*, and exceeding care was taken in 1845, when the danger of its tumbling down became imminent, to rebuild it not all at once, but one part after the other, round the four principal supports of the original structure, and to restore the beautifully

[1] About 1468, by Raden Patah.

carved lintels and posts exactly to their accustomed position. Nothing is left at Demak of Raden Patah's princely dwelling, but the graves are shown of Panambahan Jimboon, Pangeran Sabrang Lor and Pangeran Tranggana, who was killed by one of his servants on an expedition to still Sivaïtic Pasuruan.

Pangeran Tranggana had auxiliaries from Bantam among his troops and this leads us back to West Java after our slight digression in favour of Demak, the energetic central state which, at the time here spoken of, ruled the roast in matters of conquest for the propagation of the faith. The Bantamese, more than their converters, have conserved a reputation for fanaticism and it is not yet a quarter of a century since a certain Abool Karim of the district Tanara preached the holy war, the brotherhood of the Naqshibendyah fanning the flame of sedition he kindled. His *murids* (disciples) Tubagoos Ismaïl, Marduki and Wasid having spread the movement, a mob, led by a certain Haji Iskak, massacred several Europeans at Chilegon (1888). But for the Government's bayonets, rather than a course of conciliation based on a thorough knowledge of the agrarian causes at the bottom of the unrest among the population, the whole of Bantam might have blazed up and Cheribon might have followed. Seeing that they could not prevail, the dissatisfied betook themselves again to prayer, there at the grave of Hasan ad-Din, here at the grave of Sheik Noor ad-Din Ibrahim, situated not far from the capital he founded, on a hill near the sea, the Gunoong Jati, whence his title. The terraces of the *astana* so called, first home of the Islām in this region, much venerated however much defaced, savour of more ancient heathen monuments in all their odour of Muhammadan sacredness, not otherwise than the *Kitab Papakam*, the Cheribon code of laws, savours of Indian maxims and even at this date betrays its birth from the legislation introduced by the Hindu immigrants, though in 1768 (and not before that year, more than three centuries after the introduction of the law of the Prophet!), the *Kutara Manawa* has officially been abrogated in the Sooltanate. The lowest three terraces of the *astana* serve as a burial-ground for the descendants of Sunan Gunoong Jati and the men of mark in the annals of his empire; a road, winding upward, a Moslim Via delle Tombe, conducts the pilgrim to a *mesdjid* on the fourth, not to be desecrated by the feet of unbelievers;[1] above the *mesdjid*, on the fifth, the *sanctum sanctorum*, rest the mortal remains of the saint himself. Speaking of Cheribon in its relations to Hinduïsm and the Islām, a reference to Chinese influences on Javanese architecture cannot be omitted. They are most evident, of course, where the sons of the Flowery Empire have settled earliest and in greatest numbers. In several localities Chinese temples are found for the building and decorating of which renowned archi-

[1] It is told that the intrepid Governor-General Daendels once tried to invade the sanctity of this house of prayer, but even he had hastily to retire.

tects, wood-carvers and painters have expressly been summoned to Java at great expense. Reputedly the finest is the *klenteng*, situated at a stone's throw from the shed wherein Sunan Gunoong Jati's *grobak* is kept, the vehicle in which he descended from heaven to proclaim the Word. Transplanting their curved roof-trees and gaudy ornament, the Chinese brought also a taste for grotto-work, once notably conspicuous in the *kraton* of Sooltan Anom. On the road to Tagal, near the *dessa* (village) Sunyaragi, lies a rocky labyrinth belonging to the pleasure-grounds of Sooltan Sepooh's famous country-seat. Among other clever devices it contains an artificial cave so constructed that the *kanjeng goosti*, retiring thither on a hot afternoon for dalliance with his favourite of the hour, might shut himself completely off from the world by a discreet artificial waterfall, securing privacy behind its liquid screen and a refreshing atmosphere stimulative to amorous exercise. The Chinaman who elaborated the idea, had his eyes gouged out to prevent his creating another such wonder of architecture adapted to the diversions of oriental potentates.

It seems fitting that in Java, the sweet island whose air is balm and where always the delicious sound of running water is heard, where the cult of bathing is perfected by inclination as well as necessity of climate, some of the oldest signs of civilisation are found in sheltered nooks and corners still frequented by those who appreciate an invigorating plunge. Kota Batu, near Bogor, the supposed site of the capital of Pajajaran, is an instance in point. Destroyed, says the Soondanese tradition, because the illustrious King Noro Pati had lifted up his heart to boast against the message of the Prophet, his sons completed the calamity by their wrangling for the lordship over outlying, as yet unsubjugated and unconverted dependencies, and righteousness left the country. The same reasons which made Pajajaran slow to accept the Islām, had hindered her acceptance of Hinduïsm. The mountainous Priangan was sparsely populated and, even if we accept the statements of native historians who give Hindu civilisation in West Java a long life by dating the colonisation from India back to the first century of the Christian era,[1] confined to a limited area, as the antiquities discovered make clear, it remained far behind that which reared the superb temples of Central Java. To the best of our knowledge there were never any Hindu temples at all in West Java, where the people seem to have contented themselves with prayer and sacrifice in the open. While Central Java attained to the loftiest and noblest in art, West Java vegetated until improved communication, stimulated by war and trade, brought about a dissemination of more eastern artistic notions, discernible in raised levels and terraces as those of Gunoong Jati, which remind one faintly of the Boro Budoor; in earthen walls as those on the

[1] Venggi inscriptions, brought to light in West Java, go back to the sixth and fifth centuries of the Christian era and name Kalinga in India as the region from which the Hindu colonists emigrated.

Bukit Tronggool, which are arranged after a plan somewhat like that of the squares enclosing the principal temple and the surrounding smaller ones of the *chandi* Sewu. Even then Polynesian clumsiness was not shaken off. At Batu Tulis, a *kampong* in the outskirts of Bogor, where the hosts of two religions fought the battle which decided the fate of Pajajaran, are several ungainly images and impressions of the feet of Poorwakali, the spouse of one of that realm's petrified kings, who mourned him with such copious tears that she softened the very rock she stood upon, according to one legend; and, according to another legend, of the feet of a certain Raja Mantri who tarried so long in contemplation of the inscribed stone already mentioned, pondering over the meaning of its strange characters, that he sank gradually into the hard ground. There are more impressions of more feet and a coarsely carved *linga*, Siva's fecundating attribute, transformed by Muhammadan piety into the miracle working staff of a Moslim santon. Hardly greater interest is awakened by the primitive statues Kota Batu derives its appellation from, "city of stones", which form a sort of *Ruhmes Allee*, lining the path from the main road to the bath-house, with many of the same pattern scattered to right and left. All of them are petrified worthies of Pajajaran, which their own mothers would not recognise, though the natives know each of them by praenomen, nomen, cognomen and title, King Moonding Wangi, *i.e.* the nice-smelling buffalo, looking perhaps a trifle more human than the rest. Of a similar nature are the *archadomas*, a collection of about eight hundred blocks of stone on the estate Pondok Gedeh, which need a vivid imagination in the beholder to pass for the figures of men and animals. A good specimen of the Pajajaran type of sculpture, if it deserves that name, is the lachrymose Poorwakali already referred to as standing, petrified herself, at a little distance from the Batu Tulis where she solaces her widowhood by keeping company with Kidangpenanjong, forgetting her royal husband, after her paroxysm of grief, in a plebeian flirtation. Such is woman!

From these crude attempts at a representation of animate creation, sprang nevertheless an art which, in the hands of the master-builders and sculptors of Central Java, who sought the beauty of truth that is verily without a rival, flowered out in prayers of stone, visible tokens of their yearning for heavenly reward, born of communion with the divine in deep reflection, only to descend again to lower planes, to the seeking of the praise of man, in the decadent conventionality of the later eastern Hindu empires. The story of the development of architecture and sculpture in the island from the immaturity identified with Pajajaran to the luxurious grandeur of the temples of Prambanan, the Mendoot and the Boro Budoor, hides a riddle no less strange than that of the bursting forth of Arabic poetry, full-blown in all its subtleness of thought, exuberance of imagination, perfection of language. The story of decline is written in the evolution of decorative design: the significance of motives based on the observation of the earth and her precious gifts, evaporates gradually in nicely waving lines, elaborate scrolls, insipid fineries. The *kala*-head changes into the roots of a tree, figurative of the forest; the trunk of Ganapati into its bole; at last the tree, roots, trunk, branches, foliage and all, with the sun rising over the forest, with mountains touching the sky, with rivers flowing to the sea, into conventional ornament. Islāmic ideals were not conducive to a revival of artistic conceptions fading into nothingness; neither was, to repeat that too, the painful contact with Christian civilisation. When the natives were made to toil and moil for alien masters, their virtues and energies blighted into the defects and failings of apathy. How could it be otherwise where an inefficient, venal police and a slow, defective administration of justice did (and does) not protect property against depredation; where exertion beyond what is strictly necessary for bare subsistence, meant (and means) not prosperity but increased taxation. With all its pretensions to superiority and display of ethical sentiment, the Dutch Government can scarcely be said to differ much from Baron Sookmool, the personified East India Company of more than three centuries ago. Holland's wards in her rich colonies may be moulded into men, angels or devils, like the Triloka, the triple people of the Hindus, according to the treatment meted out to them and the education they receive. As far as Java is concerned, hoping in heaven's mercy, they live in their old traditions, the light of the past and the shadow of the present. What will the future bring in advance of the day on which mankind shall be scattered abroad like moths? There is no knowledge of it but with God and the secret lies behind the Banaspati,[1] in the hand of him of the budding lotus-flower, the Deliverer from Evil.

[1] Banaspati or Wanaspati is the conventional lion's (or tiger's) head, a frequent motive in the ornament of Javanese temples, especially of common use over their porches and gateways.

CHAPTER III

THE DIËNG

> Where Silence undisturbed might watch alone,
> So cold, so bright, so still.
>
> PERCY BYSSHE SHELLEY, *Queen Mab.*

WHERE five residencies—Samarang, Pekalongan, Banyumas, the Bagelen and the Kadu—meet between two seas, the wonderland of the Diëng links the eastern and western chain of volcanoes which are the vertebrae of Java's spine. The Diëng plateau, the first part created, as tradition goes, and destined to remain longest above water in the island's final destruction and submersion, is nothing but a huge crater. Nature, in her most mysterious mood, exercises here a charm of a peculiar character, well expressed by the name, according to the Javanese derivation from *adi aëng*, *i.e.* marvellously beautiful.[1] The temples in this region belong to the oldest and finest if by no means the largest of Java. The discovery of a

[1] Dr. A. B. COHEN STUART, however, derives Diëng from *dihyang*, the name found by him in old records.

stone with a Venggi inscription has led to the conjecture that the Hindu settlement to which we owe them, originated from the Priangan; other indications point to immigration directly from Southern India. However this may be, the dates ascertained (one in an inscription reproduced by me in 1885 for further examination at Batavia, leaving the stone in the place where I had found it) from 731 Saka (A.D. 809) on, witness to the lost civilisation of the Diëng having reached its apogee at the time the Abbassides flourished in Baghdad and the Omayyads in Cordova. How it rose, declined and fell, we do not know. For four centuries its memory lived only as a fantastic tale, the Diëng remaining utterly deserted, a wilderness of mountain and forest, inhabited by devils and demons of the Khara and Dushana type.

Resettled since about 1800, its villages increase in number and size, and its wild animals, big and small, disappear gradually, though the tigers are still troublesome, evincing a growing disposition to vary their accustomed fare with domestic kine and sheep. The sombre woods are gone and efforts at reafforestation gave so far no perceptible results. The ground yields abundant crops of cabbage, onions and tobacco, in which a lively trade is done with Chinese middlemen, who buy for the merchants at Pekalongan, whence the product is shipped to larger centres of trade. These middlemen congregate principally at Batoor, a prosperous village, where travellers to the Diëng, arriving from that side, will appreciate the hospitable disposition of the *wedono*, the native chief of the district. Many a one has been entertained under his roof, looked down upon from the *palupooh* (split bambu) walls by the Royal Family of Great Britain and Kaiser Wilhelm in chromolithographic splendour, while discussing a substantial lunch or arranging for sleeping accommodation if too tired to push on, or desirous of visiting the Pakaraman, the valley of death, at break of day when the uncanny manifestations of that place of horror are strongest. Another source of income for some of the Chinamen of Batoor and their henchmen of the Diëng is opium smuggling. The geographical position, commanding access to five administrative divisions of the island at once, lends itself admirably to that lucrative business. And if the smugglers cater to a low vice, they can advance an excuse logically unanswerable by those in authority who punish them when caught: they satisfy but a demand, in competition with the Government that created it, introduced the drug and encourages its use, artificially whetting a depraved appetite and demoralising the children of the land for the sake of more revenue.

Often though I went up to forget the cares of exacting duties in happy holidays on the Diëng, trying the different approaches, the impressions of my first ascent in October 1885 are freshest in my memory. Starting from Wonosobo, I preferred to a more direct route the roundabout way via Temanggoong, spending a day on the road between

II.

CHANDI PRINGAPOOS

(Archaeological Service through Charls and van Es.)

the twin volcanoes Soombing and Sindoro, enjoying the views to right and left, every new turn disclosing new wonders: mountain slopes basking in the warmth which radiated triumphantly from a sky of dazzling brightness, valleys of perfect loveliness losing their brilliant hues in the shades of evening as if a curtain fell between the world left and the world entered. The following morning early I rode from Temanggoong in a thick mist which, rolling away before the sun, uncovered a landscape more and more rugged as I passed Parakan and Ngadirejo, but always more charming, a feast to the eye. Near Ngadirejo the *chandis* Perot and Pringapoos claimed my attention. Built for the worship of Siva, his *sakti* Doorga and their eldest son, they offered a sad spectacle of decay, the former crumbling away in the baneful embrace of a gigantic tamarind, one of whose branches rose from the midst of the ruin straight up to heaven, overshadowing Ganesa, the conqueror of obstacles, in his meditations; the latter holding an image of Siva's *vahana* or *nandi*, the bull, symbol of his creative power, still an object of veneration as the *boreh* indicated, the walls of the temple being decorated with splendid bas-reliefs representing a scene from Javanese history or mythology, analogous to the rape of the Sabine women.[1] Farther on, surprise succeeding

[1] The remains of both these exquisite little temples suffered severely from a gale in 1907, which blew some of the surrounding trees down, their trunks and branches falling heavily and disjoining the still tolerably erect walls, the *chandi* Perot, according to latest intelligence, being wholly destroyed by the toppling of the tamarind it supported.

surprise, lies Joomprit, another delicious spot, sanctified by a holy grave, at the source of the Progo. The water, gushing forth from the mouth of a cavern and trickling down its sides, is immediately lost to sight in a declivity among the ferns. Curious monkeys herd round, led by their brawny chief, imperious like Hanoman, born from the wind, swinging through space, commanding the simian army of Sugriva: they constitute one of the few colonies of sacred apes which form a living link with the Hindu epoch; that of Gaja Moongkoor on the Diëng has ceased to exist.

From Joomprit on, it was pretty steep climbing to a point where, at a sudden turn, I beheld the lowlands, far beneath the clouds gathering round me, fair plains resting under their hazy veil of midday repose, calm and undisturbed. Drinking deep of the invigorating mountain air, I noticed the red cheeks of the women and girls who returned from market in little groups. After descending to the tea-plantations of Tambi, the clambering up began again, pretty hard for my pony, to which I gave an occasional rest, looking back over hills and valleys as they dissolved in soft-melting tints, impressing the beholder with a sense of eternal light in limitless space. Wonder akin to awe seized me when, panorama-like, a landscape of silent grandeur, quite different from the graceful majesty of the rose-gardens of Wonosobo and the palm-groves of Temanggoong, unfolded itself. I was on the Diëng plateau. Notwithstanding the late hour, my admiration of the scenery having made my progress slow, I could not resist the temptation to dismount and follow the trail which led me down to the source of the Serayu beside the road, and pay my compliments to the shade of stalwart Bimo by way of introduction to the regions resounding in its temples with his exploits and those of other worthies sung in the *Brata Yuda*.[1] Nor indeed only in its temples: this same delightful retreat commemorates Bimo's prowess according to a legend which in its astonishing account of his supernatural virility cannot be repeated. Enough to say that Arjuno, making him dig up the *toog* Bimo, on the advice of Samār, the wily, was the first, by determining the course of the Serayu, to direct the water from the mountains of Central Java to the sea, therewith obtaining the realm of Ngastino. And whoever takes a bath, alone and at night, in the water springing from mother earth under the *pohoon chemeti*, the weeping willow of Bimo's fountain, will have no occasion for certain elixirs largely advertised in daily and weekly papers, will retain youthful vigour into hoariest age.

It was dark when I arrived at the *pasangrahan*, the Government rest-house, received first by a shaggy, plumetailed dog of the Diëng variety, suspicious of strangers. Her name proved to be Sarama, suggesting classical associations not

[1] The *Brata Yuda Yarwa* is the Javanese version of the famous Kawi poem *Bharata Yuddha* which, in its turn, is founded on the Sanskrit epos *Mahabharata*. The war for the possession of Hastinapura is transplanted to Java; the Sanskrit proper names have passed into the nomenclature of Javanese history and geography; the Indian heroes have become the founders of Javanese dynasties, the progenitors of Javanese nobility.

sustained, I am sorry to record, by her master, mine host, a Swiss, retired from service in the Dutch colonial army and put in charge of the place. Speaking innumerable languages and every one of them as if it were a *lingua franca* composed of all the others, he showed me my room, took orders for my supper and made me comfortable, the broad, perpetual smile on his honest face illumining our polyglot conversation. Alas! Wielandt is no more. Indra, who knows men's hearts, has certainly assigned to this diamond, more polished, presumably, in its celestial than in its former terrestrial state, a worthy station among the jewels of the city of bliss, Amaravati. A man of family instincts, good Wielandt left several daughters, at the time of my visit of initiation extremely shy little girls; and a son, then Sinjo Endrik, the obliging and attentive, ever ready to act as a guide to and otherwise to assist his father's guests on their excursions, now Tuan Endrik, his father's successor in the *pasangrahan*, while one of his brothers-in-law keeps a small, private hotel, opened to meet the increasing influx of sightseers and seekers of health. The Diëng plateau, especially in the dry season, would be an ideal site for a sanatorium. The sufferer from the debilitating heat on the coast in the enervating conditions of a continuous struggle for the next dollar or official preferment with fatter salary, may find there rest and a cool climate. Going to the bath-room before setting out early on some expedition, I have often found miniature icicles pendent from the *panchuran*, the water conduit, and riding off, have often heard, in crossing a puddle, the thin coating of ice crackle under the hoofs of my pony. Sometimes, at sunrise, the few remaining temples stand out white, the whole plateau being covered with frost, which makes a strange impression on one who but the day before yesterday sweltered in the fiery furnace of, for instance, the Heerenstraat at Samarang.

Waking up the morning after my first arrival, feeling cold, though the scene my eyes met was not quite so severely wintry as that just described, my dreams seemed to continue in reality. I beheld a tranquil plain different in its bright serenity from everything I had so far seen anywhere else, the Bimo temple rising to the left and the Arjuno group to the right, sharply outlined against the hills and the sky, their dark-gray colour in wonderful harmony with the verdure of earth and the blue expanse of heaven. One moment they appeared near in the clear atmosphere as if I could seize them with my hand, and then again very, very far, never to be approached. A vapour, clinging to the slope of the Pangonan in the direction of the Kawah Kidang, reminded me of the tremendous cosmic energy entering into the composition of this soothing stillness, this tonic for the sick and worried, with the certainty of annihilation as final pledge of freedom. Once a lake of seething lava, the plateau lies enclosed by the tops of five mountains, the Prahu, Sroyo, Bismo, Nogosari and Jimat, 2050 metres above the level of the sea; the

Pangonan and Pagar Kandang are old eruptive cones, formed of the mud and sand thrown out, which accumulated at their bases and raised the surrounding ground. The plateau in its narrower sense is now a flat stretch of turf, in places, especially in the middle, a morass, called the Rawa Baleh Kambang for its northern, and the Rawa Glonggong for its southern part. Ruins have been found everywhere in the plain and up the slopes of the hills, even up to the summit of the Prahu. Here stand stone posts in a row, used by Arjuno, according to the legend, to tether his elephants, while his cows, after grazing on the Pangonan, were corralled for the night in the hollow of the Pagar Kandang, lit. "fence of the cattle-pen"; there, as in Diëng Kidool, layers of ashes among the slags and other debris, mark the situation in the past of the burning-grounds, which yield a steady harvest of bronze and gold finger-rings, bracelets, anklets and other objects of personal adornment. Ancient aqueducts, walls, staircases, foundations of secular buildings, clustered round the temples, remains of an important religious centre, so various and rich that Junghuhn did not exaggerate when calling them inexhaustible, suggest the existence, once upon a time, in those mountain wilds, of a Javanese Benares, minus the Ganges but plus a setting of unceasing volcanic activity, which demolished it by a sudden, violent outbreak. Such suggestions need only the seconding of one of the learned to be utterly ridiculed by his equally learned brethren of an opposite school. . . . We will let the matter rest at that and simply enjoy the actual calm of a landscape evidently exposed to destruction at the shortest notice, of nature recuperating from outrageous debauch.

Voices solemn and sweet summon to close communion with the power behind those manifestations, the universal soul of things human and superhuman, infernal and divine. One look more at the strip of turf which clasps the mysteries as a girdle embossed with gems, the Arjuno and Bimo shrines, shining in the splendour of early morning,—we shall return to them after our stroll of orientation. In the *dessa* Diëng Wetan, close to the *pasangrahan*, is, or rather was, the *watu rawit*, a wall constructed of big blocks of stone, two portions of which still exist with a narrow staircase, hewn on a smaller scale, leading to the coping. The structure, largely drawn upon for building material, goes also by the name of *benteng* (fort of) Buddha, an appellation incompatible with the Sivaïte origin of Diëng architecture and a contradiction in terms besides, considering the character of Gautama's teaching; but in native parlance everything connected with the Hindu period is referred to as belonging to the *jaman buda*, while the expression *agama buda* includes every pre-Muhammadan ancestral religion. Via Patak Banteng, Jojogan and Parikesit the *dessa* Simboongan may be reached, until recently the highest in Java (2078 metres). Founded in 1815 by the grandfather of the present *lurah*, or chief of the village, its inhabitants, on whose stature and colour of skin the cool climate has had a visible influence, are very prosperous, their principal occupation being the preparation of a hair-oil from the seeds of the *gandapura* (*Hibiscus Abelmoschus*). Simboongan lies on the west bank of Telaga Chebong, one of the many lakes which add to the indescribable charm of the Diëng, some possessing uncanny echoes, some being yellow and sulphurous, some of ever changing hue, some of crystalline clearness and stocked with goldfish, while the marshy shores are a favourite haunt of *meliwis*, a kind of duck much prized as food and becoming correspondingly scarce. Proceeding to Sikunang we get beautiful views in the direction of Batoor, hidden among its Chinese graves and orchards as in an airy robe of white and green ; along the mountain rills which hasten impetuously to the valley of Banjarnegara, meeting in the radiance of the sun's promise for union with the sea ; down to the ricefields of Temanggoong, resplendent at the feet of the high mountains which keep guard over the Kadu, a paradise dominated by the sister volcanoes Soombing and Sindoro, a joy to behold.

Passing Sikunang and turning round the Gunoong Teroos, a spur of the Pakuojo, we notice some trachyte steps, the head of a staircase made for the convenience of pilgrims from what is now the residency Bagelen, to the city of temples, an ascent of five thousand feet. Over a long distance, following the course of the river Lawang, that gigantic roadway can be traced far below Telaga Menjer by stones left in holes from which it was not easy to remove them for building purposes. Another of these *ondo buda* on the north side of the plateau, served the pilgrims coming from what is now the residency Pekalongan, via Deles and Sigamploong, and disappeared in the same manner. Descending, a smell of sulphur announces a lion of the Diëng of a less innocent, in fact of a decidedly satanic aspect: on this soil always the unsuspected turns up, the remains of an ancient civilisation forcing themselves upon our attention together with impressive reminders of the subterranean forces which extinguished it. From a number of cavities on the slope of the Pangonan, bare of vegetation, a picture of desolation, noxious vapours rise and bubbles of mud are blown forth and burst with a rumbling noise. High above the rest works the Kawah Kidang, the deer-kettle, spouting and growling, throwing the hot liquid round with relish, and it is advisable to keep her well to leeward on her days of gala, for she changes frequently her aim and her mood, an index of Kala's disposition when stirring the bowels of the earth. Being the pulse of the Diëng, so to speak, she is regularly excited to fiercer exertion by the rainy season, differing also in this particular from the Chondro di Muka, her rival near the Pakaraman, with whom she has been confused even by geographers of name, greatly to her disparagement since she commands a considerably wider sphere of influence, not scrupling to encroach upon the domain of her neighbours by moving about. Wherever one pokes into the ground within her sphere of action, the steam rushes out and seething puddles are formed; it is wary walking and the wise will take warning from the foolhardy Contrôleur whose curiosity prompted him a step too far: sinking through the upper crust into the boiling mud, he had his legs so badly burnt that he died of the consequences and was buried at Wonosobo instead of marrying his Resident's daughter at Poorworejo.

With its mofettes, solfataras, steam-holes, mud-geysers, sulphurous lakes, its treacherously opening and closing chasms,[1] last but not least its notorious valley of death,[2] the Diëng is the region above all others in volcanic Java, of miracles that expound the antagonism between fratricide life and death on our turbulent planet, which continuously prepares for or recovers from spasms of generative destruction. One of these spasms, on a grander scale than usual in the short span of human history, was the eruption of Krakatoa in 1883; which raised and submerged islands, shaking and altering the Straits of Soonda, a resultant tidal wave razing the towns of Anyer and Cheringin. The Diëng, some three hundred miles off, responded faithfully, as might have been expected, the Kawah Kidang roaring and splashing mud furiously, the wall of the crater-lake Chebong cracking in several places, so that part of its water, instead of flowing through the old channel, now

[1] One of those chasms, near the *dessa* Gaja Moongkoor, swallowed not merely a dancing-girl, a most common occurrence in Javanese legendary lore, but a whole village.

[2] A very active mofette which the natives call the Pakaraman, *i.e.* the "selected spot" where King Baladeva had his arms forged in the Brata Yuda war.

seeks its way through the fissures thus created, remunerative tobacco-fields being transformed into swamps. Such disasters preach an eloquent sermon on the text, hewn in stone by the builders of the temples here erected to Siva as Kala, the Overthrower, and, transmitted with the wisdom of ages by a later religion, happily expressed by the German poet:

Was hilft es Menschen seyn, was liebe Blumen küssen,
Wann sie sind schöne zwar, doch balde nichts seyn müssen?[1]

The news that a troop of strolling players had arrived, dispelled, however, ideas of that sort, unpalatable truth never proving successful against the pleasurable excitement of the moment. They were going to perform at the house of the reputedly wealthiest man of the plateau and not the less highly considered by his neighbours because caught redhanded, not once but repeatedly, in handling the forbidden, as I heard afterwards. Living near one of the enclosures traditionally associated with the pyres which were extinguished when the Hindu priests deserted their altars, he gave the *ton* to the upper ten of Diëng society, "disporting like any other fly" unterrified by daily manifestations of cosmic potency. Surrounded by his *ganadavatas*, gods of the second rank, he welcomed me to the show. Mounted on sham horses, the actors delighted their audience with a sham battle which soon became a single combat

[1] What is the use of living, of kissing lovely flowers,
If, though they are beautiful, they must soon fade into nothing?

between two valiant knights, encouraged by masked clowns, funny yet exquisitely graceful in their movements: the *savoir vivre* of this people is perfectly matched with their elegance of carriage and correctness of speech and innate propriety of demeanour. The comedians' stage-properties did not amount to much and their inventive genius shone the more brilliantly: a tiger (for a hunt of his highness our common uncle[1] followed the joust) was improvised with jute bagging and two pieces of wood, representing the jaws, snapping ferociously, perhaps a compliment to the *orang wolanda* present, his biped equivalent in native estimation, as already remarked. Or an allusion may have been intended to local events: not longer than a week before, Paman had tried to force Wielandt's stable, cooling his wrath, when baffled, on Sarama's pups.

So much for my recollections of the histrionic exercises on the Diëng, and now about the temples! If Thomas Horsfield, in his narrative of the tour he made through the island between 1802 and 1807, mentioned the so-called Buddha-roads, it was Raffles who sent Cornelius, Lieutenant in the Corps of Engineers, to survey the architectural remains on the Diëng plateau proper, which the earlier traveller had not visited. According to the official account of his mission, kept in the library of

[1] The native's deferential fear for the animal in question, makes him reluctant to pronounce its name, a liberty likely to give offence; referring to the lord of the woods, he speaks rather of his respected uncle (*paman*) or grandfather (*kakeh*), which satisfies, at the same time, his lingering belief in the transmigration of the soul.

the Museum of Antiquities at Leyden and still unpublished, he found whatever was standing of some forty groups, covered with clay and volcanic ashes up to nearly a fourth of the original height. Captain Baker, also commissioned by Raffles, worked three weeks on the Diëng after his examination of the ruins at Prambanan and the Boro Budoor. Junghuhn, whose observations date from 1838 to 1845, speaks of more than twenty temples in a wilderness of marshy woods. The woods have disappeared, the marshes hold their own and of his twenty temples only eight are left in a recognisable shape: five of them belong to the Arjuno group, including the so-called house of Samãr; the best preserved is the Wergodoro or Bimo; the Andorowati and Gatot Kocho crumble away even faster than the rest. It has already been remarked that the Diëng structures belong to the oldest in the island, the *hanasima* inscription, transferred to Batavia, furnishing a record of the Diëng civilisation which goes back to 731 Saka (A.D. 809). They are interesting to the Indian antiquary, wrote Fergusson, "because they are Indian temples pure and simple, and dedicated to Indian gods . . .; what (they) tell us further is, that if Java got her Buddhism from Gujerat and the mouths of the Indus, she got her Hinduïsm from Telingana and the mouths of the Kistnah. . . . Nor are (they) Dravidian in any sense of the word. They are in storeys, but not with cells, nor any reminiscences of such; but they are Chalukyan." Later learning accepts this statement only with cautious reserve. Whether Chalukyan or not, though, it is plain even to the unlearned that, erected to Siva, the Mahadeva worshipped principally in his character of Bhatara Guru, the divine teacher, to his *sakti* Doorga and their first-born Ganesa, these temples, radiating the all-soul in the fierce glare of the midday sun, unfolding their secrets in the mellow moonbeams of night, partake fully of their mysterious surroundings, are integral portions of the ground they occupy, as may be said of all ancient Javanese buildings. Men of great power of imagination, deep-reasoning sentiment, the builders of these marvels, working their thoughts up to the sky, rescued for us the essence of the Diëng's past existence. Their apprehension of universal happiness without beginning or end, sharpened by the desire to enjoy heaven on earth, lent immortality to the greatness of a people every vestige of whom would have disappeared but for their creative enthusiasm.

Prurient prudery, keen on the scent of the nasty, feels shocked at the *lingas* and *yonis* lying round, unable in its fly-blown purity to grasp the divinity of eternal love in the poem of generation, the union of the Deva and the Devi in causation and conception of life. The Philistine sees little more than rubbish, heaps of stone of no earthly use except as havens of refuge when out shooting *meliwis* and overtaken by rain. In the Rawa Baleh Gambang we find five such clustered together, the *chandis* Arjuno with the house of Samār, Srikandi (Ongko

III.

CHANDI ARJUNO ON THE DIËNG PLATEAU

(Archaeological Service through Charls and van Es.)

Wijoyo), Poontadewa (Trumo Kasumo or Sami Aji) and Sembrada (Sepropo), the chief hero of the *Brata Yuda* being honoured in the midst of family and friends, including his funny and faithful servant. The *kala-makara*[1] ornament of the entrance to the *chandi* Arjuno tells its tale; so do the empty niches designed for free-standing statuettes dissolved into space. Like the *chandi* Srikandi it was once surrounded by a wall and another point of resemblance is the small rectangular building called the *chandi* Samār, probably destined for secular purposes; of the Srikandi dependency, however, only the base can be traced. The *chandi* Sembrada deviates somewhat in architectural plan and detail, and the ground-idea of the decoration can be studied to best advantage in the *chandi* Poontadewa, finest of the group, exquisitely graceful on its high basement. Here again the *makara* ornament prevails, budding into leaves and flowers, chiselled with a chaste appreciation of the esthetic principle of self-control: *In der Beschränkung zeigt sich erst der Meister.* Under the tapering roofs, fallen or falling in, which give the inner chambers an air of indescribable elegance, notwithstanding the cramped dimensions, images of holiness stood on pedestals; the images have been removed, heaven knows whither, and even the pedestals have fared badly at the hands of sacrilegious robbers digging for hidden

[1] Siva as Kala, the destroyer with the lion's or tiger's head, Banaspati, devouring the sea-monster Makara: time finishing all things and alleviating all distress, in respect of which notion VOLTAIRE's short but pointed story of *Les Deux Consolés* may be profitably read.

treasure. Trumo Kasumo, supposed to keep sentinel over his *chandi* (in bas-relief, north side), cannot but be scandalised at modern methods of research and modern behaviour in general.

The morass shows, in the dry season, the foundations of buildings, regularly arranged, lining streets which intersected at right angles over a considerable part of the Rawa Baleh Gambang. Their disposition has been advanced to support the theory that the population of the Diëng lived in wooden houses, built on those substructures of stone. The theory that the superstructures of stone have been carried away and the submerged substructures left because not so easy to get at, is just as plausible; perhaps a little more so. But whatever they were, temples and priestly or private dwellings of wood or stone, the officiating clergy, their assistants and the inhabitants of the city ministering to their fleshly needs, must have suffered a good deal from the dampness of the soil, the plateau offering already in those early days a field of rich promise for the experiments of hydraulic engineers. Among canals and ditches of less importance, the Guwa Aswotomo, a *cloaca maxima* some twelve centuries old, still relieves the plain of its superfluous water. According to the legend, for nothing in this locality goes without at least one,—according to the legend then, the subterraneous passage was dug by Aswotomo on his expedition to the Diëng for the purpose of smashing the Pandawas, and nearing Arjuno's residence he pushed his way up to the surface, from distance to distance, spying how far he had yet to continue his underground march. Descending into one of the peep-holes he made, in a season of extreme drought, I was able to crawl on to the next, through mud and debris which blocked my further progress and, unable to crawl out on a level fifteen or twenty feet lower, the watercourse sloping deeper and deeper down, I had to return to my point of ingress. The glory of this feat diminishes in the light of my knowledge of the circumstance that the Diëng plateau harbours no snakes,[1] save the decorative *nagas* of temple architecture, and that a companion followed my movements above ground; had we been provided with ropes, we might have carried our work of exploration much further—but that must wait for another time. Of the rare plant which grows nowhere but in Aswotomo's burrow and owes its growth to his copious perspiration while at his task, a fern possessing rare qualities, highly beneficial to him who pulls it out by the roots, I saw or, rather, felt nothing in groping my way through mire and darkness. Taking its course in a direction inverse to the mole-man's initial tunnel boring, his Guwa begins at the Arjuno temples as an unpretentious drain and runs, for about half a mile, slanting toward the source of the river Dolok, where Junghuhn has set up two *lingas*.

The largest remaining and most beautiful temple on the Diëng is the *chandi* Wergodoro

[1] Query: Has St. Patrick ever been on the Diëng?

or Bimo,[1] where the Pangonan rises out of the Rawa Glonggong. Notwithstanding Fergusson's opinion, competent critics, deriving their conclusions from the horizontal lines of the roof-storeys, maintain its Dravidian or Southern Indian instead of Chalukyan character.[2] The niches with busts, which impress one as windows with people poking out their heads to see who is disturbing their quiet, suggest an approach to ideas further developed in the architecture of the plain of Prambanan. These curious persons look out only at the back and at the sides; the niches of the roof in front, over the projecting porch with *kala-makara* ornament, are all empty. With its entrance facing east, in contradistinction to those of the other temples on the plateau, which face west, the *chandi* Bimo possesses also notable peculiarities in the details of its sculpture: the double lotus of the cornice, lotus-buds and diminutive bo-trees of uncommon shapes, etc., while the upward tapering structural design displays a tendency to the slightly curved lines so dearly loved by Greek builders of the best period and adapted by the masters of early Gothic. The larger, lower niches have been despoiled; architraves and mouldings, festooned with foliage, flowers and seed-pods, divide the open spaces round about in a tasteful, sober manner, exciting without

[1] Or Bhimo, one of Arjuno's four brothers and avenger of the honour of the family on Kichaka, who had fallen in love with their common wife Draupadi.

[2] No buildings in the Northern Indian or Indo-Arian style have been found in Java.

IV.

CHANDI BIMO OR WERGODORO ON THE DIËNG PLATEAU

(Archaeological Service through Charls and van Es.)

fatiguing the eye. From the fact that the decoration has not been completed, it is inferred that the sculptors were interrupted like their comrades at work on other monuments of Central Java, overwhelmed perhaps by the catastrophe of volcanic or martial nature, which depopulated the Diëng and coincided with the decline of the ancient empire of Hindu Mataram. The miraculous voice heard in the *chandi* Bimo at dead of night, is silent on this point. All temples have their *shetans*, their bad, rarely good spirits, but the *genius loci* of the Bimo excels the whole Arjuno crowd of them in efficacy and unfailing attention to the business of the seekers of advice, who arrive from far and wide to consult the oracle. Entering after dusk the gate of the Dread One, Kala, one with Rudra, the Roarer (the Kawa Kidang) near by, they have but to wait in prayer at the altar of the wondrous fane. A strange whisper, mounting like the odour of *melati* and *kenanga*, tells them how to avoid the grim giant Danger if, on leaving, they are firmly determined to pursue the road of Good Desert.

The *chandis* Gatot Kocho and Andorowati, falling into hopeless ruin, will soon be remembered only by their location, like the *chandi* Parikesit, and it is a pity to think of those which left no trace at all, whose very names are forgotten. The state of affairs on the Diëng plateau, said Captain, now Major T. van Erp,[1] commissioned for the restoration of the Boro Budoor, leaves everything to be desired. . . .

[1] Reporting to the *Batavian Society of Arts and Sciences*, January 11, 1909.

Villages came into existence and expanded. The inhabitants need stone substructures in building their houses and it is a matter of course that they use temple stones for that purpose; these are here much smaller than those of the monuments in the valley of the Progo and the plain of Prambanan, easily carried off and exactly of the right size. . . . This is the case of the spoliation of the temples on the Diëng in a nutshell. But it should be added that the natives are not the only offenders. So much, indeed, is implied in Major van Erp's anecdote of a tourist who, examining the statuary adorning the grounds of the *pasangrahan*, a remarkable collection formed from miscellaneous loot, was invited to make his choice, the selected plunder to be delivered at Wonosobo in consideration of five guilders (a little over eight shillings). Many others had the same experience: numberless statues and stones carved into ornament have been appropriated by official and unofficial visitors to enrich museums and private collections. The appointment of Wielandt Sr., later of Wielandt Jr. as keeper of the *pasangrahan* and of the antiquities in a region of archaeological interest equal to Pompeii and Herculaneum, without any funds whatsoever at their disposal, was only an incident in the continuous farce performed by the Dutch East Indian Government in all its relations to monumental Java up to the date of its laborious confinement of the Archaeological Commission—and after, as I shall have abundant occasion to show: a farce with consequences sad to contemplate. This applies to antiquities of every description. I turn to my diary: In different places, when digging, layers of ashes are found with charred human bones imbedded, and often trinkets. The natives, however, keep their treasure-troves secret for fear of the Government, which has decreed, and rightly, reserving its rights, that they may not sell without asking for and obtaining permission, but appropriates everything it hears of, at ridiculously low prices; a good deal is therefore sold and bought privately, notwithstanding the prohibition, even by officials; a systematic search never having been attempted, none the less fine trifles are unearthed and not always trifles either; last night, in the *pasangrahan*, some rings were shown to me; the owner, acting very mysteriously, produced at last a statuette from under his *baju*, about six inches of solid gold, beautifully wrought; its mate, equal in height, material and workmanship, he had been forced to sell, according to his story, for seventy guilders (less than £6); he wanted more to part with this one and it is certainly worth many and many times that sum; a change in the usual sordid Government practice would result in remarkable discoveries; recently, as Dr. L. told me, an inscribed stone was laid bare; when trying to have a look at it the same day, his informant told him that it had already been spirited away to prevent *susah* (trouble); not much is necessary to be sentenced to *krakal* (hard labour in the chain-gang) at Wonosobo.

It is true the Government sent some one to the Diëng, about fifty years ago, to photograph the temples as they then existed and, fortunately, the operator chosen was I. van Kinsbergen who, having made his début in Java as a member of an opera-troupe, developed a rare artistic sense in portraying the deteriorating outlines of the ancient fanes of the island. But there the matter rested until the complaints became too loud and in 1910 hopes were held out that steps would be taken to clear the ruins of parasitic vegetation, to drain the plateau by repairing the trenches and conduits still in working order since the Hindu period, incidentally to consider the possibility of restoring the sanctuaries not yet tumbled down. Names I heard in connection with this charge, make me tremble, writes a correspondent from Batavia, for a repetition of the vandalism committed in the plain of Prambanan, particularly the criminal assaults on the *chandi* Plahosan and the *chandi* Sewu, where a Government commissioner tried to arrest further decay on the homoeopathic principle: *similia similibus curantur*. Government solicitude for conservation proves often more destructive than simple neglect and, to take an illustration from the Diëng itself (others will be culled in the course of my observations, from a plentiful supply of official *bêtises* and *bévues*, if not worse, in other localities), no sooner was general attention drawn to the enigmatic sign, described by Junghuhn and copied in his standard work from a rock between the lakes Warna and Pengilon, than it began to fade. Still quite clear in 1885 and up to 1895, despite its having been exposed to wind and weather during ten centuries (as surmised), it became fainter and fainter after that year, the process of a gradual loss of colour being duly noted at subsequent visits, until in 1902 I found it hardly distinguishable. To make up for the injury, a Contrôleur discovered, in 1889, supplementary tokens, not black but red, on the same Batu Tulis, or Watu Ketèq as the natives rather call it, "monkey-stone", because they recognise in the figure recorded by Junghuhn, a likeness to the animal referred to. The smaller red letters, or whatever they were intended for, steadily increasing in number, appearing in places where I had never noticed anything before, I could not help suspecting the little shepherds who look so innocent and shy and hardly venture an answer when spoken to, of knowing more about this miraculous growth of a hieroglyphic inscription than their artlessness implied. For all their stolid mien, the natives are exceedingly fond of a joke and what greater sport can be imagined than to get the wise men of Batavia and of European centres of erudition by the ears, inciting them to raise always more learned dust in their efforts to decipher the undecipherable characters of an impossible language, each being cocksure of the infallibility of his individual interpretation? If, however, we have not to do with Kromo or Wongso his mark, the ghost of the Batu Tulis must be held responsible for, among the incorporeal inhabitants of the many caves in this neighbourhood, the dweller beneath the monkey-stone is of greatest occult potency and the good people who come from the adjoining lowland districts, even from Surakarta and Jogjakarta, to hear and translate the voices of the Diëng, repair hither, after partaking of good advice in the Bimo temple, to *sembah* (make their salutation) before the entrance and ask *slamat* (blessing and success) on their foreshadowed undertakings. Nocturnal devotions inside the cave of the Watu Ketèq on a lucky, right lucky, carefully calculated night, means untold wealth, and whoevèr dares to brave the resident sprite of darkness with that desire in his heart, as very few do, and still remains a poor devil, has doubtless skipped a word of power in muttering his incantations or disregarded some other essential observance.

To the lover of mountain scenery it is far more profitable to wait for dawn near the triangulation pillar and point of junction of four residencies: Samarang, Pekalongan, Banyumas and the Bagelen, with a fifth, the Kadu, only a few paces off, when the Eye of Day rises to divide the waters behind the mountains and the rack of clouds, and, to the north and the south of the island, the sea begins to glimmer in the azure and orange tints sent before to meet the melting gray of vanquished darkness. Following its course in all-compassing space, the soul enters into silent communion with nature, the divine creation of the supremely divine which teaches feeble men how to worship. Such moments bring a wholesome chastening of the flesh and as we descend, goaded by the fierce darts of the conqueror overhead who makes the earth wrap herself in her vapoury robe of protection, veiling the grand vision,—as we descend where the runnels descend that feed the Serayu and the Tulis winding its way to the Kawah Kidang, we find the plain with the *chandis* one immense temple of adoration. The Vedic subtle body yearns to enter the sheath of prayer, to be moulded by its creator into the form fit for union with the spirit of the world; respiration becomes aspiration to the beatitude of manifest truth, of final rest in extinction of sin and shame and sorrow. So pass the hours in purification, in desire of a spark of the thought which breathes life into mortification of self. Then, at the passing of the light with the last flush from the West, in awe-inspiring stillness, the quivering stars lift their heads to watch the holy city of the dead; in clear-toned stillness, the night-wind moaning, the Rawa lamenting the lost civilisation of a lost religion whose symbols remain but are not understood, a mourning for humanity labouring in vain. The Diëng has been repopulated with a race between whose fanciful ideals, rooted in a forgotten past, and the rapacity of foreign rulers no lasting accord seems possible. Is it ordained that they, the thralls and the masters, shall continue in their present relations? Or will they disappear in their turn and, to quote Junghuhn, this mountain region revert to its free, natural state? Perhaps in the hour of upheaval native seers prophesy, when safety shall be found by none except to whom the Just Reckoner grants it. And mingling in one measure, which comprises the *jaman buda*, the time of bondage and the future, their dim notions of Mahadeva, the Beneficent Destroyer, and their conception of the dispensation of the Book, the leaders of religious exercise in the villages abide by their advice of submission until the true believers win the day, a day of glory for Islām, sure to arrive in the circular course of existence, which is nothing but Sansara, in attainment of Moslim brotherhood, which is nothing but Brahma Vihara, the sublime condition of love. Meanwhile, hearing is to be practised; haply it will lead to the comprehension of a lesson inculcated by each of the three creeds amalgamated in the Javanese mind and best expressed in the form borrowed from a fourth: The thing that hath been, is that which shall be; and that which is done, is that which shall be done,—or, in the version of the greatest poet of our own age: *Ciò che fu, torna e tornerà nei secoli.*[1]

[1] That which has been, returns and will return through all time.

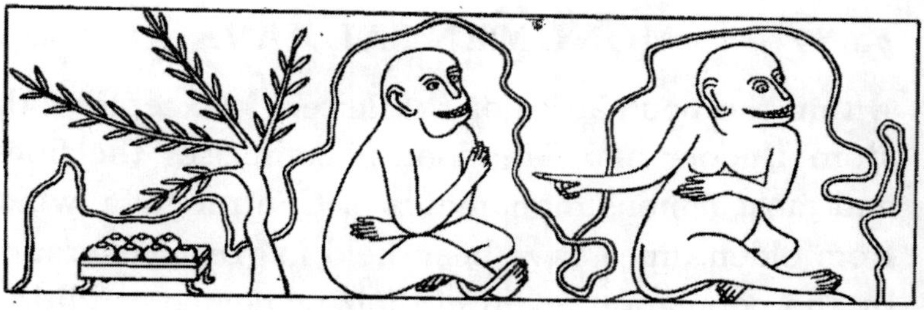

CHAPTER IV

PRAMBANAN

Queen Gertrude. . . .

. . . , all that lives must die,
Passing through nature to eternity.

WILLIAM SHAKESPEARE, *Hamlet, Prince of Denmark*, I., ii.

THE vast plain of Prambanan, which extends southward from the foot of the Merapi, one of Java's most active volcanoes,[1] is, or rather was, studded with Sivaïte and Buddhist temples. Called, in the later days of ignorance regarding their signification, after some outstanding feature (Sewu, Loomboong, Asu), after gods, demi-gods and heroes of romance (as on the Diëng), after the villages near which they were found (Kalasan or Kali Bening), or after their general position, a good many might share the appellation Prambanan. In speaking of *the* Prambanan temples, however, the group is meant which lies beside the main road between Surakarta and Jogjakarta, where the two residencies meet, but still

[1] Whence its name, derived from *api* (fire).

within the boundaries of the latter. Excepting the Boro Budoor and Mendoot, it comprises the finest and most famous monuments of Central Java, which from olden times have been held in great veneration by the population, even in their neglected condition, when reduced to little more than heaps of overgrown debris, lairs of wild animals. Freed from their luxurious vegetation and excavated, architectural remains of the first order came to light with sculptured ornament nowhere else surpassed in richness of detail and correctness of execution. Surrounded by ruins of a mainly Buddhist character, these buildings were consecrated to the Hindu Trinity with Siva leading the Trimoorti as Bhatara Guru, Master and Teacher of the World. A date recently discovered, 886 Saka (A.D. 964), or, according to another reading, 996 Saka (A.D. 1074), points to the period when Sivaïsm in Java had already become strongly impregnated with Buddhism, a circumstance fully borne out by the external decoration.

Among the natives, the Prambanan ruins go by the name of *chandi* Loro[1] Jonggrang because of the legend connected with their origin. Once upon a time Prambanan was ruled by a giant-king, Ratu Boko, possessed of an only daughter, Princess Jonggrang, and an adopted son, Raden Gupolo, whose father had been killed by command of the King of Pengging. Having sworn revenge, Raden Gupolo feigned love for the beautiful daughter of that

[1] The title Loro designates a lady of very high birth.

EAST FRONT OF THE SIVA (LORO JONGGRANG) TEMPLE OF THE PRAMBANAN GROUP IN 1895

(Cephas Sr.)

monarch and asked Ratu Boko to assist him in making her his wife. Ambassadors were despatched with instructions to negotiate the marriage. His Majesty of Pengging received them in a friendly manner and entertained them at his Court but, not wanting Raden Gupolo for a son-in-law, he sent secret agents in all directions to seek and bind to his service a hero with power to resist and subdue the giants, Ratu Boko's subjects, of whom he was in mortal fear. One of those emissaries, searching the slopes of the Soombing, met with the recluse Damar Moyo of the children of Sumendi Petoong, the chief of the *legèn*-drawers.[1] Damar Moyo's wife had blessed him with two sons, Bondowoso, a tall and strong fellow, and Bambang Kandilaras, less muscular but more favoured in outward appearance and of a gentler disposition, whom he recommended as just the man needed for the rescue of the Princess of Pengging and ready for the task, provided her royal father would consent, in consideration of the defeat of the giants, to give his daughter to the young man with half his kingdom as dowry and the other half to follow after his death—which conditions prove that even in those remote days the saintly did not despise worldly advantage. The King of Pengging consented and Bambang Kandilaras marched against Prambanan, but no weapon could harm Ratu Boko, who roared so dreadfully that the sound and his breath combined were enough to knock any human

[1] *Legèn* is the liquor prepared by fermentation of the sap drawn from some trees of the palm family.

foe down at a distance too far to distinguish a man from a woman or a giant from a *waringin*-tree. Bambang Kandilaras fled, reporting at Damar Moyo's cave, and was commanded to try once more with the assistance of his brother Bondowoso. They accomplished nothing. Bambang Kandilaras ran away even before the battle commenced, to hide himself in a ravine where the troops of Prambanan could not follow him, and Bondowoso, blown off his legs by a puff from Ratu Boko's formidable lungs, sought safety in precipitate retreat to the mountain Soombing. Then Damar Moyo taught him a magical word which, pronounced twice, would make him big and heavy as an elephant, and give him the strength of a thousand of those animals. Thus armed, Bondowoso returned to Prambanan, where he killed half of Ratu Boko's warriors in their sleep, while the other half, waking up, concentrated backward, with the enemy in hot pursuit, to tell their king what had happened. Nobody shall stir, said he ; I myself alone will settle this little business. Meeting Bondowoso near the village Tangkisan,[1] he began to roar as loud and fume as hard as he could but, to his astonishment, his breath lacked the accustomed power and so he had to fight for his life hand to hand. It was a terrible fight : houses and gardens were trampled down, forests rooted up and mountains kicked over, while the perspiration dripping from the bodies of the enraged combatants

[1] From *tangkis*, *tinangkis*, which, derived from *nangkis*, "ward off", means "to repel one another."

formed a large pool, the Telaga Powiniyan.[1] To end the struggle, Bondowoso, in a supreme effort, seized Ratu Boko round the middle and threw him into that pool, where he sank and, drowning, made the earth tremble with a last roar of anger and distress.[2] Raden Gupolo, hearing the noise, hastened to his assistance with a few drops of the water of life in a cup, an elixir prepared by Mboq Loro Jonggrang,—only a few drops, but enough to resuscitate the dead giant-king if put to his lips. Bambang Kandilaras, however, drew his bow and, from the place where he had watched the fight, shot the cup out of the hand of Raden Gupolo, who thereupon attacked Bondowoso. Bambang Kandilaras let more arrows fly at the giant-warriors of Prambanan, who now rushed up to avenge their king's death. In the general *mêlée* Bondowoso killed also Raden Gupolo and cut off his head, which he threw away in an easterly direction, changing it into a mountain, the Gunoong Gampeng; but his brains and heart he threw away in a south-westerly direction, changing them into another mountain, the Gunoong Woongkal. Thereupon he defeated the remaining half of the army of Prambanan and repaired to Pengging, claiming the reward for his brother. The king of that country, glad to be rid of the giants, was as good as his

[1] *Telaga* means "lake" and *powiniyan*, derived from *winih*, "seed", means a flooded ricefield in which the ears on the stalks, bound in sheaves, are put to serve for seeding.

[2] Not the last, as this legend has it, for Ratu Boko's roaring can yet be heard on still nights, if we may believe the people who dwell on the banks of the Telaga Powiniyan.

word, wedded his beautiful daughter to Bambang Kandilaras and appointed Bondowoso his viceroy in Prambanan, with the rank and title of *bupati*. Taking up his abode in the palace of the late Raden Gupolo, Bondowoso happened to see Mboq Loro Jonggrang, who continued living in the *kraton* of Ratu Boko, and fell in love with her. He asked her hand in marriage and she, abhorring the man who had killed her father, and one so unprepossessing in countenance too, but afraid to provoke his displeasure by a blank refusal, answered that she was willing to become his wife on condition of his providing a suitable *sasrahan* or wedding-present, nothing more nor less than six deep wells in six buildings, the like of which no mortal eye had ever seen, with a thousand statues of the former kings of Prambanan and their divine ancestors, the gods in heaven, all to be dug and built and carved in one night. Bondowoso called in the help of his father, the recluse Damar Moyo, of the King of Pengging and of his brother Bambang Kandilaras, all three of whom responded, going to Prambanan and uniting in prayer on the day before the night agreed upon by the spirits of the lower regions, who had been commandeered for the task by the saint of the mountain Soombing. The evening fell and as soon as darkness enveloped the earth a weird sound was heard of invisible hands busy laying foundations, erecting walls and sculpturing statuary. By half past three o'clock the six wells were dug, the six buildings completed and nine hundred and ninety-nine statues standing in their places. But Mboq Loro Jonggrang, roused from her slumbers by the hammering and chiselling, and suspecting what was going on, ordered her handmaidens out to stamp the *padi*[1] and to strew the ground, where the noise was loudest, with flowers and to sprinkle perfume. The spirits of the lower regions cannot bear the odour of flowers and perfumes, as everybody knows; so they had to desist and deserted their almost finished work in precipitate flight, to the consternation of Bondowoso, who pronounced this curse: Since the girls of Prambanan take pleasure in fooling a faithful suitor, may the gods grant that they shall have to wait long before they become brides![2] Having said this, yet hoping against hope, he called on his lady, who asked tauntingly whether the honour of his visit meant the announcement that the task imposed upon him by way of testing his love, had been completed. This filled the measure and he answered: No, it is not and you shall complete it yourself. The threat was immediately realised: Loro Jonggrang changed into a statue of stone, the thousandth, which terminated the labour of the spirits and is still to be seen in a niche on the north side of the principal edifice.

[1] *Padi* is rice in the hull, shelled by the women and girls, usually very early in the morning, by stamping it in blocks of wood hollowed out for the purpose.

[2] Bondowoso's curse took dire effect and the Javanese lassies of the neighbourhood, who enter the bonds of matrimony about their fourteenth year, comment with sarcastic pity on the fact that their sisters of Prambanan have, as a rule, to wait some ten rainy seasons longer—not without seeking compensation, it is alleged, after the example set by their patron saint Loro Jonggrang, whose maidenly life, according to the *babad chandi Sewu*, of which more later on, was not altogether blameless.

The reader will recognise in this legend the hoary eastern material of many others current also in western lands. It pervades the legendary lore connected with the plain of Prambanan in widest sense, and one of its many variations, to be recorded farther on, applies specially to the Buddhist *chandi* Sewu or "thousand temples", only a little distance from the Loro Jonggrang group;[1] in fact, originally adapted to account for the many ruins scattered over a vast area in that region, it has taken separate forms to meet the requirements of separate localities. Apart from tradition, we owe the oldest extant description of the Prambanan antiquities to the East India Company's servant Lons at Samarang, who wrote in 1733. The Governor-General van Imhoff referred to them in 1746 and Raffles, his successor during the British Interregnum, not satisfied with writing and talking alone, commissioned Cornelius with Wardenaar to survey them and make plans for reconstruction. After 1816 things returned to the accustomed neglect: A short stay in the plain of Prambanan, says an authority already quoted,[2] is sufficient to note that thousands of valuable hewn and sculptured stones have been and still are used for all sorts of purposes . . .; from time immemorial, great quantities of stone have been (and

[1] The very precise ridicule this appellation, which originated in the childish credulity of the natives, who persist in paying homage to a statue of Doorga as if it were actually their petrified Mboq Loro Jonggrang; but the real name of the group being unknown, why should we reject a distinction not denoted by the less definite term Prambanan?

[2] Major, then still Captain T. VAN ERP in his report to the *Batavian Society of Arts and Sciences*, January 11, 1909.

still are) taken from Prambanan by his Highness the Sooltan of Jogjakarta, generally once or twice a year . . .; this happens, if I am well informed, in compliance with a written demand, fiated by the local authorities. The foundation, in 1885, of the Archaeological Society of Jogjakarta, which undertook the excavation of the parts of the Loro Jonggrang group covered with debris and vegetation, and the clearing of the whole, did little to ameliorate the situation with respect to the carrying away from the Prambanan temples, speaking collectively, of stones for the building of houses, factories, etc., and of ornament for the decoration of private grounds and gardens. Though bills were posted all over the ruins, including Doorga's, alias Loro Jonggrang's sanctum, prohibiting, by order of that Society, the salving of gods and goddesses with *boreh* and the defacing of the walls with inscriptions, its members themselves dragged statues away to fill a so-called museum of their contrivance at the provincial capital, dislocating things of beauty, ranging the *disjecta membra* on scaffoldings in a shed as crockery on the shelves of a cupboard. The monuments of Prambanan being primarily mausolea, their first concern was to dig for the *saptaratna*, the seven treasures buried with the ashes of the dead under the images of the deities hallowing those perishable remains. The plunder consisted in urns containing, besides the ashes, coins, rubies and other precious stones, pieces of gold- and silver-leaf with cut figures (serpents, tortoises, flowers), strips of gold-foil inscribed with ancient characters, fragments of copper and glass, etc. The mortuary pits easiest to rifle, had already been emptied before the semi-official spoilers turned their attention to them. This chapter is not the most glorious in the history of the Archaeological Society of Jogjakarta which, on the other hand, started a work too long neglected by the Dutch Government, even after Raffles' vigorous initial effort. Incidentally it promoted the schemes of the superficial yet very ambitious, pushing to the front on the strength of what should have been put to the credit of more capable but, to their detriment, more modest labourers in the archaeological field: It is not always the most deserving horses that get the oats, says a Dutch proverb.

The Sivaïte character of the temples of Prambanan would be sufficiently indicated, if there were no other proofs, by the sepulchral cavities they inclose and which define them as the monuments of a graveyard consecrated to the memory of the great and mighty of Hindu Mataram, who worshipped Siva as Mahadeva, the Supreme God, Paramesvara, the Maker, the Maintainer, the Marrer to make again. Sepulchral pits or wells are, indeed, the Sivaïte hall-mark in the architecture of Java and here, at Prambanan, we find, in so far as preserved, the finest of the edifices raised to encompass and revet such pits, temple-tombs built for the glorification of the Creator in creative consciousness, highest boon granted to humanity, a glimmering of his All-

SIVA (LORO JONGGRANG) TEMPLE OF THE PRAMBANAN GROUP IN 1901

(Cephas Sr.)

Soul which, leaving the dust to return to dust, aspires to union with the Uncreated. A central group of eight shrines, once surrounded by numberless smaller ones, witnesses, in soberness of well-balanced outline, in precision of detail, to the exquisite art of those Hindu-Javanese master-builders who, like the architects of our old cathedrals, were unconcerned as to the opinion of man, but had the adoration of the godhead in mind and made the whole world partake of the divine blessing which quickened heart and hand, whether then descending from Siva's nature as the essence of the Trimoorti, or from the sublime truth symbolised in the Christian Holy Trinity. The marvels of design and execution still standing at Prambanan in their dilapidated state, on a terrace excavated in 1893–4, were arranged, with the smaller ones now altogether gone, in a square whose sides faced the cardinal points. The material used in their construction was a kind of trachyte which, originally yellowish and hard to chisel into shape, has assumed a dark gray colour and by the richness of the sculptured ornament gives an impression as if easily moulded like wax. The three western temples, of which the one in the middle, consecrated to Siva or, according to the natives, the *chandi* Loro Jonggrang proper, is the largest, correspond each with a smaller structure to the east; still smaller *chandis* bound the space between the two rows to the north and south. The buildings dedicated to the Trimoorti, set squarely with a square projection on each side, rest on basements of the same polygonous conformation, so much in favour with the architects of that period; the inner rooms are on an elevated level because of their position over the vault-like compartments saved out in the substructures, and can be reached by staircases, once provided with porches, leading to the storeyed galleries. Vestiges of 157 diminutive *chandis* outside the rampart which encircled the central group, testify to the former existence of many and many more, shut in by a second and a third demolished wall. A closer inspection of the ruins, revealing beauties not yet departed, leads to an apprehension of what has been irrevocably lost. These temples of the three gods who are but one, always reminded me in their pathetic desolation of the *capellas imparfeitas* of Santa Maria da Victoria; what is incomplete, however, unfinished at Batalha, has run to decay at Prambanan—there the budding promise and arrested blossoming of an artistic idea, here the scattered petals of the full-blown flower rudely broken off its stem.

Siva is the keynote of the Prambanan group, Siva, the Jagad, the Bhatara Guru, according to his prevalent title in the island. In the temple which bears his name, he appeared as the leader in the exterior chapel looking south; his wife, Doorga, looks north; their first-born, Ganesa, looks west. The latter, sitting on his lotus cushion, is represented as the Ekadanta, the elephant deprived of one of his tusks when fighting Parashu Rama; a third eye in

PRAMBANAN RELIEFS

(C. Nieuwenhuis.)

his forehead betokens his keenness of sight; he wears in his crown the emblematic skull and crescent of his father; one of his left hands brandishes his father's battle-axe; one of his right hands holds the string of beads suggesting prayer; his father's *upawita*, the hooded snake, is strung round his left shoulder and breast. Doorga, his mother, born from the flames which proceeded from the mouths of the gods, stands on the steer she killed when the terrific animal had stormed Indra's heaven and humiliated the immortals; her eight hands[1] wield the weapons and other gifts bestowed upon her by the deities at their delivery: Vishnu's discus, Surya's arrows, etc. etc., while her nethermost right hand seizes the enemy's tail and her nethermost left hand the shaggy locks of the demon Maheso, who tries to escape with the monster's life. This magnificent piece of sculpture, highly dramatic and yet within the limits of plastic art, the unknown maker having instinctively obeyed the rules formulated in Lessing's *Laokoon*, some thousand years after his labours were ended, is the petrified Lady Jonggrang, victim of Bondowoso's revengeful love. It does not matter to the native that Siva has always claimed her as his consort, if not under the name of Doorga then under that of Kali or Uma, ever since she, Parvati, the Mother of Nature, divided herself into three female entities to marry her three sons, who are none but he who sits enthroned as Mahadeva in the inner

[1] The sculptor showed his independence by disregarding the more canonical number of sixteen or ten.

chamber, looking east, with his less placid personifications, the *dvarapalas* (doorkeepers) Nandisvara and Mahakala, the wielders of trident and cudgel, guarding the entrance, supported by demi-gods and heroes. The colossal statue of their heavenly lord, broken into pieces by the falling roof, has been restored and replaced on its *padmasana* (lotus cushion). In this shape the god wears the *makuta* (crown) with skull and crescent, has a third eye in his forehead and a cobra strung round his left shoulder and breast; his body, decked with a tiger's skin, rests against the *prabha*, his aureole; one of his left hands holds his fly-flap, one of his right hands his string of beads; of his trident only the stick remains.

Siva, the one of dreadful charm, is everywhere, either personified or in his attributes: he dominates the external decoration of the Vishnu and the Brahma temples too, in the latter case as *guru*, even to the exclusion of all other gods; the middle *chandi* of the eastern row, facing his principal shrine, has his *vahana*, the bull; the one to the north his smaller image, while in the third, to the south, wholly demolished, no statuary can be traced. The inner chambers of the subordinate buildings show more plainly than that of Siva, which is adorned with flowery ornament, that the Sivaïte style concentrated ornamentation rather on the exterior than on the interior. The four statues of Brahma, the master of the four crowned countenances, who lies shattered among the debris of his temple, and the four statues of Vishnu in his (a large one with *makuta*, *prabha*, *chakra* and *sanka*, and three smaller ones, representing him in his fourth and fifth *avatar* and in his married state with his *sakti* Lakshmi in miniature on his left arm), are chastely conceived in the chaste surroundings of their chapels. In addition to the sorely damaged *Ramayana* reliefs, presently to be spoken of, they dwell, however simple the interior arrangement of their cells may be, among richly carved images of their peers and followers stationed outside: Vishnu among his own less famous *avatars* and supposed Bodhisatvas between female figures; Brahma, as already remarked, among personifications of the ubiquitous Siva in his quality of teacher, accompanied by bearded men of holiness. Siva's *nandi*, a beautifully moulded humped bull, emblem of divine virility, watches his master's abode, attentive to the word of command,—watches day and night as symbolised by Surya, the beaming sun, carrying the flowers of life when rising behind her seven horses, and by Chandra, the three-eyed moon, drawn by ten horses, waving a banner and also presenting a flower, but one wrapped in a cloud. The *chandis* of the eastern row, fortunately not yet despoiled of these striking specimens of Sivaïte sculpture, the statue of Siva opposite the Vishnu temple and enough to enable one to recognise that they too had once a band of ornament in high and low relief, emphasise even in the ruinous condition of their substructures, polygonous like those of the larger temples but on square foundations, the mystery attaching to the fascination exercised by the main building they supplement, and whose decoration, strictly Sivaïtic on the inside while partaking of the Buddhistic on the outside, has racked many brains for an explanation. The bo-trees and prayer-bells, profusely employed in its external embellishment, together with figures agreeable to the Bodhisatva theory, have led some to advance the opinion that it is a purely Buddhist creation, though perhaps tinged with Sivaïte notions. They were met with the objection that there is no sign of a dagob as distinguishing Buddhist feature; that the riddle of the resemblance between the statuary on the outside of the Siva temple and the conventional representation of Bodhisatvas, could find its solution in the canonisation or deification of kings and famous chiefs, a practice as old as ancestor-worship, which held its own in Java from pre-Hindu days up to our own. However this may be, if the Prambanan temples, and especially the one particularly dedicated to the great god of the Trimoorti, preached orthodox Sivaïsm to the elect of its innermost conviction, while tainted externally with the heresy of the deniers of the existence of gods, the indubitably Buddhist Mendoot reverses the process. This and the syncretism discernible in nearly all the *chandis* of Java, shows the religious tolerance of the Javanese in the Hindu period. And religiously tolerant they are still as true believers in the true faith of Islām; the fanaticism one occasionally hears of, roots rather in discontent from economic causes

VIII.

PRAMBANAN RELIEFS

(Cephas Sr.)

than in bigotry or over-zealous devotion to a creed which declares rebellion for conscience' sake against a firmly established rule that recognises it, to be unlawful.

The demi-gods and heroes with their followers on the outside of the Siva temple, occupy, counting from the base upward, the third tier of ornamentation, also the highest in the roofless condition of the building: the few niches left above are empty. Beneath, the story of Rama, an incarnation of Vishnu, is told in bas-reliefs which belong to the very best Hindu sculpture discovered in Java or anywhere else. The division of the casements is effected by bo-trees, sitting lions and standing or dancing women in haut-relief, especially the last being of exquisite workmanship. In endlessly varying attitudes, embracing one another or tripping the light fantastic toe, retreating and advancing, their measured steps being regulated by the musicians on interspersed panels, they represent the *apsaras*, nymphs of heaven, adorning the house of prayer to acquaint mortal man with the joys in store for the doer of good. The human birds and other mythical animals under the bo-trees, the prayer-bells and flowers in the garlanded foliage, enhance the charm of this ingenious decoration, the splendidly limbed virgins disporting themselves in a frame of imposing magnificence, their graceful movements being worthily seconded by the sumptuous setting. Nor does this wealth of detail, this marvellous display of artistic power, of skill perfected by imaginative thought, divert the attention from the divine idea embodied in Siva or from the introduction to its understanding provided by the *Ramayana*, initiating the beholder's intelligence by degrees. All is so well balanced that the lower guides to the higher in whetting comprehensive desire. First, on reaching the terrace, starting from the low level of vulgar interest, curiosity and sympathy are awakened by the epic which shared popular favour with the *Brata Yuda*. It is not known who enriched the literature of Java with a version of the *Ramayana* adapted to Javanese requirements; as in the case of the *Mahabharata* he was probably one of the poets living at the cultured courts of the eastern part of the island. Whatever his name, he made a hit with his tale of the god who descended from heaven, bent on flirting with the daughters of men, and won a wife, the tenderly loving Sita, by drawing Dhanusha, the mighty bow of Siva. His success may be appraised by the circumstance that scenes taken from his poem were deemed suitable to embellish the tombs of sovereign rulers. Can it be called an improvement after more than a thousand years of progressive western civilisation that we, to honour the memory of our dead, make shift with inflated epitaphs advertising virtues in life often conspicuous by an absence which the maudlin angels of our cemeteries, rather than shedding undeserved, vicarious tears, perpetually seem to bemoan on their own account?

The adventures of Vishnu in his Rama guise are

IX.

PRAMBANAN RELIEFS

(Centrum.)

told from the moment of Dasharatha, King of Ayodhya, invoking his aid to make the royal consorts partake of the blessing of motherhood. Vishnu, resting on the seven-headed serpent of the sea, Sesha or Ananta, the one without end, dispenses a potion which makes Kantalya, who drinks half of it, conceive Rama; Kaykaji, who drinks a fourth part of it, Bharata; and the third spouse, who drinks the rest, the twins Lakshmana and Shatrughna. We can follow Vishnu, reborn from mortal woman, on the reliefs of the Siva temple, which are tolerably preserved, through the first stages of his earthly career as Rama, but must renounce studying his subsequent story on the exterior of the temples dedicated to himself and Brahma, where the third tier of sculpture has altogether disappeared, save a few mutilated bas-reliefs. That is a great pity, for the illustration of the *Ramayana* by the artists entrusted with the decoration of the *chandi* Prambanan, judging from what we still possess, marks the apogee of Hindu-Javanese art; revelling in accessory ornament, it never surfeits, keeping the leading idea well in view, every embellishment adding to its intrinsic value. The heavy moulding above the lowest band of chiselled work of the Siva temple has fortunately protected it from being damaged by falling stones; here we are able to discover the sculptor's technique at close quarters and it is worthy of note that some of the curly lions are wanting in their appointed places. This, coupled with the fact that a few of the *apsaras* remained unfinished, while others, like statues of gods on higher planes, have only been outlined, and spaces, evidently contrived for ornament, present flat surfaces, has led to the conjecture of a catastrophe which surprised the builders and made them suspend their labours as in the case of the Bimo temple of the Diëng plateau.

One of the salient features of the decoration at Prambanan, indeed of all ancient Javanese art, Sivaïte and Buddhist, is the representation of animal life as an important factor in human destiny. If the Buddha was called the Sakya Sinha, the Lion of the Sakyas, and his sylvan embodiment adorns in many reproductions the Boro Budoor, his stateliest temple, at Sivaïte Prambanan we find the king of the desert extensively utilised in the general decoration, together with the beasts of the field under the bo-trees and fanciful combinations of man and his lowly friends, not dumb but of different speech, like the *kinnaris*, the bird-people. The *Ramayana* bas-reliefs echo the kindness[1] shown to those humble companions in Indian myth, history and present-day asylums for the aged and infirm among them. Attending the monkey warriors with whose help the simian deity Hanoman restored King Sugriva to the throne of his forefathers at Kishkindhya (an allusion, it is thought, to the doughty deeds of the aborigines of the Deccan), *bajings*[2] and *bolooks*[2] are

[1] Stimulated especially by Buddhist and Jaïn influences.
[2] Squirrels: *Sciurus nigrovittatus* and *Pteromys elegans* and *nitidus*.

gambolling round the house of the Most Awful and Mysterious, once worshipped here by great nations whose very names are lost, but whose art, giving a place to all creation in symbolic expression of the divine, still teaches us the lesson that the animals are also children of the gods, endowed with life not to be exterminated to serve our pleasure and our vanity, or to be abused for our profit, but to enjoy the fullness of the earth and the good gifts of heaven as we do ourselves, or might do if we were wise. Mother Nature, Siva's *sakti* Doorga, nurses at her bosom all her husband's offspring, without distinction, and at Prambanan she superintends the growing world, as the mistress of his household, in the highly finished form the artist has given her: Loro Jonggrang, daughter of Ratu Boko of the Javanese legend. Not in her outward character of the demon-steer subduing virago does she attract her worshippers here, nor in that of the woman of the golden skin riding the tiger, full of menace, but in that of Uma, the gentle goddess who sheds light on perplexing problems of conduct, to whom one turns in distress. Ideal of high-born loveliness, Loro Jonggrang is especially venerated by those of her own sex who are in trouble or have a desire to propound in the fumes of incense they burn: barren matrons praying for issue from their bodies to their lords and masters, like the wives of King Dasharatha; virgins anxious to get married; pseudo-virgins who have trusted too much in the promises of their lovers, following the *hadat* established by herself at Prambanan and diligently observed (not only, it should be noticed, in that neighbourhood, but likewise where no one ever heard of Loro Jonggrang and her *escapades d'amour*), insisting that, in the name of the precedent she set, consequences shall be warded off. When *pasar*, *i.e.* market, falls on a Friday,[1] her votaries are exceptionally numerous, mostly native women entreating deliverance from female ills or help in the attainment of feminine wishes. Chinese, half-caste and occasionally European ladies may, however, be observed among them: it is said that several happy mothers of the ruling race at Jogjakarta and Surakarta owe their husbands and children to Notre Dame de Bon Secours of Prambanan; that brides having obtained their heart's desire in union with the beloved, the bridegrooms in their turn repair to her shrine, after a honeymoon ended in storm-clouds, with an earnest supplication for means of release. This explains the sprinkling of males among the fair devotees on Fridays, dejected looking persons who smear the statue of Doorga with *boreh*, despite notices to desist, supplicating her to repeal former decrees, having different objects in view, of course, with their salvings of Ganesa and Siva's *nandi*. Favours are requested, pledges are given, votive sacrifices are performed, the gods and their attributes, Mboq Loro Jonggrang in the first place, are

[1] *Pasar* is held once every five days and once every thirty-five days it falls, therefore, on a Friday.

X.

PRAMBANAN RELIEFS

(Centrum.)

wreathed and festooned with flowers in compliance with an old Hindu custom so deeply rooted that we may notice grave, turbaned *hajis* yielding to it, unheedful of the Prophet's anathemas against those who commit the unpardonable sin of idolatry, straying more widely from the right path than the brute cattle, wicked doers, companions of hell-fire whose everlasting couch shall be on burning coals.

As the exhalations of the incense rise to the dying rays of the sun and mix with the scent of the *kembangan telon*, the flowers of sacrifice, *melati*, *kananga* and *kantil*, the soughing of the trees in the evening breeze repeats the lessons taught by an ancient inscription found near the temples of Prambanan, and a summary of which Hindu-Javanese *Libro del Principe*, taken from a translation by a Panambahan of Sumanap, may be acceptable: What has been here set down, was in the beginning an ancestral tradition, very useful if observed, but, if disregarded, it becomes a curse. This inscription was made in the year 396 (?), in the third month, on a Friday in the sixth era. Let it inform you of the most exalted, of the road to enlightenment and happiness, to attain your country's progress and prosperity. Proof thereof will be cheap food and raiment, and universal peace, that those who honour the gods may lead tranquil lives. Honouring the gods is the perfection of conduct. Whosoever strives after that will be smiled upon by them, for the practising of virtue provides access to heaven, which shines in splendour, and all gods will unite with the supreme Siva Bathara Indra to assist the practiser of virtue. But whosoever does wrong will go to perdition and his appearance will be monstrous, his shape like the shape of a dog; such a one acts unwisely because he turns away from virtue and obeys his passions, which are his enemies. It seems good to know this in life, in order to practise virtue and praise the godhead, believing in Bhatara, who has power over the world, possessing heaven and earth. The teachers must also be respected, without exception, because of their venerable charge, and you must learn of them to honour Bathara above all gods, the Omnipotent, the Ruler and Maintainer of everything. Praise him in order that you may gain happiness and bliss even while you live on earth. Honour your parents and the parents of your parents and their teachings, which are inviolable, as they before you considered inviolable the teachings which came to them from their parents and ancestors as received from the god Bathara, who opened their hearts to probity. Know that they were allowed to adorn themselves with fragrant flower-buds wherever their influence penetrated: this will also be your privilege after the purification of your minds. Conduct yourselves honestly according to divine direction, acquire discretion and try to resemble the illustrious kings of the past who compassed the felicity of their subjects. Be no regarders of persons either among the good or among

XI.

PRAMBANAN RELIEFS
(Centrum.)

the bad; all are mortals in a fleeting world. This consider: Bathara is the King of Kings who ordains the holy institutions. Fill the place of a father among his children. If there are any of your subjects who act wickedly, command them to mend their ways; if they persist in evil, teach them to distinguish between what is good and what is bad in their souls, to the advantage of the living. Excellent men must be appointed to manage the affairs of the people. These three things are of highest importance: that proper instruction be given; that your subjects become prosperous instead of poor through oppression; that every one of them know the boundaries of his fields. Persevere in honouring Bathara! Glorify him and inherit joy! Dress cleanly and keep your bodies clean. Acknowledge the omnipotence of Bathara Giri Nata and, protected by him, no one can harm you. May his superiority be reflected in you to confound the wicked doers. If you desire a change of station, seek seclusion to do penance in order that Bathara's brilliancy may become visible in you. Nothing is so beautiful and so profitable to you as the conquest of your passions, subduing them to a pure mind and lofty aspirations, vanquishing the enemies of virtue who reveal themselves: it will help to proclaim your lustrous righteousness. Glorify Bathara! He will descend in his beneficence to show you the way. Reflect seriously: some day you must die; ponder over the mystery of life and make the ignorant understand for their own salvation. Behaving in this manner, happiness cannot escape you, kings of good rule, all of whose prayers will be listened to and with whom no one can be compared: this is the sign of the eminence of the sovereign who dominates men as the tiger dominates whàtever breathes in the forest. The gods will protect such kings to the benefit of their subjects, traders and carriers of merchandise and labourers in the fields. Nothing is denied to the obedient, for the gods ward off evil from their thrones; evil is known in heaven before it touches the mortals on earth. Glorify Bathara! The men of rank and high birth who serve kings, must be of middle age. In their fiftieth year it behoves them to retire from the world into prayerful solitude to die as a child dies; let the body suffer for the soul, crowning the end of life. As you grow in knowledge your wishes will be fulfilled and your soul will leave its prison. The token of higher knowledge is evident. Where does the soul go? It gains in beatitude or, if no progress has been made, it seeks a refuge in the bodies of animals and people of mean appetites. Gaining in beatitude, it reaches heaven, the garden of rest, but hell is the abode of sin. Cleanse, therefore, your thoughts; eschew impurity! Do not favour the wealthy, nor despise the poor; all are equally confided to your care. O ye, who are kings and represent the gods in your kingdoms, listen to this admonition and know your responsibility for the ultimate lot of your subjects. Bathara, the lord of life and death, will call you to account. Woman has been created inferior to man; but many men are enticed to wrong-doing by the smooth speech of their womenfolk, who lack perception by the inscrutable decree of the gods. Woman wishes to control man, taking her caprice for wisdom, always pressing him to follow her fancies. The chronicles, however, mention the names of queens like Sri Chitra Wati, Sinta Devi and Sakjrevati Drupadi. In the days of Dhipara Jaga, Tirta Jaga, Karta Jaga and Sang Ngara bloody wars devastated the land; kings were bewitched and changed into dragons and elephants because they disregarded the ordinances of Bathara and also because they were weak, not able to restrain their burning passion for beautiful women, acting differently from that which behoves those in authority. Possess your souls in continence! Bathara watches and you are unacquainted with the hour of your death.

The shadows of evening thicken; darkness gathers, darkness in the train of Rahu, the devourer of sun and moon, robing the temples in gloom. Fire-flies, darting from between the sculptured bo-trees and festooned foliage, begin to hold their nocturnal feast but subside before a red glare, nascent in the holy of holies. They return, as if borne by strange, wild melodies, and grow into the luxurious forms of luminous nymphs, the *apsaras*, who leave their stations round the house of fear to dance their voluptuous dance of death, renouncing their allegiance to the Mahadeva to court Kama of the flowery bow, consumed by the desire to enjoy life and life's best before the approach of the mower cutting them down. Their mates, the *gandharvas*, excite them in their weird revelry with songs and the musicians urge them with the clang of tabors and cymbals. Shaped for the enchanting arts of love, skilled in the wiles of female magic, they move in a whirl of passion, like flames of fire, more redoubtable to man than the sword and arrows of his bitterest foe. Luring the unwary who tarry at Prambanan when the fates, weaving the web of the world, change the colours of day into night's blackest dyes, when the lotus-blossoms hang heavy on their stems and the air is burdened with the odour of incense and sacrificial wreaths, they intend his subversion by a mirage of delight, a hallucination of the senses, and present the gratification of carnal desire as the triumph of reason. Woe to him if he does not resist in the delirium of his infatuation! The moment he tries to grasp their flitting forms, they evade him as a mountain stream in spate, as the spray of its water dashing down the rocks, as foam on the surging brine. The *apsaras* mock, the *gandharvas* hiss him, the musicians howl, all turning again to stone, having instilled their subtle poison into his heart. He seeks in vain the joy they held out to him, begs in vain for a draught of the *soma*, the nectar of the gods. Then, shooting out from the great god's abode as a flash of lightning, the red glare takes substance and Siva appears in his most terrible aspect, Kala, destroying time, waving the skull which springs from the lotus stem,

XII.

PRAMBANAN RELIEFS

(Centrum.)

menacing men and cattle, the wild beasts of the woods, the fowl of the air and the fish of the sea, with the *trishula*, the trident of desolation. Behind him the Devi, his spouse, emerges from her niche, riding Vayu, the stormwind, not Doorga or Uma disguised as Loro Jonggrang, but Kali, the furious, of hideous countenance, crowned with snakes, dripping with blood. Lifting up her voice above the roaring of her steed, she joins the Dread One, Rudra, the Thunderer, and passion and baffled desire become a portion of the tempest she raises, the odour of the *kembangan telon* breathing agony. Mahakala, the Almighty Overthrower, deals death under his veil. But if the night of terror begins in darkness, it will end in dawn and light of day: all that lives, is born to die for new life to succeed, and so teaches Siva himself, the Bhatara Guru. In adoration of Ganesa, the fruit of his union with Parvati, wisdom will accrue to him who learns the lesson; enlightenment from the spectacle of time, the demolisher, fortifying fecund nature, reanimating the universe in anguish of decay. Wisdom is the great gift, purification of the soul in abstinence from the pleasures which drag it down, to keep the spark of the divine undefiled in its earthly sheath with the aid of the father and the son, whose distinctive qualities merge in Wighnesa, the vanquisher of obstacles. Drinking their essence, man's hearing and knowing leads to affection and commiseration, to the second Brahma Vihara, the sublime condition of sorrow at the sorrow of others, and when dissolution arrives as a reward, Yama, the judge of the dead, will find no cause for reproach. The good will enter the diamond gate, but grievous torment awaits the foolish who pamper the flesh and are ensnared by the daughters of lust.

CHAPTER V

MORE OF CENTRAL JAVA

Le bon sens nous dit que les choses de la terre n'existent que bien peu et que la vraie réalité est dans les rêves. CHARLES BAUDELAIRE, *Les Paradis Artificiels* (*Dédication*).

EXCEPT during a period of some four centuries and a half, from about 940 till the palmy days of Mojopahit, when declining Hindu civilisation, for reasons as yet unexplained, sought a refuge farther east, Central Java and especially that part of it known in our time as the Principalities, *i.e.* Surakarta and Jogjakarta, has always been the heart of the island. There lived and live the true Javanese, the people of heaven's mercy, cherishing their old traditions; these and the beautiful scenery of their fire-mountains and fertile valleys are still theirs, whatever else may fail: glory, power and freedom. They lived and live in their world of custom and formality a life unintelligible in its inner workings to the western brain, impenetrable to the western eye. There are forces hidden in the Javanese mind, the resultant of a strangely moved past, which we can never understand, though we may admire their creative energy, revealed in the now conventional designs guiding the hand of the potter, the wood-carver, the goldsmith, the armourer, the *batikker*,[1] hereditary practisers of dying arts and crafts; in the remains of a marvellous architecture long since altogether dead. No chapter in the whole history of eastern art, says Fergusson, is so full of apparent anomalies or upsets so completely our preconceived ideas of things as they ought to be, as that which treats of the architectural history of the island of Java . . .; the one country to which they (the Hindus) overflowed, was Java, and there they colonised to such an extent as for nearly a thousand years to obliterate the native arts and civilisation and supplant it by their own . . .; what is still more singular is, that it was not from the nearest shores of India that these emigrants departed but from the western coast. . . . A *linga*, erected in the Kadu in the year 654 Saka (A.D. 732), a Sivaïte symbol of generation, marks the origin of an artistic activity whose most brilliant period, the classical one of central Javanese architecture, as G. P. Rouffaer styles it rightly, begins with the construction of such buildings as the Buddhist *chandi* Kalasan or Kali Bening. The inscription of King Sanjaya in Venggi characters, and vestiges of Vaishnav tendencies in the Suku and Cheto temples of a much later date, point to the worship of Vishnu,

[1] *Batikking* is the art of dyeing woven goods by immersing them in successive baths of the required colour, protecting the parts to be left undyed by applying a mixture of beeswax and resin.

while Brahma's four sublime conditions and more subtle transcendentalism do not seem to have attracted the Javanese converts to Hinduïsm. They could grasp the unity of Siva's threefold functions much better and accepted him as Mahadeva at the head of the Trimoorti. The advent of Buddhism in its *mahayanistic* form, the creed of the northern church so called, served to emphasise native tolerance. Sivaïsm and whatever there was of Vishnuïsm, harmonised with Buddhism to the extent of borrowing and lending symbols, emblems and divine attributes; Hindu gods played puss in the corner with Bodhisatvas, as already remarked upon in the preceding chapter; the *chandi* Chupuwatu surprises us with a *stupa-linga*;[1] a Javanese prince of the thirteenth century bears the expressive name of Siva-Buddha; the old Javanese *Sang Hiang Kamahayanikan* contains the dictum: Siva is identical with Buddha.[2] If more inscriptions had been found, more light might have been thrown on the anomalous ornamentation of, for instance, the Prambanan temples and the Mendoot; but Sivaïte records of the kind leaving the matter unexplained, Buddhist information is still scantier, perhaps a consequence of Baghavat's followers not excelling in epigraphy or literary labours of any description.

[1] A *stupa*, lit. a mound, a tumulus, is a memorial structure, sometimes raised over a relic of the Buddha, one of the eight thousand portions into which his ashes were divided, or a tooth, or any other fragment of his remains. The combination of such a memento of the Most Chaste with the emblem of supreme virility is syncretism indeed!

[2] Professor Dr. H. H. Juynboll in the *Bijdragen tot de Taal-, Land- en Volkenkunde van Nederlandsch Indië*, Ser. vii., vol. vi., nr. 1.

If the backwash of great political events or religious discussion when the Islām superseded older creeds, may have aided Kala, the Destroyer, in demolishing a good many buildings of the classical period, whose sites even are sought in vain, it is certain that the pioneers of western civilisation, proud of their superiority, willfully and wantonly undid in many places work that had been spared by time and earthquakes and volcanic eruptions and enemies born of the soil, devastating with fire and sword their brethren's hearths and houses. Christian zealots regarded the ancient monuments as assembly-rooms of the Devil where the benighted heathen used to foregather in idolatry, lodges of abomination the sooner razed the better, a pious feeling often translated into action on grounds of utility: the stones offered excellent building material. Officials and *particulieren*[1] of broader views, besides acknowledging the serviceableness of *chandis* in this respect, went *recho*-hunting[2] for the adornment of their houses and gardens. Quite a collection has been formed in the residency grounds at Jogjakarta, the nucleus of which was moved thither from the estate Tanjong Tirta, whose former occupants, like most of the landed gentry, made exceedingly free with the temples and monasteries in that neighbourhood.

[1] Those not in the Government service: planters, industrials, etc., always of lower caste in general, especially official esteem, than the select who draw their salaries from Batavia. Hence the native designation of such an inferior individual as a *particulier saja*, "only" a private person.

[2] *Recho* or *rejo* is the name given to any sort of statue.

As neither they nor the others bothered about noting where they got this or that piece of sculpture, we are entirely at sea concerning the meaning of several beautiful statues. This is the case, *e.g.*, with one of remarkably fine execution, a crowned goddess, sitting on a lotus cushion and encircled by a flaming aureole, pressing her hands to her bosom. She has been fortunate enough to escape the fate of some deities who shared her sequestration and were left to the care of the convicts detailed to keep the Resident's compound in trim, a duty performed by whitewashing or daubing them with a grayish substance, excepting the hair of the head, the eyebrows, the eyeballs and the *prabha*, which the gentlemen-artists of the chain-gang are in the habit of painting black, enhancing the general effect by "restoring" lost hands and feet and damaged faces after methods nothing short of barbarous, but therefore the better in keeping with the traditional attitude of those in authority. For this infamous disfiguration and desecration, which makes any one unaccustomed to Dutch East Indian processes shudder with horror, never disturbed the aesthetic sense or equanimity of the several occupants of the residency who, during the last thirty-five years, saw it going on under their very eyes, the eyes of the representatives of a Government lavish in circulars[1] recommending the country's antiquities to their care. Neither are those eyes shocked by the

[1] From *circulus*, circle, something round, which rolls easily away into oblivion as it is intended to; but, if nothing else, *la folie circulaire* keeps the fiction of governmental guidance and control alive.

"museum" adjoining the residency, a jumble of plunder from *chandis* far and near; nor by the chaotic mass of torsos, arms and legs, fragmentary evidence of wholesale spoliation behind that pitiful exhibition of archaeology turned topsyturvy.

So much for the statuary removed from the *chandis*, as far as it can be traced. Concerning the *chandis* themselves, it should be remembered that the greater part has wholly disappeared. Hillocks, overspread with brushwood, sometimes awaken hopes that by digging foundations and portions of walls may be discovered; heaps of debris, tenanted by lizards and snakes, point to structures of which nothing that is left, indicates the former use; shattered ornamental stones speak of magnificent buildings fallen or pulled down—glimmerings of splendour that was. The temples still standing are reduced to ruins and diminish almost visibly in attractiveness and size. Rouffaer[1] gave an interesting example of their fate in the story of the spiriting away of the *chandi* Darawati: in 1889 tolerably well preserved, though two large statues of the Buddha had been dragged off to the dwelling of a European in the *dessa* Gedaren, it was gone in 1894 —vanished into air! The temples constructed of brick, like the *chandi* Abang, have suffered even more, of course, than those of stone, the memory of whose grandeur is retained in a few ghastly wrecks. Reserving the Buddhist remains for later treatment

[1] Speaking at a meeting of the *Royal Geographical Society of the Netherlands*, December 27, 1902.

and passing by the Sivaïte caves with rectangular porches in the Bagelen, mentioned by Fergusson, I shall deal here with the *chandis* Suku and Cheto, and the most noteworthy ruins in the southern mountains. The latter comprise the *kraton* of Ratu Boko, Mboq Loro Jonggrang's father, as the natives call it, and the temple group of the Gunoong Ijo. Of the legendary kingly residence little more is left than a square terrace with portions of a wall and the sill of a gate. The *chandi* Ijo consists of a large temple of the usual polygonal form with ten smaller ones and a pit which contained two stone receptacles and strips of gold-leaf with the image of a deity and an inscription; the buildings are in a sad condition, but decay has not impaired their beauteous dignity and the landscape alone repays a visit to Soro Gedoog, an estate whose gradual reclamation of the jungle led to their discovery in 1886 when ground was cleared for an extension of the plantations.

The *chandis* Suku and Cheto are situated respectively on the western and northern slope of the Gunoong Lawu, a volcano on the boundary between Surakarta and Madioon, not less expressive in its scenery of what heaven has done for this delicious island. Shortly after the mysterious pyramids of Suku had drawn the attention of Resident Johnson, in the British Interregnum, Thomas Horsfield visited them and made some drawings. The inscriptions and the sculptured ornament of Cheto were reported upon by C. J.

van der Vlis, in 1842. The groups belong to the latest, most decadent period of Hindu architecture in Java and their foundation, Suku being a few years older than Cheto, must have coincided with the introduction of the Islām. Bondowoso, the son of the recluse Damar Moyo, who assisted the King of Pengging against Ratu Boko and took such signal revenge upon the latter's daughter, Loro Jonggrang, for rejecting him, the uncouth slayer of her father, is supposed to have erected the buildings at Suku. Those at Cheto owe their origin to a prince of Mojopahit, who quarrelled with his brother, the ruler of that empire, or, according to another legend, to a certain Kiahi Patiro, who refused to become a convert to the new faith and repaired to the Lawu, where he lived as a hermit and was killed by Pragiwongso, an emissary of the Moslim King of Demak. *Linga*-worship returned in the temple groups of the Lawu to its crudest modes of expression, and Fergusson, who mentions the dates 1435 and 1440, speaks of a degraded form of the Vishnuïte religion, the *garuda*,[1] the boar, the tortoise, etc., being of frequent occurrence in the ornamentation. Junghuhn described the staircases he found, which connected the terraces, and the statues, which hardly came up to the artistic standard of Prambanan and the Boro Budoor, one of them distinguishing itself by a colossal head whose measurement from chin to crown was three feet, half of the whole height. Comparing his description with the actual state of

[1] Vishnu's *vahana* or bearer, the monster-bird.

things, much must have been removed, heaven knows whither! Notwithstanding the obvious truth of Fergusson's remark that a proper illustration of Suku and Cheto, and, I may be permitted to add, of the remains on the summit of the mountain, whether originally tree-temples or consecrated to devotional exercises in the open, *à l'instar* of West Java, promises to be of great importance to the history of architecture in the island, very little has been done in that direction or even for the conservation of the ruins where *recho*-hunters and a luxurious vegetation vie in obliterating the traces of most interesting antiquities. Junghuhn sounded a note of warning apropos of the falling in of the peculiarly constructed pyramidal temple, May 1838, but this and the other monuments have been suffered since, as before, to crumble quietly away and the easily removable sculpture to be carried off. Ganesa, in his manifold reproductions, seconds on the Lawu his father Siva, head of the Trimoorti, continuing the lead obtained seven centuries earlier in the plain of Prambanan, and a systematic study of the reliefs, now covered with moss and lichens, might shed a good deal of light on several unsettled questions. One of those reliefs, blending the human and the divine in the manner of the allusions to the *Brata Yuda* on the Diëng plateau and the Rama legend on the walls of the *chandi* Loro Jonggrang, represents a complete armoury, with Ganesa, protector of arts and crafts, between the armourer himself and his assistant who works the bellows.

If, with Rouffaer, we divide the long era during which the Hindus, first as immigrants and then as rulers, merged gradually in the aboriginal population, into a Hindu-Javanese period of Central Java and a Javanese-Hindu period of East Java, the monuments of Suku and Cheto belong evidently to the epoch of Javanese-Hindu decline, decadent art flowing back to its classical source, tarnishing original Hindu-Javanese conceptions. Leaving Buddhist architecture to be dealt with in the last chapters, and before turning to the *chandis* of East Java, a short historical review may aid in the appreciation of this decline and subsequent paralysis of the creative faculty. Kartikeya, the god of war, a younger son of Siva and Parvati, had his strong hand in this, and how he invested and divested mighty princes, who conquered or were defeated and finally passed away, causing the rise and fall of glorious kingdoms, is written in the *babads*, the Javanese chronicles, by no means such old wives' tales as Dominee Valentijn tried to make them out, but containing in their extravagance a kernel of stern reality, not the less explanatory of the condition of the fairy island Java because the *magnanimes mensonges* of a vivid imagination animate the dull facts.

Of the Hindu empire Mataram in Central Java nothing tangible is left except the ruins referred to, a few objects in metal and stone, accidentally unearthed or dug up by treasure-seekers, and some inscriptions, title-deeds, etc., the scanty "genuine charters of Java" as van Limburg Brouwer defined them. The name Mataram has been preserved on a copper plate, dating from about 900, which agrees in this respect with four other records, discovered in East Java; the capital of the *Maharaja i Mataram* is called Medang. For two centuries, from the beginning of the eighth until the beginning of the tenth, Mataram seems to have flourished as the most powerful state in the island, especially aggressive towards the east. Native tradition, in fond exaggeration of her importance, makes her sway the destinies of the world. Her star waned suddenly; by what cause is unknown; but whether it was the invasion of a mightier enemy or a natural catastrophe, the same as that which overtook the builders of the Diëng and the plain of Prambanan, forcing them to leave their work unfinished, ancient Mataram sank into insignificance. From the middle of the tenth until the beginning of the sixteenth century, the successors of her former eastern vassals, that is whichever of them happened to be on top in the continual struggle for supremacy, did in East and Central Java as they pleased, warring, intermarrying, annexing their neighbours' domains, only to lose them again and their own kingdoms to boot, to usurpers, ambitious ministers, popular governors of provinces, enterprising *condottieri* or mere adventurers favoured by Dame Fortune. In that overflowing arena of high rivalry, dynasties succeeding one another with amazing rapidity, Daha, situated in what is now Kediri, secured paramount influence after Kahuripan, situated in what is now Southern Surabaya; then Tumapel, situated in what is now Pasuruan, became ascendant; then Daha once more and, last of the great Hindu empires, Mojopahit, about 1300, to be overthrown, after two centuries of preponderance, by the sword of Islām. Jayabaya, King of Daha, from about 1130 till about 1160, has been called[1] the Charlemagne of Java, in whose reign learning and letters were encouraged; or the Javanese King Arthur, whose life among his heroes, in peace and war, is reflected in the idylls of the *Panji*-cycle, at whose Court the famous poet Mpu Sedah began his version of the *Mahabharata*, the *Brata Yuda*, finished by Mpu Panulooh, author of the *Gatotkachasraya*, while Tanakoong wrote the *Wretta-Sansaya*, a sort of *Epistola de Arte Poetica*. When Tumapel expanded, especially under Ken Angrok, troublous times arrived for Daha, which could hardly hold her own against the encroachments of that unscrupulous monarch. Ken Angrok or Arok, born in 1182 at Singosari, had seized the royal power after assassinating the old King in 1222 or 1223. The kris he used, had been ordered expressly for that deed from the famous armourer Mpu Gandring, who was its first victim because he tarried in delivering it, the tempering of the steel having taken more time than suited the usurper's patience. Dying under the murderous stroke, Mpu Gandring uttered a prophetic curse: This kris will kill Ken

[1] By G. P. Rouffaer, *Indische Gids*, February 1903.

Angrok; it will kill his children and grandchildren; it will kill seven kings. The prophecy came true with wonderful exactness. Ken Angrok having married Dedes, the widow of the old King he had despatched, was himself killed as the third victim of Mpu Gandring's kris in the hand of a bravo commissioned by their son Anusapati, the Hamlet of Javanese history. And how blood followed blood during the hundred years of Tumapel's hegemony, how Ken Angrok's descendants harassed their neighbours before the curse took effect upon each of them, appearing like luminous stars in the sky of politics and war, and then disappearing behind the shadowy cloud of untimely death, is it not written in the *Pararaton* or Book of the Kings of Tumapel and Mojopahit?

The foundation of Mojopahit has been attributed to scions of several royal families, among them to Raden Tanduran, a prince of Pajajaran in West Java which, it will be remembered, owed its origin to princes of Tumapel. The most widely accepted reading is, however, that a certain Raden Wijaya, commander of the army of King Kertanegara, great-grandson of Ken Angrok, profiting from his master's quarrels with Jaya Katong, ruler of Daha in those days, carved out a kingdom for himself, reclaiming, always with that end in view, a large area of wild land, Mojo Lengko or Mojo Lengu, near Tarik in Wirosobo, the present Mojokerto. King Kertanegara who, by branding the Chinese envoy Meng Ki, had stirred up trouble with the

Flowery Empire, was unable to punish this act of arrogance, and his violent death in a battle won by the legions of Daha, meant the inglorious end of Tumapel. This happened in 1292 and the expeditionary force sent from China to chastise him for his ungracious treatment of ambassadors to his Court, consequently found their object accomplished or, more correctly speaking, unaccomplishable when landing in 1293. But its leader indemnified his martial ardour by entering the service of Raden Wijaya who, with his assistance, subjugated Daha, which had tried to reassume her former precedence. Firmly established on the throne of the realm he had fashioned out of Daha, Tumapel and his own territory near Tarik, he refused, however, to pay the price stipulated by his Chinese ally and when the auxiliary troops asked the fulfilment of his promises, arms in hand, he proved to them that superior strength is the ultimate arbiter of right and sent them home much diminished in numbers and pride. The Emperor of China, wroth that the beautiful princesses of Tumapel, daughters of the late King Kertanegara, whom he had deigned to accept as concubines, were not forthcoming, but stayed behind to adorn the harem of the self-made King of Mojopahit, ordered his unsuccessful generalissimo to be flogged by way of example to other commanding officers. Raden Wijaya who, with the kingly title, had assumed the name of Kertarajasa, enjoyed his royal dignity only until 1295 and his ashes were entombed in two places not yet located: in the *dalem* (the inner, private part) of his palace conformably to the Buddhist, and at Simping conformably to the Sivaïte ritual, not otherwise than King Kertanegara received last honours in the guise of Siva-Buddha at Singosari and in the guise of a Dhyani Buddha at Sakala, and the remains of King Kertarajasa's successor were interred in three places according to the Vishnuïte ritual, circumstances from which we may conclude that in East as in Central Java the different creeds lived together in most amiable harmony.

The kris of Mpu Gandring might limit the earthly term of the descendants of Ken Angrok, it could not check their prowess while they were still up and doing. Overlords of East and Central Java, extending their rule to Pajajaran, they even looked for conquest to the other islands of the Malay Archipelago. Under Hayam Wurook or Rajasa Nagara, in the latter half of the fourteenth century, Mojopahit reached her zenith; a record of 1389 mentions Bali as being tributary since about 1340; Aru, Palembang and Menangkabau in Sumatra, Pahang with Tumanik in Malacca, Tanjong Pura in Borneo, Dompo in Soombawa, Ceram and the Goram islands acknowledged Nayam Wurook's suzerainty too. Seeing no more worlds to subdue, he died and, as in the case of Alexander the Great, his empire fell to pieces; in East Java itself Balambangan seceded from Mojopahit proper and the Muhammadan propaganda, fanning discord between the Hindu princes of old and new dynasties, prepared their common doom. The beginnings of the Islām in East Java have already been spoken of, with Gresik as a missionary centre, Maulana Malik Ibrahim as the first *wali* in that region and the conversion into Moslim vassal states of the dependencies of Mojopahit, whose princes, combining under the auspices of Demak against their liege lord, sealed his fate. Raden Patah of Demak was a man of war and destiny. The fire of the new faith burning fiercely within him, he hurled his defiance at the stronghold of the heathen, speaking to the last King of Mojopahit, his father or grandfather according to tradition, as Amaziah, King of Juda, spoke to Joash, the son of Jehoahaz, the son of Jehu, King of Israël: Come, let us see one another in the face,—but with a different result: the challenger from Demak came out victorious and Mojopahit ceased to exist, an issue fraught with grave consequences. This occurred about the year 1500[1] and Raden Patah, pursuing the royal family on their flight, defeated the King or one of his sons again at Malang, where a last stand was made. But Gajah Mada, the Prime Minister of Mojopahit, founded a new empire, Supit Urang, which comprised much of the territory once belonging to Singosari. The Saivas also held out at Pasuruan, which was invested by Pangeran Tranggana, a successor of Raden Patah, but after his assassination by one of his servants,

[1] The fall of Mojopahit has been put at 1478 (Javanese chronicles), 1488 (VETH's *Java*, 2nd ed.) and between 1515 and 1521 (ROUFFAER).

the troops of Demak returned home. Pasuruan and Surabaya reverted, later on, to the Regent of Madura, a son-in-law of Pangeran Tranggana. Yet, Hinduïsm lingered on in the island; its political power was only broken with the conquest of Balambangan by the East India Company in 1767, and the population of the Tengger mountain region did not commence to accept the Islām until very recently.

In the confusion which resulted after the death of Pangeran Tranggana from the disruption of his domains into Cheribon, Jayakarta and Bantam in the western, Gresik and Kediri in the eastern, and Demak proper and Pajang in the central part of the island, the latter territory absorbed Jipang and its Prince Tingkir, a scion of the royal family of Mojopahit, was proclaimed Sooltan by the spiritual authority of Gresik, the first time we find that title mentioned in the history of Java. Sooltan Tingkir appointed one of his trusted servants, Kiahi Ageng Pamanahan, governor of the tract of land which had preserved the name of Mataram. Kiahi Ageng Pamanahan improved the condition of the people and his son Suta Wijaya, who had married a daughter of the Sooltan, making himself independent by rebelling, by poisoning his father-in-law after his having been captured and pardoned, finally by taking possession of the regalia in the subsequent war of succession, became master of the situation and laid in New Mataram the foundation of another state which, in the reign of his successor Ageng,

1613–1646, gained the ascendency over the rest of Java with Madura, subjugating even Sukadana in West Borneo. Not, however, without strenuous exertion for Balambangan gave a good deal of trouble in the East and the conquest of Sumedang in the West, in 1626, taxed the military strength of the rising empire to its utmost. When the East India Company began to make its influence felt, Moslim solidarity proved a valuable asset as, for instance, in the relations with Bantam and Cheribon, whose Pangeran proposed the title of Susuhunan for Ageng (1625) before Mecca promoted him to the Sooltanate (1630). In 1628 and 1629 he ventured to attack Batavia, the new settlement of the Dutch, but had to retire and, what was even worse, by provoking those upstart strangers, he damaged his trade: they closed the channels of export to Malacca and other foreign ports of rice, the principal produce of the land. "Mataram must now become our friend," wrote the Governor-General to his masters, the Honourable Seventeen, and, indeed, Mangku Rat I., Ageng's son, found himself obliged to sign a treaty of friendship with the Company—a dangerous friendship! Differences between their "friend" and Bantam with Cheribon were sedulously fostered by the authorities at Batavia; the Company took a hand in the putting down of disturbances created in East Java by Taruna Jaya of Madura and Kraëng Galesoong of Macassar; the Company patronised and protected the reigning Sooltans, who moved their residence from Karta to Kartasura, against pretenders and exacted payment in land, privileges, concessions, monopolies, etc., shamelessly in excess of the real or pretended assistance afforded in quelling purposely manufactured anarchy—precisely as we see it happen nowadays wherever western civilisation offers her "disinterested" services to eastern countries of promising complexion for exploitation by western greed.

Mataram, trying to escape from the extortionate friendship of the honey-tongued strangers at Batavia, whose thirst for gold seemed unquenchable, has its counterparts in benighted regions now being "civilised" after the time-honoured recipe: interference which upsets peace and order, more interference to restore peace and order with the naturally opposite result, occupation until peace and order will be restored, gradual annexation. The East India Company's mean spirit of haggling was held in utter contempt by the native princes, *grands seigneurs* in thought and action, too proud to pay the hucksters with their own coin, though bad forebodings must have filled the mind, for instance, of Susuhunan Puger, recognised at Batavia as Mataram's figurehead under the name of Paku Buwono I.,[1] when near his capital a Dutch fort was built and garrisoned with Dutch soldiers to back him in his exactions for the benefit of alien usurers and sharpers. Like the rat of Ganesa, they pene-

[1] Paku Buwono, like Paku Alam, means "nail which fastens the universe."

trated everywhere and the tale of their relations to the lords of the land is one of tortuous insinuation until they had firmly established themselves and could give the rein to their sordid commercialism in always more exorbitant claims. Paku Buwono II., feeling his end approach, was prevailed upon, in 1749, to bequeath his realm to the Company, but one of the most influential members of the imperial family decided that this was carrying it a little too far: Mangku Bumi,[1] brother of Paku Buwono II., supported by Mas Saïd, son of the exiled Mangku Negara,[2] and other *pangerans* (princes of the blood), stood up in arms to defend their country's rights and inflicted severe losses on the Dutch troops in stubborn guerrilla warfare. This led to the partition of Mataram between Paku Buwono III. and his uncle Mangku Bumi, both acknowledging the supremacy of the Company, the latter settling at Jogjakarta, the old capital Karta, under the title and name of Sooltan Mangku Buwono,[3] while Mas Saïd, who did not cease hostilities before 1757, gained also a quasi-independent position as Pangeran Adipati Mangku Negara, which in 1796 became hereditary. With three reigning princes for one, the power of Mataram was definitely broken and Batavia assumed the direction of her affairs quite openly, the "thundering field-marshal" Daendels

[1] Lit. "the one who has the world in his lap," *i.e.* the supporter (ruler) of the world.

[2] Lit. "the one who has the empire in his lap," *i.e.* the supporter (ruler) of the empire.

[3] Lit. "the one who has the universe in his lap," *i.e.* the supporter (ruler) of the universe.

emphasising her state of decline and the British Interregnum bringing no change.

In 1825 the divided remnant of Mataram, viz. Surakarta with the Mangku Negaran and Jogjakarta with the Paku Alaman,[1] was deeply stirred by Pangeran Anta Wiria calling upon his compatriots to chase the oppressors away. Born from a woman of low descent among the wives of Mangku Buwono III., Sooltan of Jogjakarta, it seems that, nevertheless, hopes of his succession to the throne had been held out to him when he assisted his father against the machinations of his grandfather, Sooltan Sepooh (Mangku Buwono II.), banished by Raffles in 1812. However this may be, he resented the settlement of the Sooltanate on the death of Mangku Buwono III. upon Jarot, an infant son, and other circumstances adding to his dislike of Dutch control, he raised the standard of revolt. The Javanese responded with alacrity to an appeal which bore good tidings of delivery as the wind, ridden by the Maroots who make the mountains to tremble and tear the forest into pieces, bears good tidings of coming rain to a parched earth. Anta Wiria, under his more popular name of Dipo Negoro, and his lieutenants Ali Bassa Prawira Dirja, or Sentot, and Kiahi Maja, gave the Dutch troops plenty of bloody work in the five years during which the Java war lasted, 1825–1830. It was the last eruption on a large scale of the fire imprisoned in

[1] A fourth semi-independent domain, created at the expense of Jogjakarta for the benefit of Pangeran Nata Kusuma, ally of the British during the troubles of 1811 and 1812.

the native's heart, the last sustained effort at regaining his independence, crushed by the white man's superiority in military appliances, but occasional throbbings, ruffling the surface as in Bantam (1888), the Preanger Regencies (1902), Kediri (1910), etc., show that the volcano is by no means an extinguished one. Though "kingdoms are shrunk to provinces and chains clank over sceptred cities," the love of liberty, laid by as a sword which eats into itself, does not own foreign dominion, and the native princes, especially the Susuhunan of Surakarta and the Sooltan of Jogjakarta, remain objects of worshipful homage. Their genealogy remounts to the gods whose essence took substance in the illustrious prophet Adam who begat Abil and Kabil on the goddess Kawa; the history of their house begins with the arrival in the island, in the Javanese year 1, of Aji Soko; they are the *panatagama* and *sayidin* (*shah ad-din*), directors and leaders of religion; their Courts set the fashion in high native society, Solo[1] being more gay and extravagant, Jogja[1] more sedate and solid, as a writer at the end of the eighteenth century already remarked.

The Dutch Government recognises the imperial or royal dignity of Susuhunan and Sooltan by the superior position of its Residents in the capitals of

[1] Common abbreviations, in speaking and writing, of Surakarta and Jogjakarta; Solo is, to put it correctly, the name of the place where Paku Buwono II., after his old *kraton* had been destroyed by fire in the civil war diligently fostered by the Company, built the present one, *Surakarta Hadiningrat*, *i.e.* the most excellent city of heroes.

their Principalities, who, directly responsible to the Governor-General, correspond in rank to the general officers of the army, while the administrative heads of the other residencies have to content themselves with the honours due to a colonel; also by the institution of dragoon body-guards whose ostensibly ornamental presence can be and has been turned to good account when the mental intoxication arising from meditation on gilded disgrace, charged with the lightning of passion, produces effects irreconcilable with the fiction that all is for the best in this best of worlds. With the Government steadily encroaching on the native princes' ancient rights, bitterness grows apace and irritation at the recoiling weight of bondage lives on, though colonial reports represent it as dead. Truly, in the three centuries during which it pleased Kuwera, the fat god of wealth, to inspire the strangers from the West, rich in promise but slow in performance, exacting and pitiless, to deeds of unprincipled rapacity, the people have learned to hide their thoughts that worse may not follow, hoping that time will set things right. But as everything points more clearly to the fixed purpose of the Dutch Government to avail themselves of every pretext for swallowing the Principalities as all the rest has been gobbled up, there are those who cherish the memory of Dipo Negoro and consider the necessity of new man-offerings: the greater the need, the greater must be the propitiation. On the whole, however, better counsel prevails, deliverance being sought on planes of mystic exercise, silent submission being practised in expectation of the consummation of a higher will, and this is the native's secret as he repeats the lessons inculcated in the *Wulang Reh*, the treatise on ethics written by one of the eminent of the past, Sunan Paku Buwono IV. : May ye imitate our ancestors, who were endowed with supernatural strength, and may ye qualify for penitence, heeding closely the perfection of life ; this is my prayer for my children ; be it granted! Meanwhile taxation increases, but who can object to that when in days of old the good people had to pay for the privilege of looking at the public dancers, whether they cared to look at them or not ; when compulsory contributions to the exchequer were levied upon one-eyed persons for their being so much better off than the totally blind ; etc. . . . Fancy a Minister of Finance in Holland defending a vexatious new assessment on the ground of arbitrary cesses in the Middle Ages!

Hindu art had lost its vitality when the second empire of Mataram arose in Central Java and the cult of the ideal was effected by modernising currents from the eastern part of the island. Sanskrit, as the vehicle of thought in Venggi and Nagari characters, made place for Kawi which, related in its oldest forms to Pali and in its symbols to the Indian alphabets, evolved soon afterward into a specific Javanese type. Sivaïte literature paved the way for the *Manik Maya*, the *Bandoong*, the *Aji Saka*, the *Panji*- and the *Menak*- or *Hamza*-cycles, the

Damar Wulan; as to Buddhist literature, Burnouf's comment upon its inferiority holds also good for Java: no trace exists even of a life of the Buddha, of *jataka*-tales, except such as have originated in the eastern kingdoms at a comparatively late date. Literary culture in the seventeenth and eighteenth centuries was a continuation of and throve on the efforts of the great authors hospitably entertained at the Courts of Mojopahit and Kediri. The Javanese language with the wealth of words it acquired and the diversity of expression it developed,[1] exercised and still exercises in its four dialects[2] a vivifying influence upon the Soondanese speech in the west and the Madurese

[1] *Ngoko* is spoken among the common people, among children, by adults to children and by those of superior to those of inferior rank; *kromo* by those of inferior to those of superior rank and by people of high rank amongst themselves unless differences in social degree or grades of relationship require another mode of address; *dagellan* or *gendaloongan* (in Surakarta) and *madya* (in Jogjakarta), a mixture of *ngoko* and *kromo*, by people of equal rank conversing in an unofficial capacity, politely but without constraint, by those of superior to those of inferior rank, their seniors in years whom they wish to honour, by merchants of equal rank and the higher servants of the nobility to one another; *kromo-inggil* comprises a group of words used when referring to whatever is divine or very exalted on earth; *basa kedaton* is the language of the Court, spoken by all males in the presence of the reigning prince or in his *kraton* whether he be present or not, but in addressing him or his heir presumptive, *kromo* is used; the reigning prince employs *ngoko* interspersed with *kromo-inggil* words when referring to himself; the women in the *kraton* speak *kromo* or *kromo-madya* among themselves, *basa kedaton* to such men-folk as they are allowed to see and *kromo* to the reigning prince or his heir presumptive; *ngoko andap* is a coarse sort of speech which descends to the use of words, in relation to man, ordinarily applied only to animals; *kromo-dessa* means rustic speech in general.

[2] The central and most refined Javanese of Mataram or Surakarta, spoken in the Principalities, the Kadu, the Bagelen, Madioon and Kediri; the western Javanese, spoken in Cheribon and Banyumas; the *basa* or *temboong pasasir* (speech of the coast), spoken in Tagal, Pekalongan, Samarang, Yapara and Rembang; the eastern Javanese, spoken in Surabaya, Pasuruan, Probolinggo and Besuki.

in the east. Its script, like the people who speak and write it, and cling to their *hadat*, the manners and customs of the *jaman buda*, which, notwithstanding their Islāmitic veneer, they prefer to the law of the Prophet,—its script rejects Moslim interference and refuses to employ the Arabic characters, sticking to its equally beautiful *aksaras* and *pasangans*. Religions succeeding one another, generally without discourteous haste, Muhammadanism penetrated Central Java but slowly from the north, first by the conversion of the great and mighty who profited by the example of Mojopahit, then by grafting the idea of the one righteous god upon the godless Buddhist or pantheistic Hindu creed of the *orang kechil*, the man of slight importance who, up to this day, though fervent in his outward duties as a Moslim, shows in every act that his individual and national temperament is rooted in pre-Islāmic idiosyncrasies. The heroes of the *Brata Yuda* and *Ramayana* are just as dear to him as the pre-Islāmic saints whose legends are gathered in the story of *Raja Pirangon* and the *Kitab Ambia*, as the forerunners, companions and helpers of the Apostle of God.

The sacred *waringin*, never wanting in the *aloon aloon*, the open places before the dwellings of the rulers of the land and their deputies, what is it but the bo-tree, the tree of enlightenment? One of venerable age in the imperial burial-ground of Pasar Gedeh, planted, according to tradition, by Kiahi Ageng Pamanahan or his son Suta Wijaya, announces without fail the demise of a member of one of the reigning families either at Solo or at Jogja, by shedding one of its branches. Pasar Gedeh, Selo and Imogiri are silent spots, peopled with the dead whose lives' strength made history and is mourned as the strength of a glorious past. Selo, an enclave belonging to Surakarta, in Grobogan, residency Samarang, contains the ancestral tombs of the rulers of Mataram; Imogiri and Pasar Gedeh in Jogjakarta, which latter marks the site of the original seat of empire and was comparatively recently put to its present use, are the cemeteries common to the royalty of both Principalities, and guarded by officials, *amat dalam* with the title of Raden Tumenggoong, appointed by mutual consent. A Polynesian bias to ancestor-worship, unabated by Hinduïsm, Buddhism and Muhammadanism, accounts for the almost idolatrous adoration [1] of the graves of the Susuhunans and Sooltans, their ancestors and also their progeny that did not attain to thrones, receptacles of once imperial dust, feeding the four elements from which it proceeded and to which it returns like meaner human clay. Look, says Kumala in the Buddhist parable, all in the world must perish! The religious brethren of his faith used to repair at night to the sepulchres of those taken to bliss and spend the lone hours in pondering on the instability of conscious existence, desiring to gain the Nirvana by their undisturbed meditations, but Sivaïte

[1] A cult with a ritual handed down from the past and scrupulously observed. Cf. the account of a visit to Selo in 1849, published from papers left by Dr. M. W. SCHELTEMA, in *De Gids*, December, 1909.

associations people the old graveyards of Java with *raksasas*, monstrous giants, eaters of living and dead men and women, and santons, bent on prayer amid the last abodes of the departed, have been terrified, especially at Pasar Gedeh, by weird noises and apparitions signalling their approach, commending hasty retreat to the wise. It is advisable to distrust darkness there and rather to choose the day for acts of devotion, even if annoyed by worldlings who come to consult the big white tortoise in the tank, ancient Kiahi Duda, widower of Mboq Loro Kuning, presaging the better luck the farther he paddles forth from his subaqueous habitation. At a little distance is the *sela gilang*, a bluish stone with a more than half effaced inscription, only the lettering of the border being legible. Tradition calls it the *dampar* (throne) of Suta Wijaya, sitting on which he killed Kiahi Ageng Mangir, his rival and owner of the miraculous lance Kiahi Baru, who had been lured into his presence by one of his daughters to do homage by means of the *ujoong*, the kissing[1] of the knee; near by are a stone mortar and large stone cannon-balls, the largest possessing the faculty of granting untold wealth to those strong enough to carry it three times without stopping round the *sela gilang*, whose legend, carved by a

[1] The Javanese do not kiss in the disgusting, unwholesome, western fashion; they smell or sniff, using the olfactory instead of the osculatory organs, as sufficiently indicated by the words of the native vocabulary describing the operation referred to. In this matter again, the Hindu immigrants may have made their influence felt. Cf. Professor E. Washburn Hopkins' interesting paper on *The Sniff-Kiss in Ancient India*, in the *Journal of the American Oriental Society*, vol. xxviii., first half, 1907.

prisoner of war, either a spirit of the air or a magician, reveals in its marginal commentary a philosophic mind coupled with linguistic talents: *zoo gaat de wereld—così va il mondo—ita movet tuus mundus—ainsi va le monde.*

Selo, Imogiri and Pasar Gedeh: so goes the world indeed, and the nameless prisoner of war's motto, preserved near the *pasarahan dalam*, the imperial garden of rest, would be hardly less appropriate over the gates leading to the *kratons*, the residences[1] of the Susuhunan of Surakarta and the Sooltan of Jogjakarta, where they do the grand in the grand old way, cherishing the memories of a power gone by. A visit to the Principalities without an invitation to attend some function at Court cannot be called complete and it is a treat to watch the ceremonial exercises connected with one of the three *garebegs*[2] or with the salutations on imperial birthdays and coronation-days in the roomy *pendopos*, the open halls whose general style betrays its Hindu origin no less than the aspect, the dresses, the movements of the native nobility, officials and retainers, an assemblage of a fairy tale, betray their Hindu parentage. The *bangsal kenchono*, the

[1] Including, besides the palaces and palace grounds, thickly inhabited little towns. The *kraton* of Surakarta contains, *e.g.*, more than ten thousand people, all belonging to the imperial family and household, from the princes to their dependents, servants and hangers on: court dignitaries, court functionaries, gold- and silversmiths, wood-carvers, carpenters, masons, musicians, etc. Within its walls is also the imperial *mesdjid*, a fine, large building with a widely visible gilt roof.

[2] The *garebeg mulood*, *garebeg puasa* and *garebeg besar*, corresponding with the *maulid* (feast of the Prophet's birth), *id al-fitr* (feast of breaking the fast) and *id al-qorban* (feast of the sacrifice).

audience-chamber of the Sooltan at Jogja, is a masterpiece of construction in wood, the carved beams and joists, richly gilt and painted in bright colours, forming a ceiling of wonderful airiness and elegance; in the *bangsal witono* the Sooltan shows himself to the people on days of great gala; in the *bangsal kemandoongan*, a hall in one of the many open squares of the palace grounds, seated on his *dampar* or throne, he used to witness the execution of his subjects sentenced to death, who were krissed[1] against the opposite wall; another of these open squares was dedicated to pleasures which remind of the *munera gladiatoria*, more especially of the *ludi funebres*, and kindred amusements with a good deal of local colour: we find it chronicled of Sunan Mangku Rat I., Java's Nero, that once he beguiled a tedious afternoon in his *kraton* at Kartasura by stripping a hundred young women and letting a few tigers loose among them. The dining-hall (*gedong manis*: room of sweets) in the *kraton* at Jogja, to the south of the audience-chamber, can easily hold three hundred guests with the host of servants they require; at Solo the imperial stables and coach-houses[2] are scarcely

[1] *Krissing*, a form of capital punishment until recently still in use in the island of Bali, consisted in driving a kris to the heart of the condemned man, sometimes under circumstances of refined cruelty, the executioner not being permitted to put an end to his victim's agony before the prince, presiding in person or by deputy, had given the signal for the *coup de grâce*.

[2] A story is told of a Susuhunan of Surakarta having ordered a magnificent landau from one of the first *carrossiers* in Paris, that the favoured industrial was advised to send some cooking-pans with it on delivery. Asking: What for? he got the answer: To poach the eggs his Highness' chickens will lay in your carriage. Splendour and squalor live near together in the households of thriftless oriental potentates.

inferior in interest to the friend of horses, riding, driving and coaching, than the Kaiserlich-Königliche Marstall at Vienna or the Caballerizas Reales at Aranjuez. But of all the sights at the Courts of the Principalities of Central Java it is the human element that fascinates most, a waving mass of silent figures in the magnificent setting which reflects centuries of *Sturm und Drang*, the new to the visitor's eye being nothing but the very, very old; men taught by fate to treasure their thoughts up in their hearts, as their mountains do the hidden fire, worshipping *tempu dahulu*, sustained by *l'amour du bon vieulx tems*, *l'amour antique*, even the rising generation remaining apparently unaffected by the example of western fickleness, an inconstancy ever more pronounced since the illustrious citizen of Florence, of the Porta San Piera, commented on it:

Che l' uso de' mortali è come fronda
In ramo, che sen va, ed altra viene.[1]

The country-seats of Susuhunans and Sooltans, where they sought repose from cares of state, often contained temples erected, if not in the name then in the spirit of their kind of sacrifice, to Kama, the god of love, smuggled into the practice of a later creed. They had no wish to become the victims of their virtue like the excellent King Suvarnavarna; they did not aspire to the fame accruing to Rama in his relations to the female demon Shoorpanakha,

[1] For usage with mortal man is like the leaf
On the bough, which goes and another comes.

personification of sublunar temptations. And the manifold functions assigned to water in their pleasances, to the limpid, running water of the cool mountain rills, are characteristic of an island where a bath, at least twice a day, preferably in the open, is both a necessity and a luxury which the poorest does not dream of denying himself. Observe the crowds of men, women and children, always chaste and decent, disporting themselves in lakes and rivers, every morning and every evening; note the names of Pikataän, Kali Bening, Banyu Biru, idyllic spots and equal to the classic *chandi* Pengilon, Sidamookti and Wanasari to the lover of a plunge and a swim, screened by flowers and foliage, with the blue heaven smiling on his joy. Passing by Ambar Winangoon and Ambar Rookma, the remains of the so-called water-castle at Jogjakarta convey some notion of the manner in which royal personages sought recreation, amusing themselves in their parks of delight, fragrant and tranquil like the restful Loombini, where Maya gave birth to the Buddha; toying with their women in and round the crystalline fluid. An abundant spring within the boundaries of the palace grounds led to the conception of this retreat or, rather, these retreats, for there were two, connected by a system of canals which speaks highly for native hydraulics, though the buildings erected to obey a capricious will, show in their present ruinous state how architecture had degraded since the Hindu period, its flimsy productions being unable to withstand the first serious earthquake. Of Pulu Gedong, to the

XIII.

WATER-CASTLE AT JOGJAKARTA

(Centrum.)

northeast of the *aloon aloon kidool*, nothing is left but crumbling portions of the walls which jealously guarded the privacy of the Sooltan's watersports. Of Taman Sari and Taman Ledok, situated in the western part of the *kraton*, a good deal is still recognisable, especially the structures on Pulu Kenanga in the largest of the artificial lakes which are now dry ground, the one here meant being incorporated into a *kampong*, one of the several groups of native dwellings inhabited by the Sooltan's numerous retainers. The whilom islands convey in quite a picturesque way the lesson that human works must die like the hands that fashioned them.

The building of the "water-castle", whose pavilions, artificial lakes, tanks and gardens spread over an area of about twenty-five acres, was begun in 1758 by a Buginese architect under the orders of Mangku Buwono I., a great raiser of edifices, as Nicolaas Hartingh[1] wrote in 1761, and maker of "fountains, grotto-work and conduits which, though completed, he orders immediately to be pulled down, not finding them to his taste, thus squandering some little money." We possess a description[2] of the *kraton* at Jogjakarta, dated September 1791, from the hand of Carl Friedrich Reimer,[3] who speaks of

[1] Governor and Director of Java's northeast coast, afterwards member of the Governor-General's Council at Batavia.

[2] Published by H. D. H. Bosboom from papers in the Dutch National Archives.

[3] Titular Major, afterwards Lieutenant-Colonel of the Corps of Engineers, Director of Fortifications and Inspector of Canals, Dams, Dikes and Waterways.

"a collection of gardens, fish-ponds and pleasure-pools." He probably visited Pulu Gedong before proceeding to Taman Sari[1] and expatiates on the spaciousness of the dwelling room in Pulu Kananga, where it seems that the Court could find plenty of accommodation. But what made the greatest impression on the expert in hydraulics was the arrangement of passages and an apartment for prayer and meditation under water, as if the Sooltan deemed it an advantage to worship surrounded by the babbling stream, light and fresh air being provided through turrets rising above the surface. In the place called Oombool Winangoon, situated on a low level, with three tanks, fed from the great lake of Taman Sari, was a cool retreat where the Sooltan used to rest a while after his bath, refreshing himself with a cup of tea. Alluding to the Sumoor Gumuling, Reimer remarks that the architect must have chosen a round form for his structure to make it the better resist the pressure of the water all round. The strange building which went by that name and consisted of two concentric walls with a flat roof,[2] taken for a subaqueous house of prayer by the visitor of 1791, has also been very differently explained: some see in its remains a dancing-school, awakening visions of the Sooltan's *corps de ballet* practising in the first storey to the dulcet tones of the

[1] REIMER's description leaves Taman Ledok *in dubio* and a reason for his probable non-admittance there, may be found in the circumstance that it appears to have been the part of the pleasance reserved for the recreation of the Sooltan's concubines.

[2] Whence the name: *oombool*, like *sumoor*, means "well" or "spring", and *gumuling*, derived from *guling*, means "rolled up", "lying flat."

gamelan, the native orchestra, that ascended from the basement and aided them in going through their paces; others connect it with functions never referred to in polite society and which have nothing in common with praying, either with the heart or with the feet, more correctly speaking: with the arms, hands and hips, for Javanese dancing is no loose skipping and hopping about, but a graceful and expressive play of the body and more particularly of the upper limbs in rhythmic, undulating motion. Passing from one lake to the next, the Sooltan's means of conveyance was the *prahu* Niahi Kuning, a gorgeously decorated barge, given to him by the East India Company; other boats, plying between Taman Sari and Taman Ledok, were at the disposal of the ladies of the royal household desirous of an outing with their babies; two small skiffs left their moorings every night alternately, at a signal given on a *bendeh*, to feed the fishes, which knew the sound and assembled in shoals. The guard-rooms near the northern watergate, of which the remaining one, *i.e.* the one not altogether fallen into ruin, shelters in the morning a motley crowd of sellers of fruit, vegetables, sweetmeats, etc., witnesses to the Company's dragoons, protecting and shadowing their Highnesses of Surakarta and Jogjakarta with the princes of their blood, already having been entrusted with that task in the days of Mangku Buwono I.

Of the delicately carved woodwork hardly a trace remains, but some foliage and birds among flowers, executed in stucco, give evidence of a good taste which knew how to make old motives subservient to new requirements. Though a Muhammadan pleasance, designed by a Muhammadan architect for a Muhammadan prince, the *garuda* over one of the entrances, the Banaspatis on gables and fronts in Taman Sari and Taman Ledok, the *nagas* coping the balustrades of the staircases, show that Hindu conceptions continued to leaven Javanese art. The relations with China and the consequent influx of Chinamen have also borne their fruit in Central Java as in Cheribon and the eastern kingdoms: Reimer informs us that the galleries and tops (now gone) of the several buildings were constructed like pointed vaults, and were wrought "in the manner of Chinese roofs"; Pulu Gedong was famous for the lofty Chinese tower erected near the spring which furnished the water for the "castle", its lakes, ponds, tanks and canals, and for the irrigation of its grounds. The orchards, renowned for their mangoes and pine-apples, the vegetable-, sirih- and flower-gardens had a great reputation in the land; assiduous attention was paid to horticulture on the principle, well understood by oriental gardeners, that flower-beds, ornamental groves and bowers are like women; that however much art and pains are bestowed on their make-up, the art of arts is the concealment thereof. . . . Writing this it occurs to me how properly a western version of that universally approved maxim has been put in the mouth of *Gärtnerinnen, niedlich* and *galant*:

WATER-CASTLE AT JOGJAKARTA

(Centrum.)

Denn das Naturell der Frauen
Ist so nah mit Kunst verwandt.[1]

Though Mangku Buwono I. was a contemporary of Goethe, his knowledge of *Faust* is extremely doubtful, but being an artist in his own way, he took care that the natural scenery, assisted by art, should contribute to a pleasant general impression in the distribution of the dwellings for his retinue: native princes (and of his rank too!) do not move an inch inside or outside their *kratons* without numberless attendants at their heels. In the "water-castle" were apartments, not only for the Sooltan, for the Ratu, his first legitimate spouse, for his other wives and concubines, for the little family they had presented him with, but for the dignitaries of his Court, officials of all degrees, secretaries, servants of every description, various artificers from the armourers down to the *kebon kumukoos*, the makers of *tali api* (fire-rope), necessary for lighting his Highness' cigars. There were reception-, dining-, living- and sleeping-rooms for the Sooltan, his Ratu and female relatives, each apart; common rooms for the *selir* (wives of lower degree); rooms for the instruction of their children; rooms where his Highness' daughters spent a few hours every day in *batikking*; guard-rooms for the *prajurits*, the male guards; guard-rooms for the female guards under command of the Niahi Tumanggoong, a lady of consequence, who kept and keeps the *dalam*, the

[1] For nature in woman
Is so near akin to art.

interior of the *kraton*, under constant observation so that no illicit *amourettes* shall occur in the women's quarters, and yet—! There were store-rooms, kitchens, workshops, prisons, halls set apart for the dancers, male and female; the cream of the female dancers, the *srimpis* and girl *bedoyos*, were probably housed in or near the principal pavilion on Pulu Kananga, of which the Sooltan occupied the eastern and the Ratu the western portion. Above all there were the bath-rooms, dedicated to Kama and his wife Rati of Hindu memory; and since the parrot is the *vahana* of that frivolous god, many are the unspeakable tales of revived rites of his luxurious worship.

The etiquette at Court is fitly illustrated by the two tea-houses of Taman Sari, the eastern one for the Grand Pourer-out-of-Tea of the Right, who presided over the preparation of the delectable beverage for the Sooltan, and the western ditto for the Grand Pourer-out-of-Tea of the Left, who provided for the Ratu. A scrupulous punctilio is ingrained in Javanese habits and customs, from high to low, on great and small occasions, the native's mentality always reverting to things which were, but never more can be. The homage done to sacred objects, arms, *gamelans*, etc., by giving them a human name and a title,[1] venerating them as if en-

[1] Kiahi is a very common one. Dr. J. GRONEMAN, whose description of the water-castle at Jogjakarta contains a good many interesting particulars, mentions the name of the barge of state, presented to Paku Buwono I. by the East India Company, Niahi Kuning, as, to his knowledge, the only instance of a female appellation being given to royal paraphernalia—perhaps on the same principle as that which makes us, too, speak of a ship as of a "she".

dowed with supernatural faculties, recalls Polynesian fetishism, Hinduïsm being blended with it in Siva's *trishula*, Vishnu's *chakra*, etc., which are still carried behind the native princes among their *ampilan.*[1] The *upacharas* or imperial and royal *pusakas*[2] are treated with the utmost reverence when shown at the appearance in public of Susuhunan or Sooltan, and their bearers, the *koncho ngampil*, who hold an honoured position at the Courts of Solo and Jogja, may be considered direct successors of the envoys of King Dasharatha on the reliefs of the *chandi* Loro Jonggrang, who bore his regalia when meeting Rama and Lakshama. The strange ceremonial, preserved from the time when gods walked amongst men, seems hardly antiquated, on the contrary very germane to *siti-inggil*[3] surroundings. One need not visit the *kratons* though, to notice how the spirit of the past permeates all things Javanese; any well-dressed native getting out of his *sado*[4] at the railway station or repairing thither on foot for a journey with the fire-carriage, will do. Even if he cannot afford the few *doits*[5] necessary and must impair his

[1] Emblems of royalty; more strictly: objects of virtu belonging to the reigning family.

[2] A *pusaka* is an heirloom, generally with luck bringing properties either to the rightful owner or to any one who secures possession of it.

[3] Lit. "the high place" of the *kraton*.

[4] Short for *dos-à-dos*, a kind of vehicle naturalised in Java; offering only problematic comfort at its very best, the ramshackle specimens plying for hire in the streets of the capital towns of the island, beat everything ever invented anywhere else in the world for inflicting torture on the pretext of conveyance.

[5] *Doits* are copper coins of endless variety, demonetised more than half a century ago but still used by the natives almost exclusively and to the prejudice of the legal "cent", the hundredth part of the "guilder" or legal unit of the Dutch East Indian currency, notwithstanding the Government's

dignity by going afoot, he has his retainers to look after his box and, stuck behind, he has his magnificent kris in a sheath of gold, with a beautifully carved ivory handle, in nine cases out of ten a *pusaka*, cherished like the kris Kolo Munyang of the Prince of Kudoos or, as others allege, of a Susuhunan of Surakarta, who sent the weapon, which killed its master's enemies without human direction, to the assistance of Pangeran Bintoro, then oppressed by a king of Mojopahit. The chronology of this legend is evidently a little faulty, but, O! the wonders of Java's golden age, and, O! the superstitious honour in which their memory is held by these lovable people, whose actual existence is a dream of days gone by. And that happy dream, they ween, is a presage of the future, prophesying the restoration of their fathers' heritage. If, nevertheless, the hour draws near of unconditional surrender, the Dutch Government steadily and surely arrogating to itself the externals with the substance of power in the Principalities, they will silently submit to the *nivarana* of their ancient faith, the hindrance arising from torpor of mind appointed to them in the *sansara*, the rotary sequence of the world, and seek consolation in the promise of their new faith that the Lord will not deal wrongly with his servants. The life of nations, like the life of men, starts running as the mountain torrent and meets many

efforts (on paper) through the medium of financial geniuses, whose name is Legion and whose practical performance is Nihil, to put the monetary system and colonial finance in general on a firm, workable basis.

an obstacle before it swells to a broad river in the plains and flows tranquilly and mightily to the sea; also for Java it is written:

> . . . Non anche,
> l' opra del secol non anche è piena.[1]

---

[1] . . . Not yet, the work of (our) time has not yet reached its fullness.

CHAPTER VI

EAST JAVA

> cosi da l' ossa dei sepolti cantano
> i germi de la vita e degli spiriti.[1]
>
> GIOSUÈ CARDUCCI, *Odi Barbare* (*Canto di marzo*).

WHEN, suddenly, for reasons still unknown, the classic period of art in Central Java closed, about 850 Saka (A.D. 928), East Java awakened and entered on an era of artistic activity in every direction, which lasted until the fall of Mojopahit six centuries and a half later. In architecture it offers nothing so grand and imposing as the ancient temples of the Middle Empire, but much more diversity, and numerous inscriptions, resembling, after 900 Saka (A.D. 978), in form and contents, what we possess of old Javanese literature, enable us in many cases to determine the dates and also the character of the *chandis*, found principally along the course of the Brantas in the residencies Pasuruan, Kediri and Surabaya. Moving eastward, it was there that Hindu civilisa-

[1] So from the bones of those inhumed sing
The germs of life and of the spirits.

tion made greatest progress, no more in the vigorous enthusiasm of a young faith eager to proselyte, but modified by and finally succumbing to the influences of the soil, the climate, the idiosyncrasies of the aborigines. The oldest dates (Madioon, Kediri, Surabaya and Pasuruan) fall between 890 and 1140; then we have a good many again from Kediri (1120–1240 and 1270–1460) and from Surabaya (1270–1490); also from Pasuruan, Probolinggo and Besuki (1340–1470), Madura (1290–1440) and Rembang (1370–1390); finally, the constructive energy returning to Central Java, from Samarang and Surakarta (1420–1460), Suku and Cheto bringing up the rear. In the palmy days of Daha and Tumapel a sort of transition style was elaborated; under Ken Angrok and his descendants on the throne of Mojopahit, East Java reached its architectural zenith, never equal in the grandeur of its conceptions to the Boro Budoor or even the Prambanan temples, to the symmetrical richness of the Mendoot, but making up in fantastic decoration what it had lost in sobriety of outline. The builders pandered to the unwholesome demand for that perfection at any cost which Ruskin censures as the main mistake of the Renaissance in its early stages, the workman losing his soul in exchange for consummate finish. But, though they bear the impress of decadence, the products of eastern Javanese constructive efforts are not wholly degenerate, never coarse or vulgar and well worth looking at from more than one point of view. The evolution of the ornament alone is exceedingly suggestive: the "recalcitrant spiral" which in Central Java ascends, decking the supports, topples, as it were, in East Java, losing its character and becoming a meaningless adornment of the casements of, *e.g.*, the *chandi* Panataran; the *kala*-heads remain but the *makaras* change into a flame-like embellishment; where they are altogether dissolved, as in the *chandi* Jago or Toompang, it is safe to conclude with Dr. Brandes to late eastern Javanese influences.[1]

It has been conjectured that the migration of Hinduïsm to East Java was the effect of Buddhism gaining ground in the central part of the island; that the pronounced Sivaïte tendencies of Mojopahit were a reaction against Buddhist innovations. But it remains still to be proved that Mojopahit, though worshipping Siva as the supreme god of the Trimoorti, adhered to his overlordship in all its orthodox purity. There are, on the contrary, indications of Vishnuïte leanings, of Buddhist heresy, of a syncretism no less pronounced than that of Prambanan and the Mendoot. In the time of Old Mataram's hegemony, Buddhism must have ingratiated itself to some extent with her eastern vassals and, though not one of the temples in East Java is Buddhist after the fashion of the *chandis* Boro Budoor, Mendoot and Sewu, vestiges of the Bhagavat's doctrine are undeniable in Kediri,

[1] Cf. Miss MARTINE TONNET's article in the *Bulletin of the Dutch Archaeological Society*, 1908, on the work of the Archaeological Commission.

Southern Surabaya and Northern Pasuruan. A fusion of Sivaïsm and Buddhism has continuously controlled the construction of the larger temples of the later eastern Javanese period, says Rouffaer. Statues found in many places, *e.g.* in the *chandi* Toompang, are distinctly Buddhist and, what is most remarkable, though of later workmanship than those of Central Java and of a different style, tainted by decadent methods, they possess high merits as works of art. In their Sivaïtic surroundings they confirm the statements of the Chinese traveller Hiuen Tsiang who, perambulating India between 629 and 645, before the persecution of the Buddhists commenced, remarked upon the tolerance of the brahmins and *vice versa*, a virtue the Hindus carried with them to Java as already observed in the chapter on Prambanan. The kings of Mojopahit followed the example set in those regions: they were Saivas, Vaishnavas, Buddhists or followers of no one creed in particular, ready to protect and prefer each of them according to circumstances. In codes of law and poetry, Sivaïte priests and *sugatas*, pious brethren on the Buddhist road to perfection, are mentioned in one breath as conductors of the religious exercises on festive occasions, invoking the blessings of heaven on harvests and enterprises of peace and war; the poet Tantular calls the Buddha one with the Trimoorti.[1]

The Muhammadans were not so indulgent when

[1] Cf. Professor J. H. C. KERN's paper on Sivaïsm and Buddhism in Java apropos of the old Javanese poem *Sutasoma*, Amsterdam, 1888.

the Pangerans of Giri increased in authority as spiritual leaders of their faith, successors of Maulana Ibrahim, its first apostle in East Java. The hillock of Giri became a centre of incitement to the holy war, particularly so under Raden Ratu Paku or Sunan Prabu Satmoto, whose tomb is still an object of Moslim pilgrimage.[1] With his approval, if not on his instigation, the Muhammadan states on the north coast combined under Raden Patah of Demak to compass the extermination of heathenism and he lived to see the overthrow of Mojopahit, though dying shortly afterwards. If the Moslemin yearned to gain Paradise, sword in hand, martyrs for their Prophet's dispensation, those of the old creed remembered the power of *their* gods, blowing the *sanka*, the war-shell of Vishnu, who proved to Sugriva and Hanoman his superiority over Wali by shooting his arrow through seven palm-trunks; who, in his fourth *avatar*, as *narasinha*, the man-lion, ripped open the belly of the sacrilegious demon Hiranya Kasipu. But Raden Patah, marching with his allies, marvellously helped in the way of the Lord against the idolaters of Mojopahit, the swollen with pride, proved to be the giant in the shape of a dwarf, Vamana, known from their god's fifth *avatar*, conqueror of the three worlds. And Mojopahit, so great that the claims to the honour of her foundation, forwarded by as many princely

[1] The Pangerans of Giri continued for almost two centuries to exercise their spiritual authority, opposing the supremacy of the Princes of New Mataram until the Susuhunan Mangku Buwono II. had the last of them assassinated with all the male members of his family (1680).

houses as existed in those days, were fused in the tradition of her divine origin, her capital with its hundred gates and shining streets and palaces, the like of which had never been seen, having sprung from the earth in one night as a flower at the call of the fragrant dawn,—Mojopahit was overthrown and, laments the Javanese chronicle, the prosperity of the island disappeared. Not the last but the strongest bulwark of Hinduïsm had ceased to exist, bearing bitter fruit [1] of presumptuous pride indeed; the later Hindu empires, even Balambangan, which gave so much trouble to New Mataram and submitted only to the arms of the East India Company, leaving the ancient creed to die of slow exhaustion in the Tengger mountains, were nothing compared to her.

Like the remains, near the *dessa* Galang, of the *kraton* of the kings of the older empire of Daha, what has escaped total destruction of the capital of Mojopahit is constructed of brick. The ruins are situated about eight miles to the southwest of Mojokerto [2] in the valley of the Brantas; near Ngoomplak was the site of a royal residence in the building of which stone seems also to have been used. Raffles, visiting those heaps of debris scattered over quite a large area, found but scanty evidence of the fact that he trod the spot where great rulers had employed great architects, raising great structures for posterity to remember their great deeds by;

[1] *Mojo* means "fruit", *pahit* means "*bitter*".
[2] *Kerto* means "shining, glittering".

Wardenaar, whom he had taken with him as a draughtsman, might have stayed at Batavia, though in his *History of Java* he gives an illustration of "one of the gateways" and says that the marks of former grandeur there are more manifest than at Pajajaran, which, well considered, is saying very little. Now, a century later, a century of continued neglect, the general impression is still less calculated to prompt a vision of heroes subjecting thrones and dominions in the short space left them by their ancestor Ken Angrok's murderous kris, defying the grave, unmindful of Mpu Gandring's curse. Walking round in an effort to fit the scenery to historical dramas of love, hate and ambition, extreme care is necessary to avoid stepping on snakes coiled in dangerous repose or crawling among the brickbats which represent the foundations of princely mansions, digesting their last meal or hungry after the lizards that move restlessly in and out of chinks and crannies, lively beasties, enjoying the sunshine until snapped up, far more interesting really than the piles of rubbish bearing meaningless names. The natives one meets, will spin yarns *ad libitum* anent the numerous graves and crumbling substructures, but few have an intelligible tale to tell. Here are portions of the city-wall; there the remnant of the gate Bajang Ratu; half a mile farther the *aloon aloon*, the *taman* or pleasance, the tanks for bathing. A road, in great need of repair, leads through the Trowulan, the interior; exterior roads may be taken through ricefields and teak-plantations to the tomb of Ratu Champa, distinguished by curtains which once may have been white. Before a small building, enclosed by a fence, lies a stone supposed to cover the entrance to a subterranean apartment, the hiding-place, it is said, of the last king of Mojopahit when his capital was taken by the Moslim enemy. More graves surround that cache, graves without and, to intimate the pre-eminent importance of the elect thus honoured, graves *with* dirty curtains, narrow strips of soiled cloth, sad offerings to the dead sovereigns of an empire of celestial fame. One feels almost inclined to refuse credence to the grand past this ragged display tries to commemorate and, from sheer disappointment, to join the ranks of the sceptics who doubt of the capital of Mojopahit ever having amounted to much, and maintain that, in any case, it had come down and was of no consequence compared with Tuban and Gresik, already in 1416, a century before its falling into the hands of the Muhammadans.

At Mojopahit it is the same old story of quarrying for building material: several sugar-mills in the neighbourhood with the dwellings of managers and employees, have been wholly or partly constructed of Mojopahit bricks. In 1887 I saw them used for the abutments of bridges, foremen of the Department of Public Works superintending. A short time before, twelve copper plates had been found with inscriptions in ancient characters, which disappeared in a mysterious way. The *rechos* of Mojopahit were mostly left alone, a respectful treatment they owed to their general clumsiness. Some two or three miles from the ruins of the capital, a goodly number stand or lie together fair samples of statuary of the first eastern Javanese period, in its extravagance and exaggeration a travesty of the classic art of Central Java, crudity of conception floundering in a redundancy of form also observable at the *chandis* Suku and Cheto; after the fall of Mojopahit, in the second period, the sculptor reverted to a close study of nature as manifested at the *chandis* Toompang and Panataran; in the third, Hindu methods getting crowded within ever narrower limits, his fancy betrayed him again into lavish detail as exemplified in old Balinese imagery. At the gradual extinction of Hindu ideals of beauty, realised in decaying stone and brick, in statues defaced and vanishing like dwindling phantoms, a growing sensation of emptiness, emphasised by vague reminiscences of the artistic fullness of the *jaman buda,* claiming amends from succeeding creeds, received little from Islām and absolutely nothing from Christianity. Under Dutch rule very few attempts at style in Java and the other islands of the Malay Archipelago have been made at all, and of these few only one has resulted in an achievement not altogether ridiculous, namely the old town-hall, begun in 1707 and finished in 1710, of old Batavia, where the Resident has his office, by the natives very appropriately called *rumah bichara, i.e.* "house of talk". With one or two utterly tasteless exceptions, the rest of the Government and private buildings, including the palaces of the Governor-General at Weltevreden and Buitenzorg, descend in their architecture to the lowest grade of the commonplace. To his Excellency's ill-kept country-seat in the Preanger subverted Mojopahit seems almost preferable, notwithstanding the squalor of its threadbare *kaïn klambu* decoration ; the meanness of the viceregal reception- and living-rooms at Chipanas is not even picturesque and surely some of the public money regularly paid out for the maintenance of the "Government hotels" might be profitably expended on the improvement of the surroundings of Her Majesty the Queen of the Netherlands' representative in the Dutch East Indies, including the rickety furniture, shabby napery, etc., which has a pitiful tale of unseemly parsimony to tell: the superiority of high rank needs decorum and nowhere more than in oriental countries, a truth lately too much lost sight of by officials, high and low, who, following the example set at Buitenzorg, hoarding against the hour of their demission, presume on their "prestige" without anything to back it.

Mojopahit had ceased to exist and the Muhammadans with the Christians in their wake overran Java, despoiling the land in which toleration and art could no more flourish, but dissension throve as the tree prophetically imaged at the Boro Budoor, whose branches bear swords and daggers instead of wholesome, luscious fruit. The old quarrels over political supremacy were surpassed in violence by religious strife, and fanaticism is still held responsible in our day for disturbances conveniently ascribed to Moslim cussedness when the acknowledgment of the real cause, discontent born from over-taxation, would be tantamount to a confession of administrative impotence. It was not Hanoman, the deliverer of Sita, who troubled the repose of Ravana's garden, but the *raksasas* and *raksasis* who kept her in bonds, and there are two solutions of the Dutch East Indian problem, independent of the issue celebrated in the *Ramayana* and both suggested in the ornament of Java's temples: the devourer Time destroying all with his sharp teeth, and the lion, or tiger, to preserve the local colour, master of the fleeting moment, with a garland of flowers in his mouth, image of the clouded present holding out the promise of a brighter future. The two auguries, dark yet hopeful, belong to one old order of ideas, prefiguring things to come in dubious language, after the wont of oracles, ancient and modern, and we can choose the forecast which likes us best. So did the princes of Daha, Tumapel and Mojopahit, not to mention the lesser fry, creatures of a breath as we deem them now, doughty warriors and far-seeing statesmen to their contemporaries, who consulted their soothsayers before treading the fields of fame and blood whence they were carried to their graves, admiring nations rearing the mausoleums which now constitute the greater part of the historic monuments of East Java. The *Pararaton* mentions no fewer than seventy-three structures of that description. Such as have been left are, for various

CHANDI PAPOH

(Archaeological Service through Charls and van Es.)

reasons, hard to classify, the greatest difficulty arising from their bad state of preservation, though deciphered dates furnish important clues, for instance regarding some *chandis* in Kediri: Papoh (1301), Tagal Sari (1309), Kali Chilik (1349), Panataran (1319–1375),[1] the last named being probably the principal tomb of the dynasty of Mojopahit. Springing from the soil in amazing dissimilitude, their architects seeking new modes of expression in new forms and never hesitating at any oddity, at any audacity to proclaim the message of artistic freedom from convention, they struggled free from the sober lines and harmonious distribution of spaces always maintained in Central Java, to run riot in fantastic innovations. Yet, they held communion with nature and neither shirked their responsibility nor sinned against the proper relations between their purpose and the visible consummation of their task as those of our modern master-builders do who contrive churches like barns or cattle-sheds, stables like gothic chapels, prisons like halls of fame and cottages like mediaeval donjons. From such architectural absurdities it is pleasant to turn, *e.g.*, to the *chandi* Papoh, a temple whose corner-shrines might pass for daintily wrought golden reliquaries inlaid with jewels, when the minute detail of their exquisite decoration is shone upon by the setting sun; or to

[1] These dates are taken from Miss MARTINE TONNET's paper in the *Bulletin of the Dutch Archaeological Society* already cited, where she calls attention to the ardent religious life in that region at that time, as also attested to by the zodiac-beakers, mostly unearthed in Kediri and bearing dates between 1321 and 1369.

the *chandi* Sangrahan, when warmed to life from death and fearful decay, by the blue of a measureless sky, again budding from the earth, lovely as the lotus in the bliss bestowing hand of one of the five finely chiselled but headless statues near by.

Holiness in East Java, as everywhere in the island, took naturally to bathing. The retreat Bookti in the district Rembes, set apart for that pastime, according to the legend by Semu Mangaran, first king of Ngarawan (the later Bowerno and still later Rembang), had and has many rivals, nearly all in possession of antiquities to show their sacred character and the regard in which they were held. Some, like Bookti and Banyu Biru, the deservedly popular "blue water" of Pasuruan, are enlivened by colonies of monkeys, descendants of the apes kept there in Hindu times, beggars by profession, whose antics reap a rich reward. Sarangan in Madioon, Trawulan and Jalatoonda in Surabaya, Jati Kuwoong and Panataran in Kediri, Ngaglik and Balahan in Pasuruan, shared in olden times the renown which now is principally divided between Banyu Biru and Wendit, not to forget Oombulan, delightful spots, typical of a land where life is a continuous caress. Ngaglik has a beautiful female statue, evidently destined to do service as a fountain-figure after the manner of the nymphs which grace John the Fleming's[1] Fontana del Nettuno in Bologna and countless other waterworks of his and the succeeding

[1] More generally known as Giovanni da Bologna, though a native of Douay.

period. Wendit has Sivaïte remains: the prime god's *nandi*, statues of Doorga, Ganesa, etc.; most of the *lingas* and *yonis* that used to keep them company as reminders of their inmost nature, have been carried off. Banyu Biru has a statue of Doorga, *raksasas*, fragments of Banaspatis, etc., and a very remarkable image of Ganesa with female aspect, an object of veneration, especially on Friday evenings when flowers and copper, even silver coins are strewn round to propitiate his dual spirit, candles are lighted and sweetmeats offered to the ancient deities taken collectively. The *chandis* Jalatoonda and Putri Jawa served a double purpose: devotion and ablution, facilities for an invigorating bath playing a prominent part. The former, in the district Mojokerto, residency Surabaya, is the mausoleum of King Udayana, father of King Erlangga, and one of the oldest monuments in East Java; the latter, in the district Pandakan, residency Pasuruan, has much in common, as to ornament, with the *chandi* Surawana of the year 1365 and belongs on the contrary to the younger products of Hindu architecture. *Chandi* Putri Jawa means "temple of the Javanese princesses", and Ratu Kenya, the Virgin Queen of Mojopahit (1328–1353), who spoiled her reputation for chastity by losing her heart to a groom in her stables and making him share her throne, as the *Damar Wulan* informs us, may have repaired thither with her ladies-in-waiting to sacrifice and disport in the swimming-tank which is still replenished with water from the neighbouring river, flowing through the cleverly devised conduits; or the women of her luckless last successor, King Bra Wijaya, may have taken their pleasure there along with their devotional exercises before the Moslim torrent swamped their lord and master's high estate, harem and all.

Cave temples have been found in Surabaya (Jedoong), in Besuki (Salak) and in Kediri (Jurang Limas and Sela Mangleng). The latter, of greatest interest and Buddhist in character, can be divided into pairs: Sela Baleh and Guwa Tritis, Joonjoong and Jajar. They are easily reached from Tuloong Agoong and, though the removable statuary is gone, except the heavy *raksasas*, defaced figures on pedestals, etc., the sculpture of the interior walls of the caves remained in a tolerable state of preservation. Above on the ridge is a spot much resorted to for meditation and prayer, where the view of the charming valley of the Brantas, bounded by the beetling cliffs of the south coast, the treacherous Keloot to the northeast and the majestic Wilis[1] to the northwest, prepares the soul for communion with the Spirit of the Universe. Remains of brick structures abound in East Java; besides the ruins of Daha and Mojopahit we have, for instance, the walls of the Guwa Tritis under the jutting Gunoong Budek, the *chandis* Ngetos at the foot of the Wilis, Kali Chilik near Panataran, Jaboong in Probolinggo

[1] On the summit of the Wilis are four heaps of debris and two enclosed terraces; on its eastern slope is a place of prayer, consisting of three terraces with bas-reliefs and called Penampihan, where the natives still congregate for sacrifice.

and Derma in Pasuruan. The *chandi* Jaboong presents a remarkable instance of tower-construction applied to religious buildings in Java as further exemplified, conjointly with terraces, in the *chandi* Toompang. The surprises offered by the *chandi* Derma are no less gratifying, firstly to travellers in general who visit Bangil and, approaching the temple, which remains hidden to the last moment, suddenly come upon it in an open space adapted to full examination; secondly to archaeologists in particular because, dating from the reign of Mpu Sindok (850 Saka or before) and therefore one of the oldest monuments in East Java, if not the oldest in a recognisable state of preservation, it must be accepted as the prototype of Javanese architecture bequeathed by Old Mataram and is a valuable help to the study of the ancient builders' technique, showing, among other things, says Dr. Brandes, that the larger ornamental units are of one piece of terra-cotta, joined to the masonry by means of tenons and mortises.

About a mile to the southeast of Malang, on the top of a hill near the *kampong* Bureng, are traces of more buildings constructed in brick, the ruins of Kota Bedah. The foundation of that city is attributed to a son of Gajah Mada, chief minister of the last king of Mojopahit who, after his master's fall, fled eastward and, subjecting Singosari with adjoining territories, became the progenitor of the dynasty of Supit Urang. The Moslemin pushing on and harassing the Saivas wherever met, invested

Kota Bedah but, not prevailing against the strong defence of its commander Ronga Parmana, they caught the citizens' pigeons which flew over their camp and, attaching pieces of burning match-rope to the birds' wings and tail-feathers, they set fire to the thatch of the houses within the walls and so gained their end. Thereupon they destroyed the royal residence Gedondong, to the east of Malang, and those of Supit Urang took refuge in the Tengger mountains. This is one of several traditions explaining the existence of Sivaïte remains scattered in that neighbourhood: at Dinoyo, Karanglo, Singoro, Katu, Pakentan, etc. On the road to Toompang stands the *chandi* Kidal, one of the best preserved in Java, only the upper part of the roof having fallen down. It is the mausoleum of Anusapati, the Hamlet of Javanese history, referred to in the preceding chapter, who was killed in 1249 by his step-brother. His likeness has been sought in an image of Siva, on the supposition that some statues of deities there erected, which point to the use of living models, represent the features of exalted personages. An enormous Banaspati over the entrance with smaller ones over the niches, *garudas* and lions form the principal decoration in frames of highly finished ornament. Dr. Brandes remarks that in contrast to the decoration of the temples in Central Java, the heavy ornament of the relief-tableaux is here distributed over the parts which carry the weight of the superstructure, while the lighter ornament finds employment on the

CHANDI SINGOSARI

(Archaeological Service through Charls and van Es.)

panels and facings. The methods of construction and the treatment of details mark clearly a transition to the younger period of eastern Javanese architecture best illustrated by the *chandi* Panataran.

Somewhat older, built in 1278 as a mausoleum for Kertanegara, the last king of Tumapel, who reigned from 1264 to 1292 and was killed in battle by Jaya Katong, King of Daha, is the *chandi* Singosari, near the railway station of that name, an excellent starting-point for an ascension of the fire-mountain Arjuno or Widadaren. It has been called one of the most unfortunate monuments in the island; not, presumably, because it shared the common lot, being gradually deprived of its finest ornament while its stones were freely disposed of for building material without the local authorities minding in the least, but because the spoliation could be watched by a comparatively large number of planters and industrials, settled in the neighbourhood, none of them interfering unless to its detriment. Insurmountable difficulties of transportation opposed the removal of the colossal *raksasas* and so they were left with a *nandi*, a sun-carriage and, among fragments too defaced for recognition, a Ganesa and a female Buddhist saint, for this temple-tomb is of a mixed character in its religious aspect. A Javanese chronicle relates that Kertanegara was buried at Singosari in 1295, three years after his death, in the guise of Siva-Buddha, and at Sakala conformably to a more pronounced Buddhist rite. He was considered a wise ruler, notwithstanding his abusive attitude towards China, which had such dire results. He built an edifice, continues the *babad*, divided into two parts, the lower one Sivaïtic, the upper one Buddhistic, because in his life he prided himself on being a Saiva as well as a Buddhist. A richly ornamented *kala*-head in eastern Javanese style testifies to the admirable technique of the builders and decorators. According to popular belief a subterranean passage leads from Singosari to Polaman, about six miles away, a place of sacrifice in Hindu days, and another to Mondoroko, close by, the site of a ruin with a graceful statue of a female deity, two smaller ones which remind the beholder of Siva's and Doorga's creative faculties, and sadly damaged bas-reliefs. In 1904 an inscribed stone was recovered, at the intimation of a native, from a pond near Singosari. Confirming the data furnished by the Javanese chronicles, the inscription states that in 1351 Gajah Mada, the Prime Minister of Mojopahit, acting for King Wisnuwardhani, founded a temple-tomb, sacred to the memory of the priests, Saivas and Buddhists, who, in the year 1292, had followed their King Kertanegara in death, and of the old Prime Minister who had been killed at his feet. . . . "See here the foundation of the most honourable Prime Minister of Java's sea-girt domain."

Finest and most interesting of the Malang complex is the *chandi* Jago, about twelve miles to the east of the capital of the assistant-residency, in the *aloon aloon* of Toompang and hence more

CHANDI TOOMPANG

(Archaeological Service through Charls and van Es.)

commonly named *chandi* Toompang. It was the first taken in hand by the Commission appointed in 1901 and we owe most of the information, summarised in the following lines, to Dr. Brandes' reports on this archaeological debut. A rare example of tower-construction of the kind also observed in the *chandi* Jaboong, superposed on a raised level reached by terraces like those of the *chandis* Panataran and Boro Budoor, the extraordinary Javanese mixture of Sivaïsm and Buddhism with a dash of Vishnuïsm has affected it to such a degree that even a recent description declares it to be a Buddhist pit-temple—a contradiction in terms. Begun in the middle of the thirteenth century, *i.e.* in the time of Tumapel's political ascendency when Sivaïsm was the state religion, if we may speak of a state religion among peoples and princes whose predominant article of faith was tolerance and concession of equal rights to all religions, some of the learned investigators suppose with Professor Speyer that the Buddhist note was a consequence of the persecution of the adherents of Gautama's creed in India and the hospitality extended to the emigrants all over the island Java. However this may be, syncretism became rampant in both the ground-plan and the decoration of the *chandi* Toompang, conceived as an elevated dodecagonal structure on the highest of three irregularly shaped terraces, something quite exceptional in Javanese architecture. Apparently while the building was in progress, remarks Rouffaer, changes were made in the original project, and the more is the pity that the temple proper has fallen into almost complete ruin: not only that the roof is lacking, but the toppling back wall has dragged the greater part of the north and south walls down with it. The front or west wall has held out to a certain extent with the gateway, the chief entrance, a lofty, rectangular, monumental passage, ornamented on both sides and locked with a key-stone whose smooth middle space was destined, in the opinion of Dr. Brandes, to receive, but never did receive, the date of completion. Heaps of debris round about lead to the conjecture that the whole was encircled by a wall of brick and that the dwellings of the keepers or officiating priests were composed of the same material.

Several of the bas-reliefs fortunately escaped destruction and found an interpreter in Dr. Brandes, to whom we also owe explanations of the stereotyped decorative scrolls and flourishes. Though inferior in workmanship to the reliefs of Panataran, those of Toompang, "speaking" reliefs as he called them, are vigorously animated, gaining in interest to the devotee as he ascends the terraces, their masterly treatment culminating in what has been preserved on the portion still standing of the temple-walls. No better illustration of high and low life, of the nobility and the riff-raff portrayed in classic Javanese literature, could be imagined; the typical perfect knights and sly buffoons are there in crowds, princes and courtiers, warriors and peasants, gallivanting beaux and love-sick maidens, jealous husbands and frisky wives, worldwise sages and babbling fools, Javanese Don Quijotes riding out with their trusty squires of the Sancho Panza species, go-betweens neither better nor worse than Celestina, entangling dusky Melibeas. Every honourable soul is set off by his or her vulgar counterpart, of the earth earthy: the *panakawan* (page) and the *inya* (nurse) play most important rôles, almost equally important with those of the hero and heroine, and their characters are, conformably to the requirements of Javanese literature, clumsy and coarse but droll; their actions, whether they accomplish or fail to accomplish their tasks, reflect the performances of the born ladies and gentlemen whom they accompany, who lose each other and are reunited, who quarrel and make up, always in a comely, stately way, proud and sensitive, expressing their feelings in graceful gestures corresponding with the choicest words. When treating of Panataran, the ornamentation of the ancient monuments of East Java in its relation to Javanese literature will be more fully discussed. Here, however, belongs a reference to Dr. Brandes' ingenious explanation of the slanting stripes or bars, left uncarved at irregular intervals on the narrow tiers of bas-reliefs at the *chandi* Toompang; comparing those sculptured bands with the *lontar*[1] leaves on which the tales, whose illustration they furnish, were originally written, he saw in them the finishing strokes of the different chapters.

[1] *Borassus flabelliformis* of the palm family, which, though hardly used in these times of cheap paper as a provider of writing material, serves the natives for a hundred other purposes.

The statuary of the *chandi* Toompang has been removed, for the greater part, to the Museum at Batavia and, possibly, one or two images, with Professor Reinwardt's invoice of 1820, to that of Leyden. The deities are brilliantly executed, of idealistic design, to borrow Rouffaer's words, exuberant to the point of effeminacy. Some of them show the conventional Hindu type and we can imagine the wonderful effect they produced among the essentially Javanese scenes chiselled on the walls. For their inscriptions Nagari characters have been used, a circumstance adduced to prove the predominant Buddhist significance of this temple. The principal statue seems to have been the decapitated and otherwise damaged, eight-armed,[1] colossal Amoghapasa, Lord of the World, reproduced by Raffles, including the head, "carried to Malang some years ago by a Dutchman," he informs us, which, symbolic of unity with Padmapani, displays Amitabha, the Dhyani Buddha of the West, the Buddha of Endless Light, in the manner of a frontal. The goddess Mamakhi, scarcely less beautifully cut and also reproduced by Raffles in his *History of Java*, was carried to England *in tota* by himself. Efforts to trace her whereabouts have not met with success; she remains more securely hidden, probably in one of the store-rooms of the British Museum, than the stone with inscription recording an endowment, transported from Java to

[1] Two of the eight arms were already missing in 1815 to judge from Raffles' reproduction.

the grounds of Minto House near Hassendean, Scotland. Talking of carrying away: a little to the southeast of the *chandi* Toompang stood a temple of which hardly a stone has been left; a little to the south of the *chandi* Singosari another is visibly melting into air. The Chinese community at Malang, as Dr. Brandes informed the Batavian Society of Arts and Sciences, boast of a permanent exhibition of Hindu statuary and ornament, consisting of more than 160 numbers, gathered together in the neighbourhood and on view in their cemetery. Baba collects Sivaïte and Buddhist antiquities with great impartiality, subordinating religious scruples to practical considerations, as when he lights his long-stemmed pipe at one of the votive candles on the altars in his places of worship. Excellent opportunities for the study of Chinese influences on Javanese art are offered by the decoration of his temple in Malang with its motives derived from creeping, fluttering, running, pursuing and fleeing things: tigers, deer, dragons, bats, especially bats, shooting up and down, flitting off, swiftly turning back, circling and scudding. The mural paintings of a good many other *klentengs*, too, are of more than passing interest since they promote a right understanding of the development of the Greater Vehicle of the Law, which in Java exchanged fancies and notions with both Chinese Buddhism and Taoïsm, discarded the classic for the romantic, if the expression be permissible in this connection, and still continues to live among the island's inhabitants of Mongolian extraction, as Sivaïsm among the Balinese, their creative thought moulding old fundamental ideas in unexpected new forms. If Buddhism brought new elements into Chinese art, stimulating ideals and religious imagery, as the Count de Soissons remarks,[1] leading, for instance, to sublime personifications of Mercy, Tenderness and Love, the debt is repaid and emigrating Chinese decorators shower the graces of their benign goddess Kwan Yin on their labours in distant climes. As to Java, with which China entertained relations from the remotest Hindu period, they animated and reshaped in endless variation the ornament they found, the *makaras*, the *kala*-heads, at last, in their *saï-shiko* tracery, being gradually supplanted by the bat-motive.

The *chandi* Panataran is the most beautiful, for many reasons also the most remarkable temple in East Java and, with the exception of the Boro Budoor, the largest in the whole island. It was discovered by the American explorer Thomas Horsfield. Its foundations and the interior of its sepulchral pit are constructed in brick; its terraces are in general design not unlike those of the *chandi* Toompang; among its statues, stolen and scattered far and wide, it may have contained images of Buddhist purport and inspiration. Sivaïtic in aspect, however, as it stands now, it is the only one of the monuments in Kediri sufficiently preserved

[1] See his article, *Pictorial Art in Asia*, in the *Contemporary Review* of May, 1911.

XVIII.

CHANDI PANATARAN

(Archaeological Service through Charls and van Es.)

to determine its religious origin. Fergusson classes the *chandi* Panataran with the tree- and serpent-temples whose most peculiar feature in the residencies Malang and Kediri consists in having "a well-hole in the centre of their upper platform, extending apparently to their basement," and the suggestion occurring to him "as at all likely to meet the case, (is) that they were tree-temples, that a sacred tree was planted in these well-holes, either in the virgin soil, or that they were wholly or partially filled with earth and the tree planted in them." He compares the *chandi* Panataran with the Naha Vihara or Temple of the Bo-tree in Ceylon and bases its claim to being called a serpent-temple on the fact that "the whole of the basement moulding is made up of eight great serpents, two on each face, whose upraised breasts in the centre form the side-pieces of the steps that lead up to the central building, whatever that was. These serpents are not, however, our familiar seven-headed Nagas that we meet with everywhere in India and Cambodja, but more like the fierce, crested serpents of Central America." So far Fergusson; but the well or pit, notwithstanding the veneration of which the bo-tree was the object, seems rather to have been a receptacle for the ashes of the princes of Mojopahit whose memory the founder of this mausoleum, probably Queen Jayavisnuvardhani, the above-mentioned Ratu Kenya, immortalised in the *Damar Wulan*, intended to perpetuate. The *raksasas*, guardians of the ruins of the principal structure, bear the date 1242 Saka (A.D. 1320); a minor temple and terrace give the dates 1369 and 1375, from which it has been concluded that they were added in the reign of Ratu Kenya's son Hayam Wurook.

The edifice rose from a square base and large statues of Siva as Kala adorn the feet of the staircases which lead to the first and second terrace. Of the temple proper not a stone is left; the walls of pit and terraces are covered with sculpture, a sort of griffins on the highest, scenes from the *Ramayana* and illustrations of other popular poems and fables on the lower ones, beautiful work but irreparably damaged by official bungling. As if the apathy which suffered this noble monument to be despoiled and the providentially undemolished parts to crumble away, had not done enough harm, an amateur invested with local authority conceived a plan of restoration and preservation on official lines, that beat even the methods of the art-connoisseurs of the chain-gang to whom the care for the antiquities at Jogjakarta is entrusted, which would make reconstruction impossible for all time to come and deface the ornament in the thoroughest possible way. In obedience to a Government resolution of June 22, 1900, Nr. 18, the Batavian Society of Arts and Sciences having been consulted with a view to save the *chandi* Panataran from further decay, the Contrôleur in charge of the administrative division within whose boundaries it is situated, engaged native masons who, following their instructions, cemented, plastered and whitewashed to the tune of fl. 989.10 (about £82) with the magnificent result that the upper terrace has been transformed into a thickly plastered reception-bower for picnic parties; that everything has received a neat coat of white-wash to rejoice the hearts of housewives out for the day with their husbands, little family and friends; that the architectural detail has been hidden under solid layers of mortar and cement. Plaster, white-wash and cement everywhere: the noses and other extremities of the scanty statuary still in place but injured by time and hand of man, have been touched up with it; from top to bottom it has been smeared over whatever could be reached, making the venerable old temple hideously ridiculous—an orgy of "conservation" in the pernicious official acceptance of the word, hoary age being ravaged by cheap, destructive "tidying up". This is how the theory of Government solicitude for the ancient monuments of Java works out in practice.

It must be considered a miracle or evidence of the native masons possessing a higher developed artistic sense than their employer, that the bas-reliefs have suffered less than this extraordinary process of restoration and preservation portended, though much detail has been destroyed, thanks to their vandalism under orders from Batavia as understood by the Philistine of Blitar. In the first place we find again, divided by medallions with representations of animal life, a sculptural delineation of the *Ramayana*, the artist's buoyant fancy, blending the celestial with the human, shedding a divine light on acts of most common daily occurrence by making gods and semi-gods partake of man's estate in deeds sublimely natural. The *Ramayana* was a great favourite for the decoration of temples, as proved by the *chandis* Panataran, Toompang, Surawana and Prambanan; the *Mahabharata* or, rather, its Javanese version, the *Brata Yuda*, came as a good second; the *Arjuno Wiwaha* of the poet Mpu Kanwa has been put to use for the embellishment of the *chandis* Surawana and Toompang; the *Kersnayana* for that of the *chandis* Toompang and Panataran. We might do worse and, in fact, we are doing worse with our insipid epitaphs and tasteless lapidary pomposity in our cemeteries, than adorn the tombs of our great departed with imagery taken from our poets, tellers of good tales and fabulists, the life they knew so well aiding us to fathom death with its mysteries and promises. The promise most cherished by the Hindu Javanese was that personified in Siva: death to make new life grow and increase in beauty among mortals feeding on happiness, by reason of Kala's breath destroying the misery of tottering old age, raising man to equality with the gods. That is what the people, for whom the marvellous ancient monuments of Java were built, loved to read in the masterpieces of their literature, carved for their benefit on the mausoleums of their kings, heeding the wise lessons for whoso chooses to reflect, of their *Canterbury Tales*, *Faerie Queene*, *Paradise Lost* and *Paradise Regained*; their *Narrenschiff*, *Dil Ulenspigel* and

Faust; their *Divina Commedia* and *Decameron*; their *Romancero del Cid* and *Conde Lucanor*; their *nouvelles* and *joyeux devis*, their *vies très horrifiques* of their Gargantuas and Pantagruels. Life in their thought being intimately connected with death, which consequently inspired nothing of the abject terror the practice of western Christianity clothes it with, in curious contrast to the saving hope of its eastern origin, we discern cheerfulness, the effect of serene meditation, the true *amrita*, the rejuvenating nectar of self-existent immortality, as the keynote also to sensible earthly existence in the infinitely varied forms inviting our examination on the walls of the *chandi* Panataran. *Greift nur hinein ins volle Menschenleben!* If the beholder be a philosopher or an artist, or both, desirous to grasp the full life of man, he will receive rare instruction; and if a *lustige Person* as well, joy will accrue to him from the sempiternal relevancy of Javanese allegorical humour, at times almost prophetic: the sculptor of the pigheaded but self-satisfied peasant who cultivates his land with a plow drawn by crabs,[1] must have had a vision of the Dutch Government endeavouring, after periodical visitations of worse than customary want, misery and famine, to secure progress and prosperity in the island by appointing long commissions with long names, toiling long years over long reports that leave matters exactly where they were.

[1] Bas-relief on the remains of a small building detached from the *chandi* Panataran proper.

The skies in the scenery of the bas-reliefs on the lowest terrace of the *chandi* Panataran have something very peculiar, termed cloud-faces by Dr. Brandes, who recognised in the fantastic forms of the floating vapour as reproduced in the hard stone, demons and animals to which he drew special attention: a *kala*-head, a furious elephant threatening to charge, etc. The figures of all bas-reliefs, mostly perhaps those of the second tier from below, are notable for their departure from the smooth treatment generally accorded to Javanese sculpture of the period and best defined perhaps in the phrase of one of Canova's critics when he derided that artist's "peeled-radish" style. Angular and flat, they remind one of the *wayang*-puppets, and the obvious correspondence between the manner in which the *chandi* Panataran illustrates some of the chief productions of Javanese literature and the performances of the Javanese national theatre, has been cleverly insisted upon by Rouffaer. The *wayang*, *i.e.* the dramatic art of the island, sprang probably from religious observances of pre-Hindu origin. Dr. G. A. J. Hazeu[1] is of opinion that it formed part of the ritual of the ancient faith, and even now the *hadat* requires a sacrifice, the burning of incense, etc., before the play commences. The Javanese word *lakon*, a derivation from *laku*, which signifies both "to run" and "to act", applied to stage composition, is the exact etymological equivalent of our "drama"; the *lakon yèyèr* (*layer* or *lugu*)

[1] *Bijdrage tot de Kennis van het Javaansche Tooneel.*

confines itself to tradition, the *lakon karangan* to subjects taken from tradition but freely handled, the *lakon sempalan* to episodes from works otherwise unsuitable because of their length. The *wayang* appears, according to means of interpretation, as *wayang poorwa* or *kulit*,[1] *gedog*, *kelitik* or *karucil*, *golek*, *topeng*, *wong* and *bèbèr*, of which the *wayang poorwa* holds the oldest title to direct descent from the ancestral habit of invocation of the spirits of the dead. The epithet *poorwa* has been derived from the *parwas* of the *Mahabharata* which, together with the *Ramayana* and similar sources, offered an abundant supply of dramatic material; it is from the *wayang poorwa* that the Javanese people derive their notions of past events, as the inhabitants of another island did theirs from their poet and playwright Shakespeare's histories before eminent actor-managers set to "improve" upon his work, mutilating him on his country's stage in the evolution of a (fortunately more textual) interpretation, pointedly designated as Shakespearian post-impressionism.

A *wayang poorwa* performance knows nothing of the showy accessories devised by and for our histrions to hide poverty of mentality and poorness of acting, futile attempts to make up in settings, properties, costumes and trappings, tailoring, millinery and disproportionate finery what they lack in essentials. The performer sits under his lamp behind a white, generally red-bordered piece of cloth stretched over

[1] *Kulit* means leather, the material of which the puppets are made.

a wooden frame on which he projects the figures. He speaks for them and intersperses explanations and descriptions, directing the musicians with his gavel of wood or horn, striking disks of copper or brass to intimate alarums, excursions, etc. Formerly all the spectators were seated before the screen, as they still are in West Java, Bali and Lombok, but gradually the men, separating from the women and children, moved behind, so that in Central and East Java they see both the puppets and their shadows. The *wayang gedog*, much less popular than the *wayang poorwa*, evolved from it in the days of Mojopahit as Dr. L. Serrurier informs us; while the latter draws its repertory principally from Indian epics, the former with Raden Panji, Prince of Jenggala, for leading hero, is more exclusively Javanese and prefers the low metallic music of the *gamelan pelog*[1] to that of the *gamelan salendro*[1] with its high notes as of ringing glass. In the *wayang kelitik* or *karucil*, of later invention and never of a religious character, the puppets themselves are shown: since *wayang* means "shadow", the use of that word is here, for that reason, less correct, and the same applies to the *wayang golek* in which the marionettes lose their spare dimensions

[1] The *gamelan*, as already remarked, is the Javanese orchestra, and besides the *gamelan salendro* and the *gamelan pelog*, the *gamelan miring* should be mentioned, which varies from the former in the higher pitch of one of the five notes as produced by some of the instruments. The Kiahi Moonggang, a relic of mighty Mojopahit, the oldest, most sacred and least melodious of the royal sets of *gamelan* instruments, is played every Saturday evening and so long as its tones fill the air, all other *gamelans* must remain silent. Cf Dr. J. GRONEMAN, *De Gamelan te Jogjakarta*.

and become stout and podgy; to the *wayang topeng*[1] and *wong*[2] in which living actors perform, an innovation not countenanced by the orthodox, who are afraid that such deviations from the *hadat* may result in dread calamities; and to the *wayang bèbèr* which consists in displaying the scenes otherwise enacted, in the form of pictures. Every one finds in the *wayang*, of whatever description, an echo of his innermost self: the high-born, smarting under a foreign yoke, in the *penantang* (challenge and defiance), the lowly in the *banolan* (farce), the fair ones of all classes in the *prenesan* (sentimental, gushing, spoony speech). It is a treat to look at the natives, squatted motionless for hours and hours together, their eyes riveted on the screen, listening to the voice of the invisible performer, marvelling at the adventures of the men and women who peopled the *negri jawa* before them and faded into nothingness, even the mightiest among them, whose mausolea at Prambanan, Toompang, Panataran, bear witness to the truth of those amazing deeds of derring-do, love and hate, which will remain the wonder of the world. To them the phantom-shadows are reality of happiness in a dull, vexatious life which is but the veil of death.

From Java, says Dr. Juynboll, the *wayang poorwa* was transplanted to Bali, where it is still

[1] The *topeng* actors are masked conformably to the meaning of the word. Masques and masquerades seem to be of high antiquity in Java; the *Malat* of the *Panji*-cycle already mentions that kind of dramatic entertainment.

[2] Utilised for prose works in the *langen driya*, devised by Pangeran Arya Mangku Negara IV., and in the *langen asmara*, devised by Prabu Widaya, a son of Paku Buwono IX.

called *wayang parwa* and the puppets present a more human appearance. Beside it thrives, especially in Karang Asam, the *wayang sasak*, introduced from Lombok and more Muhammadan in character, whose puppets have longer necks after the later Javanese fashion. Apart from such influences, Balinese art, however, does not disown its Hindu-Javanese origin. The inhabitants of the island, with the exception of the *Bali aga*, the aborigines in the mountains, different in many respects, pride themselves on the name of *wong* (men of) Mojopahit and adhere to the Brahman religion, though here and there a few Buddhists may be encountered. They are divided into castes and Sivaïte rites play an important part in the religious ceremonial of the upper classes. The common people have adopted a sort of pantheism which makes them sacrifice in the family circle to benevolent and malevolent spirits of land and water, domiciled in the sea, rivers, hills, valleys, cemeteries, etc. The village temples are more specifically resorted to for propitiation of the *jero taktu*, a superior being entrusted with the guidance of commercial affairs and best approached through the guardian of his shrine, who is held in greater respect than the real priests. Every village has also a house of the dead, consecrated to Doorga, a goddess in high repute with those desirous to dispel illness, to secure a favourable issue of some enterprise, to learn the trend of coming events; the heavenly lady enjoys in Bali a far wider *renommée* than her lord and master Siva, who is honoured in six comparatively little-frequented temples. As to the decadent architecture and excessive ornamentation[1] of the Balinese houses of worship, Dr. Brandes considers both the one and the other a direct outcome of the decay of the eastern Javanese style, exemplified in the *chandis* Kedaton (1292), Machan Puti,[2] Surawana and Tegawangi. The leading ideas of the *chandi bentar* or entrance gate, and of the *paduraksa* or middle gate, adduces Rouffaer, are related respectively to those of the gate Wringin Lawang at Mojopahit and of what the present day Javanese call *gapura* in sacred edifices as old *kratons*, old burial-grounds, etc.; and to those of the gate Bajang Ratu, also at Mojopahit. These gates Wringin Lawang and Bajang Ratu, states the same authority further, can teach us moreover a few things anent the architecture of the *puris* (palaces). The temples and princely dwellings of Mataram in Lombok were completely destroyed during the inglorious war of 1894; the country-seat of Narmada, however, a fine specimen of an eastern pleasance, has escaped demolition. For how long?

In this respect it seems relevant to point to the circumstance that the monuments of the smaller Soonda islands, much more conveniently placed for the unscrupulous spoiler because under less constant observation of the general public, are exposed to even greater danger than those in Java, Government

[1] In Balinese decoration, writes Miss MARTINE TONNET (see her article already cited), the *naga-* (or *kala-naga-*) seems to flourish beside the *makara-*ornament.

[2] Lit. "white tiger", situated in Banyuwangi.

supervision counting for worse than nothing. A Batavia paper denounced quite recently a traveller who had been visiting the Dutch East Indies and, armed with letters of recommendation from personages of the highest rank and title in the Netherlands, had been collecting curiosa and antiquities on a vast scale only to advertise his collection for sale as soon as unpacked after his return to Europe. It contained carved ornament from temples, sacrificial vessels and statuary from Bali, besides woven goods, implements used in *batikking*, musical instruments, *wayang*-puppets, etc. The profit attached to this sort of globe-trotting is enormous, since the coveted objects can be acquired for a mere song by taking advantage of the influential assistance secured through letters of recommendation over high-sounding names. A hint from those in authority goes a very long way with the docile native, in fact goes the whole way of appropriation at a nominal value, and the big official who left his post in the exterior possessions, bound for home, also quite recently, with fifty boxes of antique ware of a different kind, collected in his residency, made certainly as good a haul as the distinguished, brilliantly recommended tourist.

CHAPTER VII

BUDDHIST JAVA

Was ist das Heiligste? Das was heut' und ewig die Geister
Tief und tiefer gefühlt, immer nur einiger macht.[1]

WOLFGANG VON GOETHE, *Vier Jahreszeiten* (*Herbst*).

ALTHOUGH the theory of Gautama the Sugata's life-story being only a repolished solar myth has broken down, its vital element of emancipation from Brahmanic bonds is certainly much older than Buddhism and the traditional Buddha but an incarnation of ideas long germinating and attaining fruition in his teachings, precisely as happened with other religious reformers who came and went before and after. The thirty-three gods of the three worlds, "eleven in heaven, eleven on earth and eleven dwelling in glory in mid-air," with their three supreme shining ones, Brahma, Vishnu and Siva, creating, maintaining, destroying and creating anew, began to pall on the human *trimoorti* of brain, heart and bodily wants; the moral dispensa-

[1] What is Holiest? That which now and ever the souls of men
Have felt deep and deeper, will always more unite them.

tion on which the social edifice was founded, began to need revision. Neither did the orthodox, at first, refuse admittance to the spirit of emendation. At the *sangharama*[1] of Nalanda the Vedas were taught together with the Buddhist doctrine according to the tenets of the Greater and the Lesser Vehicle *à choix*. The Buddha had to be accepted and was accepted equally by eastern tolerance and western necessity; while ranking as a divine teacher among his followers in the legendary development of his precepts, he received honour as an incarnation of Vishnu among the Hindus, says Sir William W. Hunter,[2] and as a Saint of the Christian Church, with a day assigned to him in both the Greek and Roman calendars. Truly, the Hindus regarded him as the ninth and hitherto last incarnation of Vishnu, the Lying Spirit let loose to deceive man until the tenth and final descent of the god, on the white horse, with a flaming sword like a comet in his hand, for the destruction of the wicked and the renovation of the world, but he was reckoned with and acknowledged in their mythology, and the remarkable conformity between Prince Sarvarthasiddha's lineage, adventures and achievements, and those of the seventh *avatar* of the Hindu deity in the *Ramayana* are certainly more than accidental. The law of mercy to all, preached by the blissful Bhagavat, the Buddha, the Saviour, affected the Brahman creed profoundly; so pro-

[1] An endowed convent whose inmates spent their lives in studious seclusion.

[2] *The Indian Empire: its Peoples, History and Products.*

foundly in its deductions, that apprehensive priests resolved to extirpate Buddhist heresy. But since religious persecution always defeats its purpose, Buddhism throve with oppression and holds fully its own against the two other great religions of the present day, al-Islām and Christianity.

To define the Buddhism which, parallel and entwined with Hinduïsm, preceded the Muhammadanism of Java, is no easy matter, if it is possible at all. For the sake of convenience Javanese Buddhism may be classified as *mahayanistic*, conformable to the northern canon or doctrine of the Greater Vehicle, versus *hinayanistic*, *i.e.* conformable to the southern canon or the doctrine of the Lesser Vehicle. But the geographical division proposed by Burnouf, hardly meets the case of our more advanced knowledge, which points rather to chronological distinctions. Javanese Buddhism of the younger growth was strongly impregnated with modified Brahmanic conceits,[1] in fact a compromise between the hopeful expectation of the Metteya Buddha, the Messiah promised by Bhagavat, and resignation to the decrees of the Jagad Guru whom the Saivas of Hindu Java had chosen for their *ishta-devata*, the fittest form in which to adore the Ruler of the Universe, Param

[1] After this was written a remarkable article by Dr. L. A. WADDELL in *The Imperial and Asiatic Quarterly Review* (January, 1912), insisting upon the theistic nature of Buddhism and speaking of the profound theistic development which had taken place—about 100 B.C.—in the direction of the Mahayana form of that faith, pointed to the fact of Brahmanic gods being also conspicuous in the earliest Buddhist sculptures of India, adorning, *e.g.*, the stupa of Bharhoot.

Esvara. Siva lost under Buddhist influences his terrorising aspect as Kala, and the two creeds, giving and taking, lived in perfect concord. The statues of the Dhyani Buddhas partook of Siva's attributes; those of their sons, the Bodhisatvas, the Buddhas in evolution, and of their *saktis*, showed the characteristics of other Hindu gods and goddesses; Siva, conversely, assumed the features of Avalokitesvara or Padmapani, the Buddhist lord of the world that is now. I have already spoken of the enthroned Bodhisatvas represented at the Sivaïte temples of Prambanan and the more or less Sivaïte exterior of the Buddhist *chandi* Mendoot. Also of this remarkable syncretism, born from inbred tolerance, leading to new transactions with the Islām, exacting as it may be everywhere else; of the deference still shown to deities of the Hindu pantheon in the shape of *jinn*; of the adjustment of Muhammadan institutions to usages of Hindu origin; etc. And Buddhism, doubtless, prepared the mystically inclined mind of the Javanese Moslim for the acceptance of the mild Sufism of the school of Gazali, which guides him in submission of will to *ma'ripat*, full knowledge, and *hakakat*, most hidden truth, while he lacks the conviction, to quote Professor L. W. C. van den Berg, that his neglect of the prescribed daily prayers will make him lose his status as a true believer.

Central Java is richer yet in the quality than in the quantity of its Buddhist monuments, whose

XIX.

CHANDI KALASAN

(C. Nieuwenhuis.)

builders and decorators, like the true artists they were, told what they knew and believed, nothing but that, and therefore told it so well.[1] To examine their work, beautiful even in decay, beginning with the smaller structures, we wend our way again to the plain of Prambanan. Travelling from Jogjakarta to Surakarta by rail, the first stopping-place, reached in about twenty minutes, is Kalasan, the *chandi* of that name, otherwise called Kali Bening, being visible from the train. Once it must have been one of the finest and most elaborately wrought in the island; now only the south front, nearly tumbling down, witnesses to its former splendour. It was built in 700 Saka (A.D. 778), a date preserved in a Nagari inscription which settles that point,[2] and names a Shailandra prince as its founder in honour of his *guru* (teacher), doing homage to Tara[3] who, seeing the destruction of men in the sea of life, which is full of incalculable misery, saves them by three means . . .; it speaks of a grant of land to

[1] On rereading this sentence, I see that in writing it I was with Ruskin at the Shepherd's Tower. No harm done! His observations bear repetition, notwithstanding the present fashion of pooh-poohing him, and setting myself in the pillory as a plagiarist, I improve the opportunity by making *amende* (*honorable*, I hope) also for what this book owes to many other lovers of and thinkers on art, not scrupulously acknowledged in every instance because I compose without the help of numbered and dated notes, and memory, though not failing in the essence of what has been stored from their treasures, disappoints at times in the matter of chapter and verse.

[2] The *chandi* Kalasan is the only one in Central Java of which we possess the exact date.

[3] The *taras* are the *saktis* of the five Dhyani Buddhas that occupy a place in Javanese speculative philosophy, Vajradhatvisvari pairing with Vajrochana, Lotchana with Akshobhya, Mamaki with Ratnasambhava, Pandara with Amitabha, and Tara *par excellence* with Amoghasiddha, these unions being responsible for the Bodhisatvas Samantabhadra, Vajrapani, Ratnapani, Padmapani and the coming Vishvapani.

the monks of a neighbouring monastery, contains several particulars of practical value with an admonition to keep a bridge or dam in repair, etc. The building, in the form of a Greek cross, had four apartments, reached by a terrace and four staircases, the stones of which have been carried away long ago. The four gates, judging by the little left on one of them, were profusely decorated with the *kala-makara* motive dominating the ornament. The roof bore images of Dhyani Buddhas in 44 niches and was crowned with 16 dagobs so called, the principal one rising probably to a great height. Time and rapine have reduced this magnificent realisation of a glorious conception, this masterpiece of measured luxury, as Rouffaer styles it justly, to a melancholy heap of debris. The statuary which adorned the exterior is gone, save three images in their niches, examples of the gorgeous but never too florid ornamentation; the interior pictures desolation, ruin within ruin! A disfigured elephant, driven by a horned monster, its mahout, protrudes from the wall above the throne it protects, but the cushioned seat is empty. The statue taken from it was presumably a representation of the beatific Tara glorified in the inscription, the noble and venerable one, whose smile made the sun to shine and whose frown made darkness to envelop the terrestrial sphere. It has been surmised that the mysterious female deity in the residency grounds at Jogjakarta originally filled the throne of Kalasan, but the vanished Tara left her cushion behind and the unknown goddess, whose lovely body rivals the lotus-flower in august sweetness, holds firmly to her *padmasana* in addition to her attributes defying identification as the mother of the Buddha who is to be.

The short distance between the *chandi* Kalasan or Kali Bening and the *chandi* Sari must have been often traversed by the seekers of the noble eightfold path, inquirers into the four truths and examiners of the three signs, mortifiers of their flesh in the practice of the ten repugnances. *Bikshus*, living on the alms they collected without asking by word or gesture, without unduly attracting attention, passing in silence those inclined and those not inclined to charity, avoiding the houses and people dangerous to virtue, never tarrying anywhere and never presenting themselves more than three times at the doors of the uncharitable, eating the food received in solitude before noon, the only meal allowed to them, they must have awakened a good deal of pity in their tattered robes, but one suspects that the mendicant brethren of Java, notwithstanding their individual vows of poverty, were exceedingly wealthy as a community after the wont of their kind everywhere and of whatever religious denomination. Their *viharas* or monasteries, to judge from the ruins, were well appointed and the inmates apparently well provided for by princes who took a pride or found their interest in befriending religion and the religious. If strictly adhering to their monastic rules, the Buddhist monks had to live in the open, but the wet monsoon is not a pleasant season in the woods without adequate protection against storm and rain, and *avec le ciel il y a des accommodements*, a motto acted upon long before le Sieur Poquelin formulated it. The *chandi* Sari is supposed to have been the main structure of the residential quarter destined for the accommodation of the clergy connected with the *chandi* Kalasan, the abode of the monks who knew the greater vehicle of discipline as the inscription has it, the monastery built by command of the Shailendra king for their venerable congregation and recommended to his successors in order that all who followed their teachings might understand the cause and effect of the positive condition of things and attain prosperity. The rectangular building had a lower and an upper storey, both divided into three rooms, lighted by windows; the absent roof had niches for statuary, capped with diminutive domes in the manner of dagobs. In the decoration extensive use has been made of the elephant and the *makara*, the fabulous fish with an elephant's head; images of saints with and without aureoles, of celestial beings more suggestive of the Hindu pantheon than of Buddhist atheism,[1] of the bird-people and divers animals, enliven the rich, flowery ornament of the well

[1] Here another quotation may be permitted from Dr. L. A. WADDELL'S article, *Evolution of the Buddhist Cult, its Gods, Images and Art* (*The Imperial and Asiatic Quarterly Review*, January, 1912): And notwithstanding that the Mahayana was primarily a nihilistic mysticism, with a polytheism only in the background, the latter soon came to the front and has contributed more than anything else to the materialising and popularity of Buddhism.

XX.

CHANDI SARI

(C. Nieuwenhuis.)

proportioned facings, cornices and window-frames. Rising gracefully from its solid yet elegant base, the edifice creates an impression of airiness and stability cleverly combined, the dark gray colour of the weatherbeaten andesite blending harmoniously with the tender green of the bambu-stools which transport our thoughts to the garden of Kalandra where the Buddha, preaching the lotus of the good law, made converts foreordained to rank among his most famous disciples: Sariputra, Maudgalyayana, Katyayana. . . . And the officially licensed sinners against the ancient monuments of Java, hardened, habitual criminals in that respect, expressly appointed to do their worst at the Paris Exhibition of 1900, pretended their horrid botch in the Park of the Trocadéro to be a reproduction *d'une pureté irréprochable* of this rare gem of architectural workmanship, the *chandi* Sari!

As in India, pious foundations for the benefit of those under bond to serve religion, disregarding worldly considerations, must have been numerous in Java, especially in the plain of Prambanan, once studded with *viharas* like Asoka's kingdom, the "Behar" of to-day. Passing over the monastic claims advanced for some ruins in the southern mountains, those of Plahosan cannot be ignored. There we find the remains of two buildings, formerly enclosed by a wall, portions of which are recognisable, and surrounded by smaller structures arranged in three rows, the inner ones reminding of the style conspicuous in the *chandi* Sewu, about a mile to the west-southwest. Close together, but originally perhaps divided by a second wall, they are situated due north and south from each other with their entrances to the west; the roofs have succumbed; of the two storeys only the lower ones, containing sufficient space for three rooms, are tolerably preserved. Of a composite nature, the *chandi* Plahosan was presumably rather a *sangharama* than a *vihara* and the doorkeeper at the gate, when all those scattered stones and the smashed, stolen or otherwise removed statues were still in place, may have welcomed the wayfarer, seeking shelter on a tempestuous night, with such difficult questions as barred access to the hospitality of Silabhadra, the superior of Nalanda, and his flock. Hiuen Tsiang, the Chinese pilgrim, who could answer them all and a good many more, has left us a description of the *sangharama*, the six consolidated *viharas* of Nalanda with their towers, domes and pavilions, embellished by the piety of the kings of the five Indies; their gardens, splashing fountains and shady groves, where he spent several years learning Sanskrit and the wisdom of the holy books, never thinking the days too long; their life of ease, scarcely conducive to the austere observance of pristine discipline by the ten thousand brethren under vows and novices who crowded thither to seek purification and deliverance from sin in study and meditation,—a description which, for want of any better, our fancy takes leave to apply to Plahosan. Though separated by months of travel from Bodhimanda, where Sakyamuni entered the state of the perfect Buddha and the proximity of which gave Nalanda its holy character, the zeal of its scholars and saints, no less tolerant than Hiuen Tsiang's temporary co-students, who sifted with laudable impartiality the truth from the Vedas, from the doctrines of the two vehicles and from the heresies of the eighteen schismatics, undoubtedly stimulated religious life in the best sense of the word, religion disposing the mind to kindliness and goodwill, as it should, strengthening social ties, fostering science and art.

The walls of the *chandi* Plahosan, in so far as preserved, are beautifully decorated with sculpture in bas-relief. The delicate tracery of the basement is divided by slender pilasters and the frieze beneath the symmetric cornice is richly festooned, parrots nestling in the foliage among the flowers. Bodhisatvas, standing between, formed the principal ornament of panels bordered by garlands with pendent prayer-bells; the remaining ones grasp lotus-stems springing up to their left; *gandharvas* (celestial singers) float over the *garuda*-heads of the portals. The reliefs represent scenes familiar to the observer of native life: here a couple of men seated under a bo-tree or *waringin* and saluting a person of rank, raising their folded hands to perform the *sembah*; there a *mās*[1] with his attendants, one of whom holds the *payoong* (sunshade) over his head

[1] *Mās*, meaning "gold", is used as a predicate of nobility and also as a title conferred in polite address on persons of lower birth.

while another carries a *senteh*[1] leaf. Four stone figures guard the approaches to the *viharas*, armed with cudgel and sword; in one hand they hold the snake which, after the manner of their kind, should be worn over one shoulder and across the breast, replacing the *upawita*. The statuary which adorned the inner rooms, was of large dimensions, finely chiselled and garnished with profuse detail, concluding from what we know of it. Part has been removed to the "museum" at Jogja, part has been broken to pieces by treasure-hunters who dug holes and sunk shafts, disturbing the foundations of the *chandi* Plahosan in their ignorance of the difference between Buddhist monasteries and Hindu mausolea built round funeral pits; the sorely damaged images of holiness which were suffered to keep their stations by frankly destructive and even more pernicious official or semi-official *soi-disant* "preservation and conservation," are truly pitiful to behold. It seems, indeed, as if the monuments specially recommended to official care, are singled out for the most irreparable injury. On a par with the wild feast of plaster, cement and whitewash at Panataran was the wonderful planning of a restoration of the *chandi* Plahosan after faulty drawings and the simultaneous disappearance of the staircase and a portion of the substructure of the northern *vihara*.

Less than a mile to the south of the stopping-

[1] *Alocasia macrorrhiza Schott* of the *Aracaceae* family; the leaf, which once betokened dignity, is still used to protect the head and upper part of the body against rain; other parts of the plant serve sometimes as food.

place Prambanan on the railroad from Jogja to Solo, are the ruins of a group of *chandis* which may or may not have borne a monastic character,[1] Sajiwan and Kalongan being the names connected with it. One of the structures was cleared in 1893 by the Archaeological Society of Jogjakarta and to its statuary applies what has been said of the atrocities perpetrated at Plahosan : besides downright spoliation the same errors of omission and commission. From Prambanan proper, *i.e.* from the Loro Jonggrang group, it is a short walk to the *chandi* Sewu, which means the "thousand temples". They are situated in Surakarta, the boundary between the Susuhunan's and the Sooltan's domains, indicated by two white pillars, running just behind the smaller structures which face the shrines of Brahma and Vishnu flanking that of Sîva. But, though the walk is short, it may be a trifle too sunny for comfort even if it be morning and the roads lively with the women returning from market, the surroundings of the houses of prayer and death gladdening the eye, presenting a spectacle full of colour and light, the matrons treading their way statelily and steadily, the maidens, decorous and modest, gliding behind their elders like the *devis*, the shining ones descended from the *Ramayana* reliefs, to exhibit their exquisite forms, bashful however conscious of their worth in that golden, sweet-scented atmosphere. They

[1] The pit there discovered makes the monastic character more than doubtful while it accentuates the syncretism in which also the ornament of these *chandis* does not differ from all Central Javanese religious structures of the period, except those on the Diëng plateau.

have no business at the *chandi* Sewu and on the unfrequented by-path thither we proceed alone, save for a few children with no more to cover their nakedness than the loveliest innocence—a garment quite different from the western *cache-misère* of mawkish prudery—, curious to find out what the strangers are about. Under their escort we reach the *chandi* Loomboong (*padi*-shed), thus called from the size and form of the ruins which compose it. They are sixteen in number, arranged in a square round the principal structure, its once octagonal roof, shaped like a dagob, attesting to its Buddhist character, though it is not unmixed with Sivaïte elements as the funeral pits plainly indicate. They were already empty when examined some years ago and the fine statues tradition speaks of, can nowhere be found. The little ornament left in place and one single fragment of a bas-relief give a high idea of the decoration when the beauty of these temples had not yet faded away, exactly as in the case of the *chandi* Bubrah,[1] another shrine on the *via sacra* which connects the Loro Jonggrang and Sewu groups. To quote Major van Erp again: The state of affairs here is very sad; of the *chandis* Ngaglik, Watu Gudik and Geblak, which the memory of the oldest inhabitants puts somewhat farther north, even the site cannot now be located.

By the time we reach the thousand temples, Surya, the sun-god, has driven his fiery carriage to the zenith of his daily course through the air and

[1] Best translated by "ruin".

XXI.

RAKSASA OF THE *CHANDI* SEWU

(Centrum.)

the fire-eyed *raksasas*, who guard the enclosure of holiness; two for each of the four entrances, stretch their gigantic limbs with dreadful menace in the warm brilliancy of indefinite space, tangible terror. Down on one knee to strike, snakes hanging from their left shoulders as poisonous baldrics, they seem to mark the transition between the worship of Kala, quickening destruction personified, and the creed which hails in death the portal to nirvanic nothingness, the liberation from life's miseries. Behind them reigns the stillness of a tropical noon, subduing heaven and earth to silent but intensely passionate day-dreams. The kingly sun, the sun of Java, wide-skirted Jagannath, having mounted to the summit of the fleckless sky, pauses a moment before descending, he, the light of the world, exciting to generative emotion all that dwells below. The fructifying charm of his touch is manifest in the exuberant fertility of this island fortunate; in the vitality of its people, unrestrained in creative capacity by centuries of spoliation; in their mental make-up, revealed in their history, their beliefs, traditions and legends. The legend of the *chandi* Sewu may be adduced as an instance in point, though nothing but a different version of the legend of the *chandi* Loro Jonggrang. One ancient effort to account for architectural wonders deemed of supernatural origin, by an explanation whose Indian basic idea was transplanted from the fields of eastern to those of western folk-lore too, serving at first, perhaps, for all the monuments in the plains of

Prambanan and Soro Gedoog, became the framework of different tales adapted to the requirements of different localities. Here it is the story of Mboq Loro Jonggrang repeated, and her lover Raden Bandoong Bondowoso is the son of the beautiful Devi Darma Wati, daughter of Prabu Darmo Moyo, king of the mighty empire of Pengging, whose two brothers, Prabu Darmo Haji and Prabu Darmo Noto, were kings respectively of Slembri and Sudhimoro.

The *babad chandi Sewu* describes a public function at the Court of Prabu Darmo Moyo, who sits on his throne of ivory, inlaid with the rarest gems. The *aloon aloon* outside swarms with his warriors and while he pronounces judgment and invests and displaces, ambassadors from Prambanan are announced. They deliver a letter from Prabu Karoong Kolo, in which the Boko, the giant-king, asks Prabu Darmo Moyo's daughter, Devi Darma Wati, in marriage. The Princess, acquainted with his suit, declares that she will marry no one but the man, be he king or beggar, able to rede a riddle which is given, written on a *lontar*-leaf, to the ambassadors who thereupon depart. On their arrival at Prambanan, Prabu Karoong Kolo breaks impatiently the seal of the communication; learning its meaning, his eyes dart flames, his mouth foams and, tearing the *lontar*-leaf into pieces and trampling upon it, making the earth tremble and disturbing the sky with his noisy wrath, he collects his army and marches against Pengging to raze the *kraton* of Prabu Darmo Moyo and carry Darma Wati off. The King of Pengging, warned of the approaching danger, implores his brother Darmo Noto, King of Sudhimoro, to assist him; with his brother Darmo Haji, King of Slembri, an odious tyrant, he has broken long ago. Prabu Darmo Noto orders his son, the Crown Prince Raden Damar Moyo, to lead his troops against the giant-king. Traversing the woods at the head of his men, scaling cliffs and climbing mountains, crossing rivers and ravines, attacked by evil spirits and wild animals, Damar Moyo, strenuous in the cause of his uncle and his fair cousin, hastens to their defence but, leaving every one behind, he loses his way and, tired out at last, falls asleep. A strange sensation of heavenly joy awakens him and, opening his eyes, he beholds the supreme god, Bathara Naradha, who presents him with the celestial weapons of the abode of the immortals, Jonggring Saloko, salves his forehead with the divine spittle to make him invulnerable and invincible, and puts into his hand the flower Sekar Joyo Kusumo which will enable him to rede Devi Darma Wati's riddle. Strengthened and more enthusiastic than ever, Raden Damar Moyo, having rejoined his army, engages the giants of Prambanan and defeats them, astonishing friend and foe with his acts of superhuman prowess. He redes the riddle, marries Darma Wati, and his father-in-law, Prabu Darmo Moyo, appoints him *senapati*, *i.e.* commander-in-chief of the forces of Pengging.

The legend being too long for insertion in full,

besides its containing details too candidly illustrative of the generative emotion engendered by the wide-skirted Jagannath, a summary of the events which led to the foundation of the *chandi* Sewu must suffice. Boko Prabu Karoong Kolo, King of Prambanan, loses his life in another attempt at the subjugation of Pengging, and Raden Damar Moyo, having nothing more to fear from that side, but naturally inclined to strife and contest, resolves to take part in the wars then raging among the kings of the Thousand Empires, Sewu Negoro. So he leaves his wife and the son born to them, Raden Bandoong, who grows into a comely youth. Arriving at manhood and still in complete ignorance of his sire's name and lineage, the prince questions his mother on that subject but, in obedience to an express order from the gods, she refuses to tell him. Vexed and suspicious, he equips himself from the armoury of his grandfather, Prabu Darmo Moyo, and eludes maternal vigilance, escaping from the *kraton* in search of his father. After many adventures, culminating in a conflict with his parent in the Sewu Negoro, the two meeting and exchanging hard blows and parting as strangers, he reaches Prambanan, kills Tumenggoong Bondowoso, left in charge of that realm, and falls in love with Devi Loro Jonggrang, daughter of the late Boko Prabu Karoong Kolo. But he has been forestalled in her favour by his cousin Raden Boko, who is to become her husband on condition of the overthrow of Pengging and Sudhimoro. Suspecting a rival while maturing his plans for conquest, this Raden Boko takes a mean advantage of the lady by a trick learnt from a recluse who lends him a *tesbeh* (string of prayer-beads) which possesses the power of transforming its temporary owner into a white turtle-dove. So disguised, he flies to the women's quarter of the *kraton* of Prambanan and attracts the attention of Loro Jonggrang, who responds to the lovely bird's advances, puts it in her bosom and pets and fondles it to her heart's content until, alas! it is killed by an arrow sped from the never erring bow of Raden Bandoong, thanks to the busybodies of the palace having informed him of the idyllic progressive cooing. Woman-like, the bereaved Devi submits to the inevitable after a period of passionate mourning, and promises her heart and hand to the stronger if not more dexterous suitor on condition of his building a thousand temples in one night between the first crowing of the cock and daybreak. With the help of the gods of Jonggring Saloko he accomplishes the task, but at the moment that he whispers *astaga*[1] *chandi Sewu*, struck by the sight of the moonlit plain blossoming into a city of holiness, the immortals change him for his arrogant prayer into a monster of horrible aspect. Woman-like again, the Devi declines to keep her promise, pleading that she engaged herself to a man and not to a brute, and seeks refuge on the banks of the river Opak. Frightened by the persecution of Raden Bandoong, who tracks her from cave to cave,

[1] An exclamation of wonder and surprise.

she gives untimely birth to a daughter, the fruit of her affection for turtle-doves, and dies. The brutal, baffled lover still haunts the neighbourhood, which therefore native mothers-to-be scrupulously avoid, though it is not observed that the virgins derive much instruction from the legend as far as concerns the consequences of Devi or Mboq Loro Jong-grang's *amours* at an earlier stage.

From legendary lore we return to fact in the matter of the foundation of the *chandi* Sewu by taking cognisance of an inscription, *mahaprattaya sangra granting* or *sang rangga anting*, unearthed near one of its 246 (not thousand) temples,[1] extolling the munificence of the magnanimous Granting or Anting. The style of writing justifies the conjecture that the buildings date from about the year 800 and are consequently of one age with the Boro Budoor. If not erected by one architect at the command of one bounteous prince, and the gifts of several pious souls who possessed the wherewithal for devotional works, they were at least constructed according to one plan steadily kept in view, a good deal more than can be said of many religious edifices in western climes, which owe their existence less to co-operative than to contentious piety. In respect of area the largest of the temple groups in Java, the first impression received from it is that of a chaos of ruins, confusion being worse confounded by the quarries opened here and there, and partly filled again with earth and rubbish, while a luxuriant

[1] And removed to the "museum" at Jogjakarta.

vegetation, regaining on the inroads of mattock and pickaxe, quickly covers what they disturbed. Looking closer, the separate shrines with their elaborate tracery appear in the fiery embrace of the sun like sparkling jewels, trembling with delight in the luminous atmosphere beneath the immaculate sky; the very marks of decay and ravaging time are beautiful; the weeds clustering round the broken ornament, the toppling walls, rouse to fanciful thought. No sound is heard; nothing stirs while we make our way to the principal structure, once lording it over the smaller ones which stood squarely in four lines, 28 for the inner, 44 for the next, 80 for the third, 88 for the outer circumvallation. Excepting those of the second row, their entrances faced inward and amidst their scanty remains the foundations have been uncovered of five somewhat larger ones: two to the east, two to the west and one to the north; like the outlying buildings, these are, with regard to their superstructures, as if they never existed. Of the terraces and staircases no other trace is left than the telltale unevenness of the ground. The resemblance in constructive methods between the *chandi* Sewu and the *chandi* Prambanan strikes one at the first glance; the same builders, it is surmised, strove here to do for the Triratna[1] what there they did for the Trimoorti; and if not the same, they discerned equally the one truth bound up in the old creed and the new, and expressed it with equal skill and conviction in these twin litanies of stone—so the

[1] The three gems: the Buddha, the law and the congregation.

workers wrought and the work was perfected by them.

The decorators in charge of the finishing touches, embellished this city of temples with a wealth of ornament which in the quivering glare of day, despite ravage of time and pillage, clothes sanctity in robes of encrusted winsomeness. The sculpture of the *chandi* Sewu, says a visitor of a century ago, is tasteful, delicate and chaste. Much of what he based his judgment on, has since been carried off or demolished, but what remains fully bears him out: foliage and festoons, garlands and clustered flowers, distributed over facings divided into lozenges and circles by pilasters and fantastically curved lines, with lions, tigers, cattle and deer in ever varying abundance, awaken reminiscences of the carvings which excited our admiration at Prambanan and lead to the question: Did the richly framed panellings of the twenty-four external wall-spaces of the central temple exhibit scenes from the epics and fable-books, besides this sumptuous adornment, to match the almost uniform bas-reliefs of the lesser structures? If so, they must have rivalled the artistic excellence of the *Ramayana* reliefs which beautify the shrines of Siva, Brahma and Vishnu. And a second question arises: Was the central temple the depository of a relic? In connection with this query it deserves to be noticed that, generally speaking and excepting statuary, the internal wall-spaces of the *chandi* Sewu lack ornament, evince a soberness in marked contrast to

DETAIL OF THE *CHANDI* SEWU

(Archaeological Service through Charls and van Es.)

the extravagant representations of the abode of bitterness, as if sign- or house-painters had been entrusted with the illustration of Dante's *Inferno*, repulsive attempts à la Wiertz minus the talent to be admired in the Rue Vautier at Brussels, nightmares of crude drawing and cruder colouring to depict perverse torture, I found in eastern edifices raised to satisfy priestly conventions, even in Ceylon, the island of the doctrine that the Buddha next to dwell on earth is the Metteya Buddha, the Buddha of Kindness. More in harmony with the soul's yearning for his kingdom to come, is the lotus motive happily adapted to the decoration of the *chandi* Sewu, especially in one of the partially preserved small temples of the outer file, to the east of the southern entrance: from a strong stem which separates into three branches, on three of the sides, the entrance taking up the fourth, three lotus-flowers spring from the soil to carry, in a finely chiselled niche, the (vanished) image of the expected one, the gone-before and coming-after. A few of the outlying buildings have plain facings without any ornament at all, from which it has been concluded that here too something happened to stop the labour in progress. Where completed, the plump-bellied flowerpot, a familiar feature in Javanese ornament, enters largely into the decorative design and its frequent repetition bestows on the sculpture of the *chandi* Sewu, otherwise so very similar to that of Prambanan, a character all its own.

It has already been remarked that the interiors of the structures which together form this group, are almost bare of decoration. The recesses of the central temple, whose external ornament surpasses in luxuriance everything met elsewhere in Java, three small interconnected apartments projecting on the west, north and south, while the eastern front is broken by the porch, have only empty niches[1] framed by pilasters with flowery capitals. The inner chamber, no less soberly decorated and stripped of the statuary it possessed, *en négligé* as it were,

Belle sans ornement, dans le simple appareil
D'une beauté qu'on vient d'arracher au sommeil,

has on its western side a raised throne of ample dimensions, once perhaps occupied by the large image without head and right hand, dug out of the debris and carried off to the "museum" at Jogja. It still awaits identification and the difficulty is increased by the impropriety of speculating on the likelihood that representations of the universal spirit were admitted in a temple built for the ritual of a creed which acknowledges neither a god nor a soul aspiring to communion with the divine essence in prayer, desiring nothing but annihilation. Yet the Buddhists did learn to pray and to give transcendental ideas a tangible expression in human shape, though they never sank to idolatry. And in Java, mixing freely with Brahmanism, not imperme-

[1] Offering accommodation, inclusive of the holy of holies, for 42 statues, which had already flown in 1812.

able to the Sankhya doctrine, Buddhism seems to have swerved occasionally from its longings for extermination in the Nirvana to entertain vague, confused notions of something more hopeful, witness the oft repeated Banaspatis. Herein lies, perhaps, the explanation of otherwise embarrassing peculiarities observed in the conception, the attributes and attitudes of many Buddhist statues in the island which, for the rest, are distinguished by great simplicity of execution. So is the throne which extends over half the floor of the inner room of the central temple of the *chandi* Sewu, and the same applies to the few headless Dhyani Buddhas lying round, sundered from their stations where they faced the cardinal points, the four quarters of the world, and the first of them, the very elevated, facing the sky. A gigantic finger of bronze, found in the chapel of the throne, supports the theory that the principal statue was of that alloy, an additional incentive to plunder—ancient images of bronze have become scarce indeed: the form of the cushioned pedestal in the *chandi* Kalasan too betokens a captured metallic Tara, to the further detriment of the domiciliary rights there claimed for the homeless Lady of Mystery in the residency grounds at Jogja.

Although the bulky *raksasas* which keep her company in that place of exile, prove that official vandalism did not hesitate to avail itself of facilities of transportation afforded by forced labour, the uncommonly heavy guardians of the *chandi* Sewu balked even the absolute decrees of local despotism. Everything desirable that could be detached and removed, is, however, gone. Those in authority having exercised their privilege by helping themselves, mere private individuals gleaned after their reaping, with or without permission, and exceedingly interesting collections of antiquities were formed by owners of neighbouring sugar-mills. What they appropriated, did, at least, remain in the country, but, among other sculpture, the lion-fighting elephants which lined the fourteen staircases, ten feet high and eight feet wide, still in place as late as 1841, cannot even be traced—they are dissolved, battling animals, staircases and all. It is always and everywhere the same story: statuary and ornament are stolen, treasure-seekers smash the rest, the stones are prime building material and who cares for the preservation of worthless, because already looted and demolished, tumble-down temples? The monuments in the plain of Soro Gedoog have suffered exceptional outrages; at this moment hardly anything is left because there exists absolutely no control, says Major van Erp. His investigations disclosed that stones taken from the *chandi* Prambanan and, when this was stopped, from the *chandi* Sewu, were used for the building of a dam in the river Opak. Had not public opinion made itself heard, both these temples might have shared the fate of the *chandi* Singo, once one of the finest in that region, whose gracefully decorated walls excited the admiration of Brumund in 1845, whose substructure with damaged ornament still held out until 1886, while now the ground-plan cannot even be guessed at and deep holes, dug to get at the foundations, are the only indications of the razed building's site. To give an idea of the quantity of material used for the dam in the river Opak, I transcribe the measurements of its revetments: 35 metres on the left and from 50 to 60 metres on the right bank; the facings, running up to a height of 6 metres, make it evident beyond doubt where the stone for that work was quarried. Neither are we quite sure that such frightful spoliation belongs wholly to the past. The value of Government solicitude, so eloquently paraded in circulars and colonial reports, can be gauged from the fact, stated by Mr. L. Serrurier, that, during officially sanctioned excavations among the ruins of the *chandis* Plahosan and Sewu, the stones brought to the surface were simply thrown pell-mell on a heap without their being marked as to locality and position, quite in keeping, it should be added, with the prevailing custom.

This accounts for the sad desolation, more pitiful since *soi-disant* archaeologists got their hands in, shone upon at the *chandi* Sewu as at the *chandis* Plahosan, Sari, Kalasan, Panataran, to restrict myself to one name from East Java,—shone upon by the sun, the egg of the world, whose yolk holds the germ of creation. Surya, the solar orb personified, is a companion wonderfully, grandly suggestive among the "thousand temples" of life accomplished, decaying into new birth, whether he scorches the earth and withers the drooping flowers, or climbs a dim, hazy sky to attract the vapours that descend again in precious showers when the clouds collect and cover the stars, charming from darkness the lovely dawn and budding day. The meditations he disposes the mind to are mostly directed to the future, dreams of coming happiness, and even the contemplative Buddhist images under the Banaspatis seem agitated by their knowledge of a promise excelling the hope of Nirvana, which cannot satisfy the aspirations of the children of this island, full of the joy of existence. What will the future bring to them, the people cradled in tempest, who were taught forbearance by a creed profoundly imbued with the inner nature of things, and submission when misery of war and pestilence came as the harbingers of bondage to an alien race? Too trustful, they sacrificed their birthright for a mess of pottage and after the encroachments of the Company, past ages crowding on their memory, the felicity of the *jaman buda* assumes to their imagination a tangible shape in the ancient monuments founded by the rulers of their own flesh and blood, edifices so widely different from the meretricious Government opium-dens and Government pawnshops in which the predatory instinct of the present masters manifests itself—*layin dahulu, layin sekarang.*[1] Resigned to fate, which wills the mutability of earthly relations, the Javanese philosopher—and

[1] Different of yore, different now.

all Javanese are philosophers in their way—takes the practical view of the Vedantins, considering that calamities mean purification to the victor in moral contest, and looking for a serene morning after a night of distress. He has more beliefs than one to draw upon when seeking refuge in his cherished maxim, his phlegmatic *apa boleh buwat*,[1] and doubts not the possibility of obtaining a Moslim equivalent for the Buddhist *arahat*, the perfect state, irrespective of outward conditions, by the help of a Hindu deity, Ganesa, who knows what is to happen and, as Vinayaka, the guide, conquers obstacles hurtful to his votaries in the course of events preordained according to their Islāmic doctrine—syncretism yet more complex than that of their forefathers of Old Mataram! Watch well the heart, commanded the master. As to the watched heart dominating the senses, the Javanese, rather a mystic than an ascetic, and predominantly a child of nature, whence he proceeds and whither he returns in his search of the divine, prefers enjoyment of the world's fullness to mortification of the flesh. He feels much more closely drawn to Padmapani, the lord of the world that is, than to any other of the emanations of the essence of the Universe, be it Diansh Pitar or the One, the Eternal, who sent Muhammad as a mercy to all creatures, or the Adi-Buddha, the primitive, the primordial, the incarnate denial of god and soul together. Whatever he prays by, the deity involved is one of overflowing gladness, who presents a flower

[1] There is no help for it; lit. "what can be done?"

with each hand, like Surya when circling land and sea and air in three steps; and, notwithstanding his sorrows, he rests content with his portion for, though the light of day sets, it will rise again in glory.

CHAPTER VIII

THE APPROACH TO THE BORO BUDOOR

> The goodly works, and stones of rich assay,
> Cast into sundry shapes by wondrous skill,
> That like on earth no where I reckon may ;
>
> EDMUND SPENSER, *Faerie Queene*, Canto X.

AMONG the ancient monuments of Insulinde[1] the *chandi* Boro Budoor stands *facile princeps.* Situated in the Kadu, it is easily reached from Jogjakarta, about twenty-five miles, or from Magelang, about eighteen miles distant, by carriage or, still more easily, by taking the steam-tram which connects those two provincial capitals and leaving the cars at Moontilan where an enterprising Chinaman provides vehicles, at short notice, for the rest of the journey via the *chandi* Mendoot on the left bank of the Ello, just above its confluence with the Progo. No better approach to the most consummate achievement of Buddhist architecture in the island or in the whole world, can be imagined than this one, which leads

[1] The very appropriate name bestowed on the Dutch East Indies by EDUARD DOUWES DEKKER (MULTATULI), Holland's greatest writer of the preceding century.

past the smaller but scarcely less nobly conceived and conscientiously executed temple, a commensurate introduction to the wonderful, crowning edifice across the waters, portal to the holiest in gradation of majestic beauty. The Kadu has been well styled the garden of Java, as Java the pleasance of the East, full of natural charms which captivate the senses, abounding in amenities soothing to body and soul; but if it had nothing more to offer than the Boro Budoor and the Mendoot, it would reward the visitor to those central shrines of Buddhism far beyond expectation.

Behind the horses, a mental recapitulation of the characteristics of Hindu and Buddhist architecture in the golden age of Javanese art will not come amiss, and there may be some wonder that with so much veneration for the Bhagavat in friendly competition with the Jagad Guru, nowhere in the *negri Jawa* an imprint is shown of the blessed foot of promise, with the deliverer's thirty-first sign, the wheel of the law on the sole. If, in explanation, it should be adduced that he never travelled to those distant shores, what does that matter? Has he been in Ceylon? And how then about the *sripada*, the record left there as in so many other countries, with the sixty-five hints at good luck? While we revolve such questions, our carriage rolls on; the coachman cracks his whip, evidently proud of his skill in turning sharp corners without reining in; the runners jump with amazing agility off and on the foot-board and crack *their* whips, rush to the front to encourage the leaders of the team up steep inclines, fall again to the rear when it goes down hill in full gallop. The exhilarating motion makes the blood tingle in the veins. How lovely the landscape, the valley shining in the brilliant light reflected from the mountain slopes, . . .

Another turn and we dash like a whirlwind past the *kachang*-oil[1] and *boongkil*[2] mill of Mendoot; still another turn and, with a magnificent display of his dexterity in pulling up, our Jehu brings us to a sudden standstill before the temple. Opposite is a mission-school conducted for many years, with marked success, by Father P. J. Hoevenaars, in his leisure hours an ardent student of Java's history and antiquities, ever ready to apply the vast amount of learning accumulated in his comprehensive reading on a solid classical basis, to the clearing up of disputed points, though his modesty suffered the honours of discovery to go to the noisy players of the archaeological big drum. His large stock of information was and is always at the disposal of whoever may choose to avail himself of it and, writing of the *chandis* Mendoot and Boro Budoor, I acknowledge gratefully the benefit derived from my intercourse with this accomplished scholar, lately transferred to Cheribon.

The exact date of the birth of the *chandi*

[1] General name given to various plants of the bean family; the *kachang* here meant, is the *kachang china* or *tanah* (*Arachis hypogaea*) the oil of which is used as a substitute for olive-oil.

[2] The beans or nuts pressed into cakes and used as manure, especially in the cultivation of sugar-cane.

Mendoot is unknown but there are reasons for believing that it was built shortly after the *chandi* Boro Budoor, at some time between 700 and 850 Saka (778 and 928 of the Christian era), in the glorious period of Javanese architecture to which we owe also the Prambanan group, the *chandis* Kalasan, Sewu and whatever is of the best in the island. There are additional reasons for believing that the splendour loving prince who ordered the Boro Budoor to be raised and under whose reign the work on that stupendous monument was begun, founded the Mendoot too as a mausoleum to perpetuate his memory, and that his ashes were deposited in the royal tomb of his own designing before its completion. If so, he was one of the most prolific and liberal builders we have cognisance of; but his memory is nameless and all we know of him personally, besides the imposing evidence to his Augustan disposition contained in the superb structures he left, rests upon two pieces of sculpture at the entrance to the inner chamber of the mortuary chapel, if such it be, which represent a royal couple with a round dozen of children, just as we find in some old western churches the carved or painted images of their founders' families.[1] We are perhaps indebted for the preservation of these suggestive reliefs to the circumstance of the *chandi* Mendoot having been covered, hidden from view during centuries and to a certain extent protected

[1] According to another explanation they represent King Sudhodana and Queen Maya with Siddhartha, the future Buddha, as a baby in her arms, which leaves us in the dark about the other children.

XXIII.

CHANDI MENDOOT BEFORE ITS RESTORATION
(Cephas Sr.)

against sacrilegious hands by volcanic sand, earth and vegetation. Almost forgotten, its slumbers were, however, not wholly undisturbed for, when Resident Hartman, his curiosity being excited by wild tales, began to clear it in 1836, he found that treasure-seekers, out for plunder, had pierced the wall above the porch and that by way of consolation or out of vexation at missing the untold wealth reported to be buried inside, they had carried off or smashed the smaller, free standing statuary. The process of cleaning up rather stimulated than prevented new outrages: stripped of its covering of detritus, which had shielded it at least against petty, casual pilfering, the *chandi* Mendoot excited by its helpless beauty the most injurious enthusiasm. Fortunately, the statues which formed its chief attraction were too big for the attentions of the long-fingered gentry whose peculiar methods in dealing with native art strongly needed but never experienced repression by the local authorities.

Speaking of the statuary and comparing it with Indian models, more particularly a four-armed image, seated cross-legged on a lotus, the stem of which is supported by two figures with seven-headed snake-hoods, Fergusson says: The curious part of the matter is, that the Mendoot example is so very much more refined and perfect than that at Karli. The one seems the feeble effort of an expiring art, the Javan example is as refined and elegant as anything in the best age of Indian sculpture. Of the Mendoot carvings, however, more anon. I shall first endeavour to give a general idea of this temple which, according to the same writer, though small, is of extreme interest for the history of Javanese architecture. Rouffaer calls it the classic model of a central shrine with substructure and churchyard, while observing that the principal statue of the Boro Budoor, the rest of whose statues are turned either towards one of the cardinal points or towards the zenith, faces the east and the Mendoot opens to the west, the two temples therefore fronting each other. Closely observed, the latter proved of double design since it consists of a stone outer sheath, built round an older structure of brick, the original form with its panellings, horizontal and perpendicular projections, having been scrupulously followed. The neatly fitting joints, both of the hewn stones and of the bricks of the interior filling, show a mastery of constructive detail rarely met with at the present day and certainly not in Java. To this wonderful technique, adding solidity to a graceful execution of the groundplan, belongs all the credit for the Mendoot holding out, notwithstanding persistent ill-usage. An ecstatic thought brightly bodied forth by a daring imagination and astonishing skill, a charming act of devotion blossoming from the flower-decked soil as the lotus of the good law did from the garden of wisdom and universal love, it must have looked grandly beautiful in its profuse ornament, which taught how to be precise without pettiness, how to attain the utmost finish without sacrificing the ensemble to trivial elaboration. Yet this gem of Javanese architecture seemed destined to complete destruction. Its pitiful decay did not touch the successors of Resident Hartman. When, in 1895, after several years' absence from the island, I came to renew acquaintance, it had visibly crumbled away; official interference with "collectors" limited itself to notices, stuck up on a bambu fence, warning them of the danger they ran from the roof falling in. It needed two years more of demolition, the walls bulging out, the copings tumbling down, before the correspondence, opened in 1882 anent a desirable restoration, produced some result; before the Mendoot, the jewelled clasp of that string of pearls, the Buddhist *chandis* pendent on the breast of Java from the Boro Budoor, her diamond tiara, was going to be refitted.

And how? It is an unpleasant tale to tell: after two decades of consideration and reconsideration, in the fourth year of the preliminary labours of restoration, the local representative of the Department of Public Works, put in charge of the job as a side issue of his already sufficiently exacting normal duties, aroused suspicions concerning his competency in the archaeological line. An altercation with Dr. Brandes, followed by more controversy *de viva voce*, in writing and in print, led to compliance with his request that it might please his superiors to relieve him from his additional and subordinate task as reconstructor of ancient monuments. From that moment, January 2, 1901, until

May 1, 1908, absolutely nothing was done and the scaffoldings erected all round the building were suffered to rot away, symbolic of the extravagant impecuniosity of a Government which never cares how money is wasted but always postpones needful and urgent improvements till the Greek Kalends on the plea of its chronic state of *kurang wang*.[1] When most of the fl. 8600, fl. 7235, fl. 25142 and fl. 4274, successively wrung from Parliament for excavations and restoration, had been squandered on what Dr. Brandes considered to be bungling patchwork, the expensive, useless scaffoldings, becoming dangerous to the passers-by in their neglected state, necessitated the disbursement, in 1906, of fl. 350 for their removal. On the continuation of the work, in 1908, by other hands, of course a new one, also of teak-wood, had to be erected. And, the restoration once more being under way on the strength of fl. 6800 grudgingly allotted, Parliament decided finally that no sufficient cause had been shown to burden the colonial budget with the sum which, according to an estimate of 1910, was required to bring it to an end! The profligately penurious mandarins of an exchequer exhausted by almost limitless liberality in the matter of high bounties, subsidies, allowances, grants for experiments which never lead to anything of practical value; in the matter of schemes which cost millions and millions only to prove their utter worthlessness,—the penny-

[1] Lacking money and wanting money, always more money: a summary of Dutch colonial policy as it strikes the native.

XXIV.

CHANDI MENDOOT AFTER ITS RESTORATION

(Archaeological Service.)

wise, pound-foolish heads refused, after an expenditure of fl. 52401 to little purpose, to disburse fl. 21700 or even fl. 7000 more for the completion of the work commenced, this time under guarantee of success. Arguments advanced to make them revoke their decision, were met with the statement that the Government did not intend to deviate from the line of conduct, adopted after mature deliberation in regard to the ancient monuments of Java, restricting its care to preservation of the remains . . . a characteristic sample of Governmental cant in the face of grossest carelessness and the kind of preservation inflicted on the *chandi* Panataran or wherever its officials felt constrained by public opinion to act upon make-believe circulars from Batavia and Buitenzorg before pigeon-holing them. And so the perplexing inconsistencies of Dutch East Indian finance, parsimony playing *chassez-croisez* with boundless prodigality, are faithfully mirrored in the tribulations of the *chandi* Mendoot: the reauthorised work of restoration was stopped again, on the usual progress killing plea of *kurang wang*, after the adjustment of the first tier above the cornice, and the temple, bereft of its crowning roof in dagob style, calculated to fix the basic conception in the beholder's mind, has in its stunted condition been aptly compared to a bird of gorgeous plumage, all ruffled and with the crest-feathers pulled out.

The operations were hampered by still other contrarieties. A tremendous battle was waged apropos of the question whether or not gaps in the layers of stones of the front wall above the porch pointed to the existence of a passage or passages for the admittance of air and light to the inner chamber; if so, whether or not those passages inclined at an angle sufficient to let the sun's rays illumine the head of the principal statue in that inner chamber. To rehearse the heated dispute is not profitable: as usual, after the *chandi* had fallen into ruin and an endless official correspondence had lifted its ruin into prominence, archaeological faddists of every description tried to acquire fame with absurd suggestions and crazy speculations. Leaving their theories regarding the inclinations of the axes of probable or possible transmural apertures for what they are, more instruction is to be derived from the decorative arrangements. The inherent beauty of the ornament survived happily the injurious effects of changing monsoons, of ruthless robbery, of preservation in the Government sense of the word. When the sun caresses it, the Friendly Day, under the blue vault of the all-compassing sky, smiling at this gem of human art, offered in conjugal obedience by the earth, which trembles at his touch, it seems a sacrificial gift of reflowering mortality to heaven. In art, said Lessing, the privilege of the ancients was to give no thing either too much or too little, and the remark of the great critic, as here we can see, applies to a wider range of classic activity than he had in mind. Wherever the ancient artist wrought, in Greece or in Java, we find moreover that he drew his inspiration directly from nature; that his handiwork reflects his consciousness of the moving soul of the world; that the secret of its imperishable charm lies pre-eminently in his keenness of observation. To Javanese sculpture in this period may be applied what Fergusson remarked of Hindu sculpture some thousand years older in date: It is thoroughly original, absolutely without a trace of foreign influence, but quite capable of expressing its ideas and of telling its story with a distinction that never was surpassed, at least in India. Some animals, such as elephants, deer and monkeys, are better represented there than in any sculptures known in any part of the world; so, too, are some trees and the architectural details are cut with an elegance and precision which are very admirable. Turning to the Mendoot we notice how the sculptors charged with its decoration, always truthful and singularly accurate in the expression of their thoughts and feelings, portrayed their surroundings in outline and detail, wrote in bas-reliefs, ornament and statuary the history, the ethics, the philosophy, the religion of the people they belonged to and materialised their splendid dreams for. What conveys a better knowledge of the Tripitaka, the Buddhist system of rules for the conduct of life, discipline and metaphysics, than their imagery, coloured by the very hue of kindliness and effacement of self in daily intercourse; what inculcates better the *paramitas*, the six virtues, and charity the first of them, than their carved mementos of the reverence we owe to the life of all sentient creatures, our poor relations the animals, striving on lower planes to obtain ultimate delivery from sin and pain but no less entitled to benevolence than man?

As in the decoration of the younger *chandis* Panataran and Toompang, fables occupy a prominent position in that of the *chandi* Mendoot. Among the twenty-two scenes spread over the nearly triangular spaces to the right and left of the staircase which ascends to the entrance, eleven on each side, partly lost and wholly damaged, are, for instance, reliefs illustrative of the popular stories of the tortoise and the geese, of the brahman, the crab, the crow and the serpents, etc. Of one of them only a small fragment is left, representing a turtle with its head turned upward, gazing at something in the air, whence Dr. Brandes infers its connection with the following tale, inserted in the account of the concerted action of the animals which conspired to kill the elephant, as rendered in the *Tantri*, an old Javanese collection of fables: Once upon a time there were turtles who took counsel together about the depredations of a ravenous vulture and their *kabayan* (chief of the community) asked:—What do you intend to do to escape being eaten by that bird? Accept my advice and lay him a wager that you can cross the sea quicker than he; if he laughs at your conceit, you must crawl into the sea where the big waves are, except two of you, one who stays to start on the race when he begins to fly, and one who swims across the day before and waits for him at the other side. What do you think, turtles? You cannot lose if you manage this well.—Your advice is excellent, answered they, and while the *kabayan* was still instructing them, the vulture arrived and demanded a turtle to eat.—What is your hurry, spoke the *kabayan* for them all; I bet you that any one of us can swim quicker across the sea than you can fly.—I take that bet, replied the vulture, but what shall I have if I win?—If you win, you will be at liberty to eat me and my people and our children and grandchildren and great-grandchildren and so on and so on to the end of time; but you must pledge your word that if you lose, you will move from here and seek your food elsewhere. It is now rather late but to-morrow morning you can choose any one of my people you please to match your swift flight with.—All right, said the vulture and he went to his nest to sleep, but the *kabayan* sent one of his turtle-people across the sea. The vulture showed himself again a little after dawn, not to waste time, for he felt pretty hungry and the sooner he could win the race, the sooner he would have breakfast. He did not even take the precaution to select an adversary among the decrepit and slow, so sure was he of his superiority, and, besides, all the turtles were so much alike. The *kabayan* counted one, two, three, go! and the vulture heard one of them plunge into the water and he unfolded his wings and alighted at the other side in an instant, when, lo! there he saw the beast calmly waiting for him. The vulture felt ashamed and moved to a distant country for he did not know that he had been cheated. And there was only one vulture but there were many turtles. And the boar told this event to his friends, exactly as the reverend Basubarga saw it happen.

Another fable, still more widely distributed and clinching the same moral, is that of the *kanchil* (a small, extremely fleet species of deer) and the snail; travelling to Europe, it is there best known in its German form recorded by Jakob and Wilhelm Grimm. Of its many variants in the Malay Archipelago we may mention the wager between a snail and a tiger as to which could most easily jump a river; the snail, attaching herself to one of her big competitor's paws, wins, of course, and convinces the terror of the woods by means of his hairs adhering to her body, that she is accustomed to feed on his kind, two or three per diem, freshly killed, whereupon the tiger leaves off blustering and sneaks away.[1] The prose version of the *Tantri* which, somewhat different from the two metrical readings known to us, contains the vulture and turtle incident, dates probably from the last half of the Mojopahit period and is therefore at least four centuries younger than the *chandi* Mendoot, so that

[1] The influence of eastern fables on western literature and art in all its branches cannot be overestimated as exemplified for instance, with special relevance to the one just referred to, by the late EMM. POIRÉ (CARAN D'ACHE) when he made our old friend Marius imitate the snail's braggadocio in his delightful cartoon *Les Pantoufles en peau de tigre* (*Lundis du Figaro*). And the story of the vulture and the turtles found its way, via American plantation legends, into J. C. HARRIS' tales of Uncle Remus. Concerning the manner of the "Migration of Fables" from East to West, most interesting particulars can be found in MAX MÜLLER's *Chips from a German Workshop*, iv., p. 145 ff.

its author and the sculptors of the scenes from popular beast-stories on the temple's walls, must have had access to a common stock of ancient fables. All turned it to best advantage and the decorators of this splendid edifice seized their opportunity to let the men and animals they carved in illustration of their national literature, express what they had to say in their passionate overflow of the creative instinct. They gave their narrative a frame in ornament of dazzling beauty, sweetly harmonious with the moral of the lessons they taught, stirring to deepest emotion ; they cased thoughts of happiest purport in shrines embossed and laced with fretwork more suggestive of ivory than of stone. They adorned the Mendoot as a bride, to be displayed before her husband, the Boro Budoor, revelling in the fanciful idea which makes the *saktis* of the Dhyani Buddhas carry budding flowers to honour incarnate love. The wealth of statuary, while orthodox Buddhism did not admit the worship of images either of a saintly founder of temples or of his saintly followers ; the deities with the attributes of Doorga, Siva and Brahma, who diversify the ornament of the exterior walls, from which right distribution of lines and surfaces may be learnt in rhythmical relation to contour and dimension, are further indications of the syncretism signalising the tolerance, the fraternal mingling of different creeds in the distant age of Mataram's vigour and artistic energy.

The religious principles underlying that empire's

greatness and providing a basis for a firm sense of duty to guide a temperament of fire, are nobly embodied in the three gigantic statues placed in the inner chamber of the Mendoot or, to be quite exact, round which that *chandi* was reared, for the entrance is too small to let them through, especially the largest of them which, miraculously undamaged save one missing finger-tip, has slid down from its pedestal and consequently occupies a lower station between the subordinate figures than originally intended. All three are seated and the first in rank, of one piece with his unembellished throne, measures fourteen feet; the two to his right and left, of less grave aspect, wearing richly wrought necklaces, armlets, wristbands, anklets and tiaras, measure eight feet each. If the *oorna*,[1] more excellent than a crown, identifies the master among them, the position of whose fingers reminds of Vajrochana, the first Dhyani Buddha, the others have been taken respectively for a Bodhisatva and for a devotee who attained by his meritorious life a high degree of saintliness but whose Brahmanic adornment flatly contradicts the Buddhist character of such perfection. This explanation is therefore considered unsatisfactory and unacceptable by many, as, for instance, his Majesty Somdetch Phra Paramindr Chulalongkorn, the late King of Siam, who, by the way, when visiting the *chandis* Mendoot and Boro Budoor in 1896, claimed those masterpieces of *mahayanistic* art for his own, the southern church,

[1] The Buddha's characteristic tuft or bunch of hairs between the eyebrows.

XXV.

INTERIOR OF THE *CHANDI* MENDOOT

(Cephas Sr.)

to use the incorrect but convenient distinction. According to this royal interpreter, the idea was to represent the Buddha in the act of blessing the Buddhist prince who ordered the Boro Budoor to be built, here placed at his right with an image of the deliverer in his *makuta* and carrying no *upawita* but a monk's robe under the insignia of his dignity; the third statue, directly opposite, at the Buddha's left, without Buddhist accessories but with an *upawita* hanging down from its left shoulder, might impersonate him again in his state before conversion, or his unconverted father on whom, after death, he wished to bestow a share in the deliverer's benediction. However this may be, there is no doubt of the Enlightened One's identity in one of his many personifications and, leaving the eighty secondary marks unexplored (three for the nails, three for the fingers, three for the palms of the hands, three for the forty evenly set teeth, one for the nose, six for the piercing eyes, five for the eyebrows, three for the cheeks, nine for the hair, ten for the lower members in general,—without our entering into further detail!), the thirty-two primary signs are all present: the protuberance on the top of the skull; the crisped hair (of a glossy black which the sculptor could not reproduce) curling towards the right;[1] the ample forehead; the *oorna,* which sheds a white light (also unsculpturable) as the sheen of polished

[1] In consequence of the young enthusiast Sarvarthasiddha cutting his long locks with his sword when leaving his father's palace to adopt the life of a recluse as Sakyamuni, the solitary one of the Sakyas, and meditate upon the redemption of the world.

silver or snow smiled upon by the sun; etc. Though the colossal statue of the welcome redeemer, like those of the worshipping kings, does not recommend itself by faultless modelling, it breathes the spirit which sustains the *arahat*, him who becomes worthy; it radiates the tranquil felicity of annihilation of existence, sin, sorrow and pain; it promises the final blowing out of life's candle, the Nirvana, when the understanding will be reached of the Adi-Buddha, the primitive, primordial, immeasurable. And the lowest of the four degrees of the Nirvana, it seems to say, is already attainable on earth by emancipation from the bondage of fleshly desire and vice, by avoidance of that which taints and corrupts. . . . The noonday glare, subdued by the heavy shadow of the porch, fills the sanctuary with a golden haze and upon its dimly gleaming wings a faint music descends, a song of deliverance. The psalmist's visions of the covering of iniquity compass us about and invite to recognition of a common source of divine inspiration in mankind of whatever creed. The scent of the *melati* and *champaka* flowers, strewn at the feet and in the lap of the deity—the image of him who taught that there is none such, and revered by professed believers in the Book which consigns idolaters to hell-fire!—mingles with the pungent odour of the droppings of the bats, fluttering and screeching things in the dark recesses of the roof, disturbed in their sleep. Truly there ought to be a limit to syncretism and this last mentioned mixture of heterogeneous elements soon affects the visitor in a manner so offensive that retreat becomes a matter of necessity.

As we step outside, our eyes are blinded by the burning light inundating the valley, the fiery furnace ablaze at the foot of mountains flaming up to the sky, a terror of beauty: Think of the fire that shall consume all creation and early seek your rescue, said the Buddha. It speaks to us of the cataclysm which shook Java on her foundation in the waters and upset the work of man, killing him in his thousands and burying his temples, the Mendoot and many, many more, under the ashes of her volcanoes, some such upheaval as when the conflict began between the Saviour of the World and the Great Enemy, to quote from the sacred scriptures; when the earth was convulsed, the sea uprose from its bed, the rivers turned back to their sources, the hill-tops fell crashing to the plains; when the day at length was darkened and a host of headless spirits rode upon the tempest. Though the ground has also been raised by the drift down the slopes of the Merapi, by the overflowing runnels discharging their load of mud into the Ello and the Progo, the magnitude of volcanic devastation can be gauged from the difference in level between the base of the *chandi* and the site of the *kampong* higher up, under which the platform extends whereon its subsidiary buildings stood. Excavations in the detritus have already resulted in the discovery of portions of a brick parapet once enclosing the temple grounds; of vestiges of smaller shrines in the east corner of the terrace and of a cruciform brick substructure to the northeast with fragments of bell-shaped *chaityas*;[1] of a Banaspati, probably from the balustrade of the staircase, and detached stones with and without sculptured ornament, which revealed the former existence of several miniature temples surrounding the central one. At the time of my last visit (which came near terminating my career in my present earthly frame, through the rotten scaffolding giving way under my feet when ascending to the roof), more than half of the space conjecturally encompassed by the parapet, still awaited exploration, and since then restoration, within the limits of the scanty sums allowed, seems to have superseded excavation. In connection with both, the names should be mentioned of P. H. van der Ham, who did wonders with the little means at his disposal, and C. den Hamer, who showed that the decoration of the Mendoot too was not completed before the great catastrophe which devastated Central Java and stopped architectural pursuits.[2]

Reviewing the history of the ancient monuments of the island, not one can pass without a repetition of the sad tale of spoliation. However unpleasant it be to record in every single instance the culpable negligence of a Government stiffening general indifference and almost encouraging downright robbery, the rapid deterioration of those splendid

[1] The words *chaitya* and *dagob* are often used indiscriminately and every *dagob* is, in fact, a *chaitya*, but a *chaitya* is a *dagob* only if it contains a relic.

[2] *De Tjandi Mendoet vóór de Restauratie*, publication of the *Bataviaasch Genootschap*, 1903.

edifices allows no alternative in the matter of explanation. When officials and private individuals of the ruling race set the example, the natives saw no harm in quarrying building material on their own account for their own houses, and they had no time to lose in the rapid process of the razing of their *chandis* for the adornment of residency and assistant-residency gardens, the construction of dams, sugar-mills and indigo factories. Temple stones have been found in many villages round the Mendoot and particularly in Ngrajeg, about two miles distant on the main road, there is no native dwelling in the substructure of which they have not been used.[1] Though the wealth of the *dessa* Ngrajeg in this respect may be explained by its once having boasted its own *chandi*, of which nothing remains but the foundations, there is abundant proof that the chief quarry of the neighbourhood on this side of the river was the Mendoot as the Boro Budoor on the other. From a juridical standpoint, the natives in possession of such spoil, acquired by their fathers or grandfathers, have a prescriptive right on it not disputable in law, averred the administration at Batavia, and so whatever the architects in charge of the restoration needed, had to be bought back and diminished still further the disposable funds. Leaving the doubtful points of this legal question and the enforcement in practice of the theoretical decision for what they are worth to

[1] Major VAN ERP, in the *Tijdschrift voor Indische Taal-, Land- en Volkenkunde*, 1909.

Kromo or Wongso, ordered to part with his door-step or coinings, there is *no* doubt that it is illegal and highly censurable to demolish temples, and temples like the Mendoot at that, to secure building material for Government dams and bridges. What happened in Mojokerto with the bricks of Mojopahit and has been complained of elsewhere, I saw happen in 1885 with Mendoot stones, freely used for abutments, piers, spandrel fillings, etc., when near by the spanning of the Progo was in progress. That bridge has since succumbed like the railway bridge then in course of construction farther down the Progo, a warning which, if heeded, might have prevented, for instance, the chronic misfortunes of the railway bridge in the Anei gorge, West Coast of Sumatra.

With Government bridges lacking the strength to resist the impetuosity of more than ordinarily boisterous freshets, there may always be a surprise in store for the pilgrim to the Boro Budoor who has arrived at the first station, the Mendoot: will he or will he not find the means to cross? For, in time of *banjir*, *i.e.* when the river is in spate, the primitive ferry which maintains the communication in lieu of better, a bambu raft or two frail barges fastened together, fails as to both comfort and safety, and after heavy rains large groups of men and women can often be seen waiting for the turbulent waters to quiet down a bit. Lord Kitchener visited the Mendoot in December, 1909, during a bridgeless spell and conditions generally inauspicious to his

XXVI.

THE *CHANDI* PAWON AND THE RANDU ALAS

(C. Nieuwenhuis.)

proceeding a mile and a half farther to the Boro Budoor. Otherwise the being ferried over in company of gaily dressed people going to or coming from market with fruit, garden produce and all sorts of merchandise for sale or bought, has its compensations; rocked by the eddying stream which glides swiftly between its steep banks, our dominating sensation is one of joy in the splendour of unstinted light, of freedom from the petty torments of everyday routine,—and let worry take care of itself! As we climb the opposite shore, comes the mysteriously grateful feeling of being enveloped in the soil's genial exhalation of warm contentment, the fertile earth's response to the passionate embrace of the sun. Their espousal, their connubial ardour appears incorporate in the *chandi* Dapoor,[1] a petrified spark of universal love, a wonder of structural and decorative skill in a shady grove some hundred paces to the right of the road.[2] And again the *spiritus mundi* is symbolically interpreted in the story of yond temple betrothed and wedded to the tree. They were very much smitten with each other, the *chandi* Pawon and a *randu alas*[3] living in the hamlet Brajanala. They married and the pretty comedy of affection turned into tragedy: as chances very often in the case of a weaker and a

[1] *Dapoor* means "a producer of heat", "a place where things are produced by heat", hence an oven, a kitchen, the priming-hole of a gun.

[2] Before the road was relocated to correspond with the relocation of yet another new bridge after the last but one's tumbling down, the *chandi* Dapoor stood almost at the wayside; its having been smuggled out of sight has not improved its chances of preservation.

[3] *Bombax malabaricum* of the numerous *Malvaceae* family.

stronger partner in the matrimonial game, the latter throve and prospered at the expense of the former. Now of his brothers there were and still are many exactly like him, but of her sisters there were only few and none of her peculiar kind of beauty, and since it seemed a pity that she should waste her singular comeliness in supporting a husband of no particular worth for all his bigness and parade of protecting her, a divorce was resolved upon which meant his sentence of death. Voices in favour of reprieve or commutation of the penalty were disregarded: what did one *randu alas* more or less matter compared with the preservation of the exquisite *chandi* Pawon, sole surviving representative of her class? So the tree was cut down and she escaped happily the fate which overtook the *chandis* Perot and Pringapoos. The *chandi* Pawon was even wholly restored; its foundations, sapped by a tangle of roots, relaid; its roof reconstructed.[1] In its graceful proportions a striking illustration of the truth that a great architect can show the vast range of his art in a very small building, may it stand many centuries longer between Mendoot and Boro Budoor as the typical expression of Javanese thought in Dravidian style!

All is quiet and still in the stately avenue of *kanaris*[2] and few wayfarers are likely to be met, except after *puasa*.[3] "Than longen folke to gon on pilgrimages," and the Boro Budoor attracts a

[1] By the architect VAN DER HAM.

[2] *Canarium commune*, fam. *Burceraceae*.

[3] Or *ramelan* (*ramadhan*), the great yearly fast.

XXVII.

THE *CHANDI* PAWON DIVORCED AND RESTORED

(Centrum.)

goodly crowd bent on sacrifice to the statue in the crowning dagob or to lesser images held in special veneration. Such travelling companions, merrily but sedately intent on devotional exercise conformable to ancestral custom, notwithstanding Moslim doctrine, their forefathers' imaginations tingeing their conceptions of life seen and unseen because of their forefathers' blood running in their veins, increase the cheery solace of abandon to nature, facilitate the attainment of a higher sublime condition than reached as yet, the third Brahma Vihara improved upon by the Buddha, joy in the joy of others while earth and vapoury atmosphere mingle in fullness of delight,

> *. . . in un tepor di sole occiduo*
> *ridente a le cerulee solitudini.*[1]

We turn a corner and the road winds up a hill. That hill is the base of the Boro Budoor, the long desired, suddenly extending his welcome, majestic, overwhelmingly beautiful. It is a repetition on a much grander scale, much more magical, of the effect produced by the *chandi* Derma bursting upon our view in its sylvan frame, reality taking the semblance of a glorious dream. In the waning light of evening the polygonous pyramid of dark trachyte appears as a powerful vision of the mystery of existence shining through a veil of translucent gold. Gray cupolas, raised on jutting walls and projecting cornices, a forest of pinnacles pointing to heaven, gilded by

[1] . . . in the soft rays of the setting sun
Smiling at the cerulean solitudes.

the setting sun, reveal perspectives of boundless immensity, vistas of infinite distance. The brilliancy of heaven, reflected by this mass of forceful imagery, this conquering thought worked in solid stone, receives new lustre from the dome-encircled fundamental idea so mightily expressed. Nowhere has art more ably availed herself of the possibilities of site and more felicitously combined with natural scenery, created a more harmonious ensemble than in the amazingly original design and delicate execution of this puissant temple, this gift of the Javanese Buddhists to posterity, a source of spiritual quickening to whoso tries to understand.

CHAPTER IX

THE STONES OF THE BORO BUDOOR

. . . la vérité rendue expressive et parlante, élevée à la hauteur d'une idée. ERNEST RENAN, *Vie de Jésus* (*Introduction*).

THE *pasangrahan*, built for the convenience of visitors to the Boro Budoor, offers fair accommodation to the student of oriental architecture and lover of art in whatever form. Also to a good many who feel it incumbent on them to be able to say: "I have taken everything in," or who have quite other ends in view than communion with the thought of distant ages: foreign tourists whose principal care is to exhibit trunks and travelling-bags covered with labels of out-of-the-beaten-track hotels while their brains remain hopelessly empty; junketers of domestic growth, often in couples whose irregular relations seek shelter behind the excuse of "doing" the island, and heartily disinclined to practise the virtues preached in the reliefs of the shrine of shrines, particularly down on continence. So even the Philistines derive advantage, after the notions of their kind, from the ramshackle fabric of vile heathenism, as this magnificent temple has been called by one of their number, and its visitors' book tells a sorry tale of irreclaimable vulgarity; the wit, laboriously aimed at in many entries, but widely missed, partakes altogether too much (minus the element of *badinage*) of the answer given by a young naval officer to an old aunt when she asked him where, in his opinion, the most striking natural scenery of Java was to be found: At Petit Trouville,[1] said he, on Sunday in the dry season.

The *pasangrahan's* guests of that ilk are generally no early risers and their company is therefore not likely to mar the impression received of the Boro Budoor at second sight after supper, supplied by the army pensioner in charge of the place, and a night's sound rest. Looking tranquillity itself, the vast pile charms and soothes the heart, notwithstanding its enormous size, before the intellect, scrutinising its outline, begins to marvel at the unaccustomed form the builder has chosen to proclaim his idea. Save one or two temples in *hinayanistic* Burmah, which present a faint resemblance, nothing else can be named as producing the same effect, but then, wrote Fergusson for the land where the creed was born that inspired its founder, it must be remembered that not a single structural Buddhist building now exists within the cave region of Western

[1] Such is the name given to a stretch of beach, not far from Tanjoong Priok, the harbour of Batavia, much resorted to, for bathing and advertisement, by that city's frail sisterhood, and Batavians will appreciate the young naval officer's *bon mot* better than did his aunt, a provincial spinster, when at length she fathomed it.

India. Rising light and airy for all its grandeur, it expresses more strength than a mere massing together of the ponderous material in huge walls and buttresses and towers could have done; its quiet consciousness of power is enhanced by its strange beauty of contour in perfect harmony with its setting of living colour. There it lies, clasping together the sapphire sky and the emerald garden of Java.

The *mahayanistic* character of the Boro Budoor is well attested by the Dhyani Buddhas among its statuary, despite the opinion of Siamese connoisseurs, and by its further ornamental sculpture, of which more anon. Meant for a reliquary, it may or may not be, in the absence of historical proof pro or contra, one of the 84,000 *stupas* consecrated to receive and hold a fractional portion of the Indian Saviour's remains after King Asoka had opened seven of the depositories of his ashes in the eight towns among which his remains were originally divided, to make the whole world share in their blessed possession. Who has not heard of the transfer, in the ninth year of the reign of Sirimeghavanna, A.D. 310, of the Dathadathu, the holy tooth, from Dantapura to Ceylon, where it became the *mascotte*, so to speak, the pledge of undisturbed dominion to the rulers of the ísland who should control its guardians. The sacrosanct yellow piece of dentin, about the length of the little finger,[1] enclosed in nine concentric cases of gold,

[1] A description, dated October 12, 1858, informs us that the piece of ivory, supposed to have garnished the jaw of Gautama, is about the size of the little

inlaid with diamonds, rubies and pearls, is but rarely shown, far more rarely than even the seamless coat at Treves, and then under conditions of excessive adoration. But, notwithstanding all this pomp and circumstance, who that has visited the Dalada Malagawa at Kandy and the Boro Budoor in Java, can fail to prefer the latter, though sacrilegious robbers have carried off its relic, leaving the desecrated shrine to decay.

The wordy war waged around the etymology of the name Boro Budoor, did not solve the mystery of its origin; all derivations thus far suggested are mere guess-work and unsatisfactory, whatever reasons be adduced for Roorda van Eysinga's explanation that it means an enclosed space, or Raffles' surmise that it is a corruption of Bara (the great) Buddha, or the late King of Siam's that it refers to the (spiritual) army of the Buddha, if not to the several Buddhas, as alleged by others. One of the oldest existing monuments in the island, the foundation of the *chandi* Boro Budoor has been attributed by native tradition to Raden Bandoong, already known from the legends connected with the *chandis* Prambanan and Sewu, who, as King of Pengging, assumed the name of Handayaningrat. Professor Kern[1] puts the date of the substructure at about 850, allowing several years for its completion

finger, of a rich yellow colour, slightly curved in the middle and tapering. The thickest end, taken for the crown, has a hole into which a pin can be introduced; the thinnest end, taken for the root, looks as if worn away or tampered with to distribute fragments of the relic.

[1] Reports and Communications of the Dutch Royal Academy, 1895.

—if ever it was fully completed, for this temple, like the *chandi* Mendoot near by, the *chandi* Bimo on the Diëng plateau and so many more, shows traces of the work having been suspended before the decoration was quite finished. Sculpture just commenced or little further advanced than the bare outlining, found on the walls, especially of the covered base; divers blocks of stone half transformed into ornament and statuary, Dhyani Buddhas and lions, very illustrative of the methods followed at different stages of the carving, lying forsaken on the slope and summit of a neighbouring hillock, disclose an interruption of the labour by some event of tremendous consequence.[1] Rather than accept the theory that the ancient temples of Java were left intentionally defective from religious motives, viz. to emphasise the sense of human imperfection as an incentive to humility and prostration before the divine, we may believe in the Merapi, that wicked old giant, having asserted himself in one of his destructive moods, belching forth flames and ashes, shaking and burying the handiwork of Hindu and Buddhist pygmies with strictest impartiality. Standing on the first of the highest terraces on the south side, says an article[2] in the *Javapost* of December 5, 1903, one observes

[1] According to another explanation these incompleted pieces of sculpture, found lying about, were rejected in the building because they did not come up to the architect's requirements.

[2] *The Ruin of the Boro Budoor or Vandalism*, signed GOENA DARMA. It is no indiscretion, I believe, to reveal behind this significant pseudonym Father P. J. HOEVENAARS, of whose sagacious observations I shall avail myself repeatedly in the following account of the temple's history.

a bulging out of the lower terraces, best accounted for by a violent earthquake in a southerly direction. When the galleries were cleared in 1814 and 1834, the volcanic character of the detritus which filled them (ashes from the Merapi, wrote Roorda van Eysinga in 1850) and also forms the substratum of the rubbish still unremoved from the once enclosed grounds of the *chandi* Mendoot, furnished strong evidence in support of an eruption of the nearest fire-mountain having been the cause of the precipitate flight, perhaps the death in harness, of the builders. Of the preservation of their work too, in so far as finished, for, to speak again with the writer in the *Javapost*, the very fact of its having been embedded has saved much of its artistic detail; and the reason why some of the sculptured parts are damaged to a far greater extent than others adjoining, is probably that they were exposed earlier and longer. Deterioration and demolition set in rapidly when wind and weather began to ravage the wholly unprotected edifice, when unscrupulous collectors wrought havoc unchecked.

The Boro Budoor was never hidden from view to the point of blotting out its existence from memory. I shall have occasion to refer to native chronicles mentioning it in the eighteenth century. To speak of its rediscovery by Cornelius is therefore inaccurate though we owe to that clever Lieutenant of Engineers, purposely sent to the Kadu by Raffles, in 1814, the first scientific survey and description with elucidating drawings. Except for the publication, in 1873, of Dr. C. Leemans' book with an atlas containing illustrations after drawings by F. C. Wilsen, and the mission of I. van Kinsbergen to obtain photographic reproductions of the reliefs, the Dutch Government left the matchless temple entirely to its fate until very recently. An official correspondence, kept trailing indefinitely to invest ministerial promises regarding the antiquities of Java with a semblance of sincerity, had the usual negative effect. Whenever a colonial Excellency declared with unctuous pomposity that the most conscientious care would be taken of the Boro Budoor, a monument of incalculable value considered from the standpoint of science and art, most brilliant memento of the island's historic past, etc., etc., those versed in the phraseology of Plein and Binnenhof at the Hague trembled in expectation of bad news of criminal negligence, theft and mutilation to follow. The later history of the "brilliant memento" agrees but too well with the ominous prognostics derived from such dismal parliamentary fustian. A great poet sang of things of beauty scarce visible from extreme loveliness: the readily movable things of beauty constituting the loveliness of the Boro Budoor, became invisible *sans phrase.* We are told in legendary lore of statues which flew through the air to take domicile at enormous distances from their proper homes, or vanished altogether, dissolving into space: the statues of the Boro Budoor developed that faculty in an astonishing degree; if handicapped by great weight or solid attachment to the main structure, bent on travelling *à tout travers*, they sent their heads alone to seek recreation and instruction in the varying ways of the world, and their heads did never return, either because they were amusing themselves too jollily away from the austerities of the eight-fold path or because they found themselves unavoidably detained in durance vile.

The remaining, mostly headless statues are sad to behold, and the fishy account given of their defective condition, that, namely, the Buddhists, beleaguered in the sanctuary by the Muhammadans, battling *pro aris et focis*, drove the enemies off by bombarding them with the Lord of Victory's noble features, hewn in stone, smacks of a too ingenious evasion of the disgraceful facts.[1] The chronicles are silent on such a desperate struggle in that locality between the conquering hosts of Islām and the followers of him who pleaded peace, love and goodwill, whose doctrine and example alike forbade strife and armed resistance. Not that there has been no fighting round and even within the walls of the Boro Budoor among the Javanese engaged in internecine warfare and during the insurrection of Dipo Negoro,[2] but the story of the using up of the statuary in the shape of

[1] Invention being stimulated by quasi-historical novels like GRAMBERG'S *Mojopahit*.

[2] Vide *De Java-Oorlog*, commenced by Captain P. J. F. LOUW, continued by Captain E. S. DE KLERCK and published under the auspices of the *Batavian Society of Arts and Sciences*, vols. i. and ii.

missiles, has no leg to stand on. In the Java War (1825–1830) the Dutch troops erected a temporary fort near the temple, but it is improbable that *chandi* material entered into its construction, not because the warriors of the Government would have scrupled to destroy any ancient monument, but because the Boro Budoor stones are exceedingly heavy and earthen fortifications amply sufficed against native bands without artillery. Though cavalry in particular never enjoyed a high reputation in respect of their relations to art,[1] there does not seem to be any more substance in the confession of a *ci-devant* commander of a squadron of hussars, cited by Brumund, that his men used to try the temper of their swords on the ears and noses of the silent host of Dhyani Buddhas when the rebels of Sentot and Kiahi Maja were not available.

The true misfortune of the Boro Budoor was official indifference and negligence; and far more injurious than the fretting tooth of time or even the merciless hand of the spoiler combined with the provoking *laissez aller* yawned in periodical circulars from the central administration, from Sleepy Hollow at Batavia, was the dabbling in archaeology of ambitious persons who posed as discoverers, the less their aptitude to digest their desultory reading, the more arrogant their cock-

[1] This holds good for western as well as eastern lands and, whether true or false, the story of Napoleon's dragoons converting the refectorium of Santa Maria delle Grazie at Milan into a stable and adjusting their horses' mangers against da Vinci's *Cena*, expresses very well what cavalry on the warpath are capable of.

sureness where famous scholars reserved *their* conclusions. A little knowledge is a dangerous thing and might have proved disastrous to the venerable temple in combination with one of their vaunted discoveries, which established beyond doubt what not a few knew well enough and never had doubted of, viz. that there was a gallery lower than its lowest uncovered terrace, wisely filled up to increase the stability of the building, very probably soon after or even before the erection of the upper storeys. The removal of the supporting layers of stone impaired, of course, the general condition of the structure and the good news of its being again in its former state, was received by many with a sigh of relief. This happened in 1885 with great flourish of trumpets, and the only benefit derived, certainly not of sufficient importance to balance the inevitable weakening of the foundations attendant on such excavations, consisted in the bringing to light of rude, scarcely decipherable inscriptions or rather scratchings,[1] and the intelligence that of the photographed sculptures, in which, so far, no representation of connected events has been recognised, twenty-four are unfinished and thirteen damaged—six wholly smashed. In 1900 new shafts were sunk for new discoveries of the long and widely known, and while this pernicious dilettantism was going on, pseudo-archaeologists vying with professed iconoclasts who should do most harm to the Boro Budoor, the Government

[1] The form of the characters, etc., according to Professor KERN, points to about the year 800 Saka (A.D. 878).

BASE OF THE BORO BUDOOR SHOWING THE (FILLED UP) LOWEST GALLERY

(C. Nieuwenhuis.)

confined itself to antiquarian pyrotechnics at the yearly debates on the colonial budget in Parliament.

The Boro Budoor being undermined and gradually scattered to the four winds, it was but natural that the natives, following the example set by the elect, even by the elect of the elect acting in this or that official capacity, who used, for instance, *chandi* stones for the flooring of the Government *pasang'rahan*,—that the inhabitants of the neighbouring *kampongs* should carry off what appeared suitable for their own ends, and the least heavy *jataka* reliefs claimed their first attention. So things went from bad to worse and the most disastrous year, a veritable *annus calamitatis* for the Boro Budoor, arrived with 1896, when the late King of Siam paid his second visit to Java. Much interested, as was to be expected of a ruler of a Buddhist country, in the Buddhist monuments of the island, so interested, in fact, that his Majesty tried to put the *mahayanistic* temples of the Kadu to the credit of his own, the *hinayanistic* church, his endeavours in this kind of mental annexation inspired authorities, eager to share in the honours of Siamese Knighthood (White Elephant, Crown of Siam, etc.) distributed with right royal generosity, to urge him to annexation in deed. If foreign visitors of little account had been permitted to help themselves in a small way to "souvenirs" for a consideration to keepers' underlings left without control, why should foreign visitors of distinction not be served wholesale? His Majesty Chulalongkorn, to whom no blame attaches for gratifying his desire where he found Dutch functionaries, high and low, more than willing to oblige, was invited to make his choice and we must still thank him for his moderation, which limited the quantity of sculpture selected to eight cart-loads: there is scarcely a doubt that if he had requested them to pull part of the Boro Budoor down in consideration of Knight Commander- or Grand Masterships in this or that Order, the official conscience would have raised no objection. This came to pass, of course, after a more than usually fine flow, at the Hague, of ministerial rhetoric anent the priceless heritage Holland has to protect in the "brilliant mementos of Java's historic past," and the lover of ancient Buddhist architecture who wants to make a study of its acknowledged masterpiece, must now of necessity travel on to the banks of the Meynam to get an idea of some of its most characteristic imagery, not to speak of fragments of ornament and statuary removed by tourists of commoner complexion and dispersed heaven knows where.

This instance of the ancient monuments of Java being officially despoiled to please crowned heads and other visitors in exalted stations, *pour le bon motif*, seemed so incredible that, when I censured it in the Dutch East Indian Press, the Dutch Press, over-zealous in hiding colonial enormities, also *pour le bon motif*, considered it an easy task to deny, waxing eloquently indignant at the denunciation until in regular, normal sequence, always observable

DETAIL OF THE BORO BUDOOR
(C. Nieuwenhuis.)

in the perennial case of Dutch whitewashing versus colonial boldness of speech, the correctness of the statement could no longer be assailed, new evidence accumulating steadily, Mr. J. A. N. Patijn, for one, describing, in the *Kroniek* and the *Tijdschrift voor Nederlandsch Indië*, a collection displayed near the Wat Pra Keo at Bangkok and brought thither from Java in 1896.[1] The frolicking monkeys doubtless, the people of the large cheek-bones, represented on some reliefs thus transferred, prompted an enthusiastic, genuine archaeologist's imprecation on the heads of the guilty official and non-official toadies, inasmuch as he wished them, if there be anything in the dogma of Karma, which provides for our sins being visited on us in lives to come, that their least punishment might be their transformation, when called to new birth, into apes abandoned to ceaseless squabbles over their *kanari*-nuts (honours, dignities, preferment with big salaries, fat pensions, etc.), clawing one another with their sharp nails, to find at last that all the shells are empty. Desisting from a profitless discussion on the possibilities of retribution in a future existence, it requires to be stated that the official mind needed several years' reflection in this before reaching the conclusion that really, in the matter of the conservation of the Boro Budoor something more was wanted than the periodical outbursts of gushing sentiment, grossly disregarded in practice, which are *le moyen*

[1] See also the *Westminster Review* of May and *The Antiquary* of August, 1912.

de parvenir of Dutch colonial politicians. The independents of the colonial Press, however, had at last the satisfaction that Captain T. van Erp of the Engineers was detailed to take the work of restoration in hand, building himself a house in the shadow of the *chandi* confided to his care, anxious to direct the necessary labours on the spot. Stationed there since August, 1907, his promotion to the rank of Major fortunately did not result in the withdrawal of his services from the archaeological field and, the climax of laxness with regard to the Boro Budoor having been capped in the Siamese episode, brighter days may dawn for that venerable edifice.

One of the rooms of the *pasangrahan*, reserved, under the old dispensation, for the storing of detached pieces of sculpture, was called the sample-room because, according to current report, orders were taken there for the delivery of such still undetached ornament and statuary as might have struck the visitors' fancy. Other images lined the path from the *pasangrahan* to the temple, among them two Dhyani Buddhas, a fine Akshobhya and a still finer Amitabha, and lions, the poor remainder of those which once adorned the steps leading to the raised level of the building, whence the name: Avenue of Lions. Seemingly commanded to descend from the places where they kept guard as solitary sentinels, and to unite for defence at the point of greatest danger, terrible havoc was wrought in their ranks by the onslaught of souvenir-hunters, and one of their large-limbed,

DETAIL OF THE BORO BUDOOR

(C. Nieuwenhuis.)

beautifully chiselled chiefs, who himself watched the entrance with a vauntful air as if proclaiming to foe and friend alike: *Et s'il n'en reste qu'un, moi je serai celui-là*, had to suffer the ignominy of being captured and carried off to Siam—which proves his Majesty Chulalongkorn's good taste: it was the best specimen of animal carving on that scale in Java. These are no cheerful reflections when approaching the eminence skillfully converted into a *stupa* whose equal, both in originality of design and cleverness of execution, can nowhere be found. Though India furnished its prototype, the style here evolved baffles, on close examination, all comparison. The only building it can be likened to is the Taj Mahal at Agra, and only in this single respect while differing in all others, that, conceived by a titanic intellect, the delicate decoration suggests the minute precision of the jeweller's craft. Opening and closing a distinct chapter in architecture, this admirable production rises in terraces which form galleries round the hill-top, enclosed by walls, spaced on the outside by 432 niches for statues of the Buddha with *prabha* (aureole) and *padmasana* (lotus cushion), on the inside with representations illustrating sacred and profane writings in bas-relief; the galleries of the superstructure raised on the square ground-plan, become circular and are bounded by 72 bell-shaped *chaityas* containing statues of the Buddha without either *prabha* or *padmasana*, or any ornament whatever. The profuse decoration of their surroundings never detracts from the powerfully expressed central idea of praise to the Enlightened One, the one who has fulfilled his end; the repetition of the motives manifesting the religious purpose, directs rather than confuses the attention of the worshipper in their multiformity of application. The spiritual father of the Boro Budoor must have been a man of strong mental grasp, of honest masculine endeavour stimulated by a highly sensitive temperament; his work, "a goodly heap for to behold," growing in dignity and beauty the closer it is observed, a realisation of the sublimest aspirations of Buddhist Java, will perpetuate also, as long as it can endure, the memory of his own superior mind.

The constructive ability of this gifted builder was no less wonderful than his mastery of detail in aid of his main intent. A clever system of drainage attests to the foresight of his workmanship; but the gutters remaining filled up and the gargoyles (open-mouthed *nagas*) choked after the excavation of the galleries in 1814 and 1834, without any one thinking of clearing them too, the water had to flow off as best it could in the torrential rains of successive west monsoons, filtering through the fissures between the stones, passing down to the foundations and adding, in oozing out, to the causes of decay by washing the supporting layers of earth and gravel away. The staircases and passageways to the different terraces and galleries are constructed with the accurate

XXXI.

DETAIL OF THE BORO BUDOOR

(Centrum.)

sense of right proportion which distinguishes the natives of the island up to this day, and their *naga*- and *kala-makara* ornament belongs to the most impressive part of the graceful decoration. In our ascent from lower to higher planes of understanding, increasing in perception of the mysteries of life and death, the Banaspati shows the road, the Hindu-Javanese Gorgon's head as Horsfield called it, appropriated by Buddhist architecture, figurating the terrors of error it faces while budding forth in the promise of further guidance for whoso shall leave the world's delusions, a loved wife, a young-born son, to seek the truth in pursuance of the Buddha's ordinance: no intimidation which threatens with the pains of hell all who dare to disobey the dictates of priestly ambition, but an assurance of beatitude gained by self-purification. The staircases of the superstructure correspond with the four approaches leading up the hillock to the temple-yard; in the course of the excavations, undertaken to facilitate the work of restoration, one of them, very much out of repair, has been laid bare. The reconstruction of the lower principal staircase, whose original position has now been determined, will result, it is hoped, in the removal of the unsightly flight of uneven steps masquerading as the main entrance at the corner opposite the *pasangrahan*; and, perhaps, to provide one worthy of site and building, the Government will not haggle over the modest sum required for the re-erection of the monumental gate whose remains were discovered adjoining the balustrade of the spacious elevated platform.

On entering the galleries, establishing contact with this symmetrical embodiment of highly spiritualised thought in the strongly knit language of chiselled stone, to mount to the state of the perfect disciple, spurred by the figured evolution of the four degrees of Dhyana which lead to supreme happiness, the pilgrim must have experienced, as we do, the sensation of physical well-being imparted by the splendour of nature wrapping human longings in sunshine and the delicious odour exhaled by mother earth. The luxurious emotion increases, despite nirvanic chastening, and among the serene images of the higher terraces, who can remain unmoved in contemplation of the ancient temple lifting its dagob to the blue heaven, of its hoary walls touched by the golden light, quivering in desire of sacred communion! Nor do we cease to marvel when turning from the general idea of universal solidarity, enunciated in an irreproachable architectural form, to the expository details of decoration. The ornament accommodates itself with amazing facility to the characteristic tendencies of the ground-plan, never perverting the central purpose, which dominates in a most felicitous combination of the two principles separately developed for western ends in the classic and gothic styles: the horizontal expansion to allow thinking space to the brain and the mystic pointing upward to satisfy the cravings of the heart. Both found application in the Boro Budoor, their unity of thought in diversity of expression being consolidated by an inexhaustible wealth of imagery, elucidating accessories, filled as it is "with sculptures rarest, of forms most beautiful and strange." Faithful in choice of subject and manner of representation to the notions of its time, bodying forth things unknown to our age, the ornament surprises by its fanciful invention and peculiar treatment, though always in the best of taste. The heavy cornice which protects the lowest uncovered tier of external, so far not yet satisfactorily explained reliefs, carries the niches for the statues already mentioned. The shape of these niches and of the temples delineated in the scenery of the carved tales and legends, here as at Prambanan, Toompang, etc., afford us material assistance in determining after what model *chandis*, long fallen into ruin, were built; they are especially helpful in explaining the often puzzling arrangement of the superstructures, hardly one being found, even among those best preserved, with the roof still intact. Leaving archaeological problems alone, modern architects and decorators can further derive a good deal of profit from a study of the gradation observed in the downward radiation of both the architectural and decorative conceit centred in the crowning dagob, or, rather, the upward convergence in a nobly devised distribution of spaces connected and entwined by cunning ornament, the luxuriant fantasy of the sculptor being unerringly controlled by the staid design of the builder. A fervent imagination may revel in miles of bas-reliefs without surfeit, the salutary restraint of a sober outline and a proportional disposition of the component parts being such that the eye never gets tired or the faculty of perception cloyed.

Fergusson, pointing to the identity of workmen and workmanship in the sculpture and details of ornamentation at the Boro Budoor and at Ajunta (cave 26), Nassick (cave 17), the later caves at Salsette, Kondoty, Montpezir and other places in that neighbourhood, computes that at the former the decoration extends to nearly 5000 feet, almost an English mile, and, as there are sculptures on both faces, we have nearly 10,000 lineal feet of reliefs. They numbered 2141 in all, counting what is damaged and altogether lost, but omitting the decoration of the ornamental niches: on the lowest wall 408 in the upper and 160 in the lower tier outside, 568 inside; on the second wall, 240 outside and 192 inside; on the third wall, 108 outside and 165 inside; on the fourth wall, 88 outside and 140 inside; on the fifth wall, 72 inside. Regarding their noble qualities of style and decorative value as a component of the general project, the opinion of a writer in the *Quarterly Review*[1] may be quoted, who discusses the Boro Budoor's straight lines, its untroubled spaces of flat stone, its mouldings of classic simplicity, its intricate and elaborate bands of ornament, held in place by the nice choice of

[1] ROGER FRY on *Oriental Art*, January, 1910.

DETAIL OF THE BORO BUDOOR
(C. Nieuwenhuis.)

relief, being low and unaccented, in opposition to the deep cutting and full modelling of the panels they surround; and in these panels, he continues, in spite of the full roundness of the modelling and the wealth of ornamental detail, the unity is maintained by a fine sense of rhythm and discreet massing and spacing. The upper tier of carvings on the inner wall of the first gallery, haut-reliefs in contradistinction to the rest, represents the life of the Buddha from his birth until his death and is the best preserved. Many of the others have suffered so badly that they baffle explanation; taken on the whole, they treat of traditional occurrences in connection with the Buddha himself or his predecessors, of gatherings under bo-trees, pilgrimages to reliquaries, alms-giving, exhortations to observe the law, admonitions to virtue: abstinence, tolerance and charity. Animal fables are interwoven with *jataka*-tales, *i.e.* narratives concerning the Buddha before he appeared as the perfect man, tracing his path to holiness in his adventures as a hare, a fish, a quail, a swan, a deer, the king of monkeys, an elephant, a bull, a wood-pecker, a tortoise, the horse Balaha, every metamorphosis serving to illustrate his zeal to sacrifice himself for his fellow-creatures and, incidentally, stimulating the kindness we owe to our poor relations without the power of speech. Professor Speyer's translation of legends collected in the *Jatakamala* (wreath of *jatakas*) enables us to recognise in a good many of the reliefs of the Boro Budoor the successive stages of the Buddha on the road to supreme excellence, the figuration of his progress being largely influenced by ancient Hindu folk-lore.

If Ruskin compared St. Mark's at Venice so aptly with a vast illuminated missal, bound with alabaster instead of parchment, studded with porphyry pillars instead of jewels, and written within and without in letters of enamel and gold, in the Boro Budoor, a sacred book of volcanic stone, the life of the Buddha, before and after he became a son of man and man's saviour, lies opened before us: the flowery earth and the shining heaven are its binding; Surya, the sun himself, gilds and enamels the letters, the images which, in their sculptured frame, not too deeply cut and not too rich for a setting, but precisely adequate, tell to all creatures the story of wisdom and elevation of spirit. The illustration of the *Lalita Vistara* occupies, as already mentioned, the upper tier of the inner wall of the first open gallery. Walking round in the proper direction, *i.e.* keeping the dagob to the right while moving with the sun, we have first a few introductory scenes, leading up to the Buddha's advent and preparing us for the mystic teachings of an imagery which expands simply and naturally between the flowing lines of harmonious ornament and speaks to the heart as does the sound of running water or the soughing of the wind in the tree-tops. Immediately after his birth, rising from the white lotus-flower which has sprung from the earth at the place touched by his feet, Siddhartha, in token of his power over the several worlds, paces seven steps to each of the

XXXIII.

DETAIL OF THE BORO BUDOOR
(C. Nieuwenhuis.)

cardinal points and to the abode of sin, announcing his mission: I shall conquer the Prince of Darkness and the army of the Prince of Darkness; to save those plunged into hell, I shall cause rain to descend from the huge cloud of the law and they will be filled with joy and happiness. He grows and marries and leaves his father's palace, moved by the misery of the lowly and lost, to gather knowledge as Sakyamuni, until, compassing all wisdom, he becomes impersonated truth and the great renunciation takes place. The closing scene refers to his death, to the adoration of the mortal remains of the immortal Tathagata, symbolising his course among men not as a succession of past acts but as a constant one to be imitated by whoso desires the reward. Increasing in excellence of design and execution the nearer we approach the Holy of Holies, the touching tale of a life of sacrifice is told with that straightforward simplicity of which only the consummate artist possesses the secret. All appears so human and real, so inspiringly animated by the extreme of vital motion, to use an oriental expression, the individuality of the figures being always preserved in minutest personal detail without the least affectation. Plastic triumphs, emphasising the lessons of the sacred books, bring up unto us the people of the *jaman buda*, heroes tall and strong as palm-trees, virgins lithe and slender as bambu-stems, with drooping eyes, shrinking from a too inquisitive gaze, with limbs modelled as if they would tremble under the pressure of a caressing hand.

The statues, watching the ascent of the seeker of purification, second the impulse received from the reliefs by their tranquil composure, that is in so far as they remained at their stations, for their ranks are sadly thinned. Aspiring to the holiness figured in the images of the higher terraces, to the priceless boon of the Nirvana as final blessing, the Dhyani Buddhas, sunk in meditation, girding themselves with virtue, longing for the ecstasies vouchsafed to the Adi-Buddha's meditation, reflect the five salient features of his understanding, as indicated by their gestures. Divided into three or twice three groups, according to the position of their hands, and in intimate relationship with their Bodhisatvas, Vajrochana, Akshobhya and Ratnasambhava are supposed to have swayed, during thousands of years, the three worlds which successively disappeared, as Amitabha, whose Bodhisatva is Padmapani, sways since twenty-four centuries the present world, in closest spiritual union with the historical Buddha, to be succeeded by Amoghasiddha, whose Bodhisatva is Vishvapani, the ultimate Buddha, the Buddha of universal love. Facing the four cardinal points and the zenith, they sit with crossed legs,[1] clothed in a thin robe which leaves the right shoulder and arm bare, and have the distinctive protuberance of the skull, generally also the *oorna*, the symbol of light, be it then produced by the sun or by lightning. A sixth Buddha, represented

[1] In the position called *silo* by the natives, but with the body straight, not bent forward.

XXXIV.

A DHYANI BUDDHA OF THE BORO BUDOOR

(Cephas Sr.)

by the statues of the fifth and highest wall, is supposed to refer to a power which dominates the other five, swaying in last resort the destinies of all worlds without exception; but this theory still needs confirmation. The statues of the circular terraces stood, or rather sat, in bell-shaped *chaityas*, four to five feet high, capped with tapering keystones which carry conical pinnacles—no *lingas*, though this oft recurring motive of Hindu decoration may have suggested the idea. These *chaityas*, 72 in number [1] and for the greater part in ruin, shattered shells of sanctity, were closed all round and the images inside, without aureoles, like the Buddhas lower down, only visible through openings in the form of lozenges. Their peculiar contour has led to the conjecture that they were constructed after the holy *padma* or lotus-flower, a hypothesis to which their *padmasana*-like bases and the numerous peepholes, which might figurate empty seed-lobes, lend some colour. Of the 72 Buddhas they protected, eighteen are wholly lost and no more than ten escaped grievous hurt.

Winding our way upward, passing through the galleries whose profound silence, imbued with the intensely religious spirit radiating from their sculptured walls, becomes more and more eloquent; circling the terraces where the attitude of ecstatic elation of the world's pre-eminently venerable ones in their *chaityas* exalts the mind in tremulous

[1] The lowest circular terrace has or ought to have 32, the second or middle one 24, the highest and last 16 of them.

expectation, we arrive at the dagob, the shrine of shrines, the temple's coronet, glittering in the bright glow of day. This is the reliquary proper, the centre into which the holiness of the hallowed building converges. It rises, similar to the smaller cupolas, but perpendicular to a height of several feet, from a substructure in the guise of a lotus cushion; it was also closed round about, without any aperture so far as can be concluded from its present state, for a portion of it has tumbled down and the base of the crowning pinnacle, reached by ill-matched, rickety steps, a recent, outrageously discordant addition, serves for a bench, the whole, about 25 feet above the topmost terrace, having been transformed into a crude belvedere, enabling visitors to enjoy the magnificent view. The interior space seems originally to have been divided into an upper and a lower chamber; there is nothing deserving mention in the matter of decoration save an inscription to remind posterity of the late King of Siam's visit in the disastrous year 1896—a delicious memorial, at the same time, of official vandalism and servility. The golden letters affect one unpleasantly in the spoliated sanctum, whose ruinous condition dates from a previous call, some sixty or seventy years ago, permitted if not encouraged by previous authorities, when looting pseudo-archaeologists broke into it and carried off the relic, which consisted, assuming the credibility of local reports regarding their disappointment, in a small quantity of ashy substance, enclosed in a

XXXV

RELIEFS OF THE BORO BUDOOR

(C. Nieuwenhuis.)

metal urn with lid; furthermore in a small image of metal and a few coins. The large statue they unearthed too, would have impeded the movements of the marauders on their return voyage and so it remained in place, half hidden in the hole they had dug, undisturbed, for the same reason, by subsequent collectors. Left unfinished by its sculptor, designedly or not,[1] resembling in the position of its hands the Dhyani Buddhas which face the East, does it personify the Adi-Buddha, a purely abstract entity, a metaphysical conception hitherto defying even symbolic utterance? The learned and especially the quasi-learned never lacked weighty arguments pro or contra, and, without prejudice to all they proved and disproved,[2] it does not appear improbable that the lively imagination of the Javanese artist aimed at a tangible expression of him who ran his course as the spirit and source of the Buddhist conception of happiness, resuscitated from his ashes, dominating East and West, North and South, the blissful abode of those progressing in self-negation and the infernal regions of prolonged earthly existence, by the strength of the divine rays proceeding from the *oorna*, illumining the path trodden by the virtuous toward annihilation,

[1] M. A. Foucher points out in the *Bulletin de l'Ecole Française d'Extrême Orient*, iii., that the Chinese pilgrim Hiuen Tsiang found another unfinished statue in the Mahabodhi temple near the Bo-tree of Enlightenment, a statue which, according to the description, represented the Buddha in the same position, his left hand resting in his lap, his right hand hanging down, etc.

[2] The literature concerning this statue, says Goena Darma in the *Javapost* of December 5, 1903, is extensive and rich in curious conjectures but poor as to scientific value.

terrifying the children of darkness, dwellers in passion and sin, pervading all creation with his saintliness, the one of the Paranirvana whose essence flowers in the beauty of the Boro Budoor. And the Moslim native worships him as the god of his ancestors, caught in stone; smears him with *boreh* and performs acts of sacrifice before him in spite of the Book fulminating against idolaters and of the almost contemptuous familiarity intimated by the otherwise very appropriate nickname bestowed on this heterodox deity, namely *recho belèq*, which means "statue in the mud".

The work of restoration, started with excavations and the removal of heaps of accumulated debris, has led to important discoveries, also in relation to the dagob. Among shattered *naga*-gargoyles, antefixes, carved detail of every description, fragments have been found of a triple *payoong*, an ornament in the form of a sunshade which capped it; of a statuette supposed to have adorned its second storey, the upper compartment of the cella. To quote from Major van Erp's last published report,[1] the excavations shed new light on the design of some minor parts of the building, the decoration, *e.g.*, of the lowest three staircases on each of the four sides; notwithstanding the existing drawings, the *kala-makara* motive seems to have entered into the ornament of the entrance gate in the principal outer wall; the design of the balustrade which enclosed

[1] Proceedings of the *Batavian Society of Arts and Sciences*, January 11, 1910.

XXXVI.

ASCENDING THE BORO BUDOOR

(Cephas Sr.)

the platform of the temple and disappeared altogether, has been determined and a portion of it will be rebuilt to show how things must have looked; slabs belonging to the different series of bas-reliefs, mostly of the *jataka* variety, have been unearthed or detected in neighbouring *kampongs*. Especial care is taken to retrieve those missing from the upper tier in the first gallery: if the recovered reliefs are not always complete, the recognisable principal figure explains generally the idea which the sculptor intended to convey, with sufficient clearness to be grasped by the trained archaeologist. And as to the rest of the detached pieces of architectural value, dug up or otherwise revealed to the searching eye, the symmetric unity of the Boro Budoor is such that place and position of each component part, however subordinate in the mighty fabric, are easily ascertained. Every new find discloses new excellence, so far undreamt of, in the constructive ability of the master-builder whose illuminated brain conceived the idea of this temple wherein he wrote the history of a religion,

Whose goodly workmanship far past all other,
That ever were on earth, all were they set together.

His name is unknown, though native fancy, descrying his likeness in the profile of the Minoreh mountains, a fine conceit worthy of his genius, has baptised him Kiahi Guna Darma. Another tradition calls him Kiahi Oondagi and makes him chisel the statue which, up to the time of the late King of

Siam's visit in 1896, stood near the *pasangrahan*, facing a damaged Amitabha and seemingly heartening the diminishing ranks of the lions mounting guard. It had been brought thither from a place known as Topog, about a mile distant, and was certainly a portrait-statue, beautifully cut and with its extraordinarily clever features a rare work of art. The story goes that, like Busketus, the architect (with Rainaldus) of the Duomo at Pisa, his dearest wish was to have his remains carried to rest under the stones of the edifice he had raised to the honour of the unseen; that, baffled in his hopes and reincarnated after his death because of some venial offence which made him fail in attaining the Nirvana too, he fashioned this effigy to be set up at the entrance of his *magnum opus*, anticipating an idea of the equally nameless artist who put the Byzantine stamp on San Marco in Venice. It is an additional proof of the late King Chulalongkorn's discrimination in favour of the very best that, making the permitted choice, his Majesty included Kiahi Oondagi, but O! the official cringing and the little piety shown to the memory of the illustrious labourer who wrought this wonderful monument.

On the hillock of Topog, the *deva agoong's* primitive home, two wash-basins in the form of *yonis*, one of them of colossal dimensions and resting on a crouched figure, testify to the worship of Siva's *sakti*, the female principle of life personified in the Mahadeva's Devi. Hindu motives in the ornament of the Boro Budoor avouch syncretism having influenced the highest expression of Buddhism itself: there is a four-armed image with *padmasana* and *prabha*, which, carrying a Buddha in its *makuta*, may hint at Vishnu's ninth *avatar*; there is a four-armed figure seated on a throne supported by Siva's *vahana*, the bull; there is a goddess crowned with five *trishulas*; etc. All this illustrates again native tolerance in matters of religion as in other respects, a result of the ancient habit of the Javanese in particular, to meet widely different races and civilisations half-way, which has preserved them from the narrow-mindedness consequent on isolation, as observed by a scholar who knows them well and whose study of special subjects has in nowise impaired his breadth of vision.[1] The modification of this easy-going temperament in contact with western greed, offers abundant food for thought when we return to the cool cave of refuge from passion where the *recho belèq* symbolises deep contemplation and meditation terminating in absorption of self by participation of the Spirit of the Universe, under the gaudy memorial tablet, *Koning van Siam: 1896*, which, in its glaring incongruity, symbolises the inverted process.[2] The feeling of annoyance it

[1] Professor Dr. C. SNOUCK HURGRONJE, *Nederland en de Islām.*

[2] Since this was written, the information reached me that the *recho belèq* has been taken out of its hole to give it a place somewhere in the temple grounds where it will be open to inspection, which the reconstruction of the dagob would have made impossible if left in its original station. The sacrilege may be condoned to a certain extent if it implies the disappearance of the tablet intended to keep alive the memory of the disastrous royal visit.

The illustration opposite page 280 shows the upper terraces and the dagob after their restoration: the pinnacle of the dagob having been reconstructed with its crowning ornament, this was afterwards taken away because of some uncertainty as to its original arrangement.

produces, soon passes when the mind begins to expand with admiration of the scene of calm splendour beheld from the dagob containing the pollen of the lotus of the law. The hues and harmonies of evening dispose to a quietude nowhere else experienced or enjoyed in that measure. The only sound heard is a faint humming of insects circling the pinnacles of the *chaityas* which divide the panorama of the plain below into views of separate interest and beauty, bounded by the graceful outline of the terraces and the distant hills. Ricefields and palmgroves stretch as far as the eye can reach, with villages between, sheltered by their orchards, earth's tapestry, embroidered in all gradations of green from that of the sprouting *bibit padi* of the young plantations to that of the thick foliage of centenarian *kanaris*. The shadow of the temple, kissing the drowsy eyelids of the Kadu, lengthens towards the Merapi over whose crater, gilt by the setting sun, hangs a cloud of dark smoke which drifts slowly in the direction of the Merbabu, while the Soombing, to the northeast, looks tranquilly on. The darkness, ushered by the smoke of the ill-tempered old fire-mountain, mingling with the pink and purple of the western sky, spreads over the land, envelops forests and gardens in gray, hushing all that breathes to sleep. One parting smile of the sun's gladness and night descends in her sable robes. Nothing stirs; the toils of day are forgotten in wholesome repose; it is the hour of Amitabha, ruler of the region of sunset and spiritual father of the present world's

XXXVII.

REACHING THE CIRCULAR TERRACES OF THE BORO BUDOOR

(Cephas Sr.)

ruler, the one whose hands rest in his lap after the completion of a laborious task. Morning will come and in time the creation of a new world, the world of loving-kindness, Vishvapani's, the Metteya Buddha's own—in time, long time! A *gardu*[1] strikes seven; another answers immediately with eight strokes on the *beloq*;[1] far away no more than six respond,—what is time to the native! Silence reigns again, silence emphasised by the high-pitched notes of a *suling*,[2] quavering indistinctly as the evening breeze speeds the lover's complaint or refuses its aid. A noise of revelry in the *pasangrahan* distracts the attention from this tuneful courtship; the visionary beings that were taking life from the germ of thought hidden in its shrine, petrify into mute statues or vanish altogether: the spell of the Boro Budoor is broken.

[1] *Gardus* are guard-houses erected for the accommodation of the men who take their turn in watching the roads at night; near the entrance of each hangs the *beloq* (block), a piece of wood which, being hollow, is beaten with a stick to proclaim the hour or to signal fire, amok, the appearance of *kechus* (armed thieves), etc.

[2] The Javanese reed-pipe.

CHAPTER X

THE SOUL OF THE BORO BUDOOR

> Ciò ch' io vedeva, mi sembrava un riso
> Dell' universo ; . . . . [1]
> DANTE ALIGHIERI'S *Commedia* (*Paradiso*, Canto 27).

IT has already been remarked that the natives knew of the existence of the *chandi* Boro Budoor long before Cornelius' discoveries or, rather, that they never lost sight of it, and the place it occupies in the Javanese chronicles appears from the *Babad Tanah Jawa.*[2] In the early years of the eighteenth century Ki Mas Dana, son-in-law of Ki Gedeh Pasukilan, incited the people of Mataram to a rebellion, which broke out in the *dessa* Enta Enta, a centre of sedition it seems, since only a short time before a certain Raden Suryakusumo, son of Pangeran Puger, had chosen the same village for his headquarters when rising against Mangku

[1] That which I saw, seemed to me
A smile of all creation ; . . .

[2] J. J. MEINSMA, *Babad Tanah Jawa*, text and notes, 1874–1877, commented upon by Dr. J. L. A. BRANDES in *Het Tijdschrift voor Indische Taal-, Land- en Volkenkunde*, 1901.

Rat II., who captured him and put him in an iron cage without, however, killing him, because the omens were unfavourable.[1] Ki Mas Dana had many followers and appointed *bupatis* and *mantris*. Ki Yagawinata, *bupati* of Mataram, marched against him but was defeated and fled to Kartasura, acquainting his Majesty with what had happened. Thereupon Pangeran Pringgalaya was sent to suppress Ki Mas Dana's revolt, with instructions to capture him alive because his Majesty had made a vow that he would exhibit him publicly as an example to the inhabitants of Kartasura and let him be *rampokked*[2] with needles. Pangeran Pringgalaya departed and with him half of the *bupatis* of Kartasura. When he arrived at Enta Enta the battle began. Many rebels were killed. Ki Mas Dana fled to the mountain Boro Budoor. He was surrounded by the troops of Pangeran Pringgalaya and made a prisoner. Then they brought him to his Majesty at Kartasura, who ordered all the inhabitants of the town to assemble in the *aloon aloon*, each of them with a needle. It lasted three days before all the inhabitants of Kartasura had had their turn. When he was dead, his head was

[1] The insurrection headed by Raden Suryakusumo broke out in 1703 and, according to letters from the Governor-General then in function at Batavia, to the Honourable Seventeen at home, this Javanese Hotspur gave a good deal of trouble. Having regained his liberty, he rebelled again at Tagal, was captured once more and brought to Batavia, whence the Dutch authorities sent him into banishment at the Cape of Good Hope, agreeably to the request of Mangku Rat IV. Cf. J. K. J. DE JONGE, *De Opkomst van het Nederlandsche Gezag over Java*, vol. viii.

[2] To *rampok* is to attack one, crowding on him, generally with lances. The *rampokking* of tigers after they are caught and again set free in a square formed by rows of men with pikes, is still a favourite amusement.

cut off and exhibited on a pole. After the execution of Ki Mas Dana, the news was received that his father-in-law Ki Gedeh Pasukilan had also revolted. His Majesty ordered the repression of that revolt too. Ki Gedeh Pasukilan was defeated and killed.

Dr. Brandes, observing that the *chandi* Boro Budoor must have been meant because there is no other place known of the same name and its strategical value, given ancient modes of warfare, is obvious, puts the date of its investment by Pangeran Pringgalaya to seize Ki Mas Dana, at 1709 or 1710. A native reference to the Boro Budoor of half a century later, is found in a Javanese manuscript, used by Professor C. Poensen for a paper on Mangku Bumi, first Sooltan of Jogjakarta.[1] The conduct of the Pangeran Adipati, son of that Sooltan, grieved his father very much. Besides his ignorance in literary matters, he was proud and arrogant; he disdained his father's advice and associated with the women of the toll-gate, which caused all sorts of annoyance. He went also to the Boro Budoor to see the thousand statues, notwithstanding an old prediction that misfortune would befall the prince who beheld those images, for one of them represented a *satrya* (a noble knight) imprisoned in a cage; but it was the Prince's fate that he wished to see the statue of the *satrya*. Having gratified his desire, he remained in the

[1] *Bijdragen tot de Taal-, Land- en Volkenkunde van Nederlandsch Indië*, vi., 1 and 2.

Kadu, where he led a most dissolute life. This gave great sorrow to his father, the Sooltan, because the scandal reached such dimensions that the (Dutch) Governor at Samarang heard of it and reprimanded him. Ashamed and angry, he sent a few *bupatis* with armed men to order the Pangeran Adipati to return to Ngajogja (Jogjakarta); if he refused, they had to use violence and were even authorised to kill him. The Pangeran Adipati obeyed and was kindly received by his father, but soon after he fell ill, spat blood and died. A letter of the Governor-General J. Mossel, dated December 30, 1758,[1] contains the passage: "His Highness' eldest son, the pangerang Adipatty Hamancoenagara, having departed this life, . . ." and the profligate Crown Prince's visit to the Boro Budoor may therefore be put at a few years less than fifty after Ki Mas Dana's rebellion.

It is clear, says Dr. Brandes, that at the time referred to in this second record, the Boro Budoor was something more to the natives than simply a hill; they knew of the building with the thousand statues —a round number like that of the *chandi* Sewu, the "thousand temples"—and they knew of the images in the bell-shaped *chaityas* on the circular terraces. And though any one of those 72 statues or even the principal statue in the central dagob may have been meant, in which last case, however, another expression than *kuroongan* (cage) would appear more appropriate, we think involuntarily

[1] J. K. J. DE JONGE, *op. cit.*, vol. x., p. 329.

of the Sang Bimo or Kaki Bimo so-called, a statue of the Buddha promoted or degraded by popular superstition to the rank of a Pandawa, Arjuno's chivalrous brother, seated in the *chaitya* of the lowest circular terrace, next to and south of the eastern staircase, still venerated by the natives, by the Chinese community and by more women and men of European extraction than are willing to confess it. Bimo or Wergodoro, to use the name given to him in the *wayang lakons* when they extol his youthful exploits, is the archetype of the *satrya*, the pattern of ancestral knighthood. Most probably it was Sang Bimo who, conformably to the *ilaila* or ancient prediction, executed the decree of fate on Pangeran Adipati Hamangkunagara. Disregarding the example set by the invisible power which resides in the Boro Budoor, a later Crown Prince of Jogjakarta visited that temple in 1900 without, so far, coming to grief. Has then the *ilaila* under special consideration lost its efficacy? We must presume so, notwithstanding that the occult forces identified with Sang Bimo and other statues of the ancient fane, are affirmed still to work miracles in plenty when propitiated by adequate sacrifice.

The greatest miracle of all is the elation of man's thought by the irresistible charm which goes out from it. A night with the Boro Budoor is a night of purification, when Amitabha offers the lotus of the good law and the gift is accepted; when the wonderful edifice, rising to the star-spangled sky,

ASCENDING TO THE DAGOB OF THE BORO BUDOOR

(Cephas Sr.)

unfolds terrace after terrace and gallery after gallery between the domed and pinnacled walls, as his flower of ecstatic meditation spreads its petals, opens its heart of beauty to the fructifying touch of heaven; when tranquil love descends in waves of contentment, unspeakable satisfaction. The dagob loses its sharp, bold outline and melts into boundless space, a vision of fading existence in consummation of wisdom. A mysterious voice, proceeding from the shrine, urges to search out the secret it hides. The summons cannot be resisted and going up, trusting to the murky night, mounting the steps to the first gate as in a somnambulistic trance, the seeker of enlightenment discerns the path, guided by his quickened perception when the voice dies of its own sweetness, the fragrant stillness appeasing the mind and extending promise of pity for passion and fleshly desire, the garment of sin left behind. Surely, it was the supreme wisdom, forgiving all things because it understands, which inspired a human intellect to devise, directed human hands to achieve in the delineation of mercy such powerful architectural unity, sustained by such sublimely beauteous ornament. Aided from above, the spirituality of the builder, creating this masterpiece, needed not the laborious tricks passed off on us in our days of feverish *effect-hascherei* by artists who dispense with the rudiments of their art to strive after the sensational. Neither was his originality of the cheap kind which tries to cloak crass technical ignorance and hopeless general ineptitude with paltry though pretentious artifices, displaying a deplorable lack of the conceptive faculty into the bargain. Proclaiming the doctrine glorious in veracity of thought and utterance, the Boro Budoor typifies honest endeavour and sincerity of purpose.

Entering the first of the porches through which from four sides the successive galleries and terraces are reached, we come under the spell of the rapture symbolised by those vaulted staircases, leading upward from reason to faith, constructed, it seems, to match the "evident portals" of the perfect state: composure, kindness, modesty, self-knowledge. The Banaspati, terrifier of the evil spirits, shelters him who proceeds on the path they indicate in clemency and charity. As we pass on, confiding in his protection, the sculptured walls gleam softly, impregnated by the sun's light embedded in the stones, and the germ of truth, treasured in the dagob, radiates down in luminous substantiation of the word, making the invisible visible by degrees. The air hangs heavy and warm in the galleries and throbs with the emotion excited by the lustrous reliefs which picture the life of the Buddha. A flush of indescribable splendour, clear exhalation of his virtue and holiness, lifts veil after veil from the bliss this initiation portends. The transparent atmosphere lends new significance to the gestures of the Dhyani Buddhas, seated on their lotus cushions as stars half quenched in golden mist, while we feel more than see the serene calmness of their features still wrapped in obscurity. Their contemplation is the beginning of the highest; their ecstasy pierces eternity, opens the regions of infinite intelligence, complete self-effacement, absolute nothingness. Too much absorbed in abstract cogitation to occupy themselves with matters of mundane interest, they leave the government of the created worlds to their spiritual sons, and Padmapani is the Mahasatva on whom our age depends. Out-topping human knowledge, they teach the meaning of the universe: the Buddha of the East dreaming his dreams as the sun rises, the Buddha of the South blessing the day, the Buddha of the West unfolding the secret of the all-spirit as the sun sets, the Buddha of the North pointing the way from darkness to light, the Buddha of the Zenith lifting his hands to turn the wheel of the law. The statues smile beatitude in happiness at losing the consciousness of existence when they will be worthy of the Nirvana, the solution of life in non-being, death which disclaims resurrection in any form. And the highest attainable blessing, the Paranirvana, the Nirvana Absolute, is signified in the image of the central dagob: however interpreted as solitary indweller of the shrine of shrines built over the remains of the flesh which embodied the word, the Tathagata, the self-subsisting, preceded and to be succeeded in fullness of time, it figures the immanence in bodily imperfection of the energy for good which sanctified Ayushmat Gautama, who modified his carnality by dominating his senses; who, when questioned by his first disciples, could declare that he was the expected teacher of lucid perception and replete comprehension, the discerning monitor, the destroyer of error, the spotless counsellor impelled to release them from the bonds of sin and make them deserve the manifest favour of annihilation.

The rudely interrupted sleep of the *recho bèlèt* formulated, intentionally or not, a confession of faith in the reward of righteousness by complete dissolution, cessation of continuance, eternal rest undisturbed by gods or men, by feeling or thought. The pilgrim to the Boro Budoor, longing for the *arahat*ship, accomplished in the science of conducting himself, must have hesitated before ascending to the highest terrace and seeking direct communion with the pure spirit of the son of virtue, born of a woman truly, but whose mother died seven days after his birth, in token of his eminence; the venerable one whose moral strength stands paramount, overcometh even the innate fear of extinction. The essence of the Triratna lies here within the grasp of the earnest inquirer, the precious pearl whose lustre divulges the principle of causation, the beginning and the end of all things, the primary source of what is and shall be. How to obtain it? By offerings to the symbolic stone? Not so, but by good works and self-examination which excels prayer and makes any place a Bodhimanda, a seat of intelligence. The Buddha was a man, no god surpassing the limits of humanity, who has to be propitiated by adoration. Whoso wishes the Rescuer's saving grace, should remember the story of Upagoopta and the courtesan Vasavadatta, and ask: Has my hour arrived?[1] Penance for errors committed, not by

[1] The story points a moral not less relevant to western than to eastern ethics and runs as follows:

Once upon a time there lived in Mathura a courtesan renowned for her beauty and her name was Vasavadatta. On a certain day her maid, having been sent to buy perfume at a merchant's, who had a son called Upagoopta, and having stayed out rather long, she said:

—It appears, my dear, that this youth Upagoopta pleases you exceedingly well, since you never buy in any shop but his father's.

—Daughter of my master, answered the maid, besides being comely, clever and polite, Upagoopta, the son of the merchant, passes his life in observing the law.

These words awakened in Vasavadatta's heart a desire to meet Upagoopta and she bade her maid go back and make an appointment with him. But the youth vouchsafed no other reply than:—My sister, the hour has not yet arrived.

Vasavadatta thought that Upagoopta refused because he could not afford to pay the high price she demanded for her favours, and she bade her maid tell him that she did not intend to charge him a single cowry if only he would come. But Upagoopta replied in the same words:—My sister, the hour has not yet arrived.

Shortly after, the courtesan Vasavadatta, annoyed by the jealousy of one of her lovers, who objected to her selling herself to a wealthy old voluptuary, ordered her servants to kill the troublesome fellow. They did so without taking sufficient precautions against discovery; the crime became known and the King of Mathura commanded the executioner to cut off her hands, feet and nose, and abandon her thus mutilated among the graves of the dead.

Upagoopta hearing of it, said to himself: When she was arrayed in fine clothes and no jewels were rare and costly enough to adorn her body, it was a counsel of wisdom for those who aspire to liberation from the bondage of sin to avoid her; with her beauty, however, she has certainly lost her pride and lustfulness, and this is the hour.

Accordingly, Upagoopta went up to the cemetery where the executioner had left Vasavadatta maimed and disfigured. The maid, having remained faithful, saw him approach and informed her mistress who, in a last effort at coquetterie, told her to cover the hideous wounds with a piece of cloth. Then, bowing her head before her visitor, Vasavadatta spoke:

—My master, when my body was sweet as a flower, clothed in rich garments and decked with pearls and rubies; when I was goodly to behold, you made me unhappy by refusing to meet me. Why do you come now to look at one from whom all charm and pleasure has fled, a frightful wreck, soiled with blood and filth?

—My sister, answered Upagoopta, the attraction of your charms and the love of the pleasures they held out, could not move me; but the delights of this world having revealed their hollowness, here I am to bring the consolation of the lotus of the law.

So the son of the merchant comforted the courtesan doing penance for her transgressions, and she died in a confession of faith to the word of the Buddha, hopeful of rebirth on a plane of chastened existence.

fasting and self-torture, but by persevering in the eight-fold path of right views, right aspirations, right speech, right behaviour, right search of sustenance, right effort, right mindfulness of our fellow-creatures, right exultation, should ward off the dire punishment of remorse which in well-balanced spirits cannot dwell. Self-restraint, uprightness, control of the organs of sense, makes the fell fire of the three deadly sins—sensuality, ill-will and moral sluggishness—die out in the heart by a proper arrangement of the precious vestments, the six cardinal virtues: charity, cleanness, patience, courage, contemplative sympathy with all creation and discrimination of good and evil. This leads to perfection, advancement to the highest of the four sublime conditions, the Brahma Viharas on which Buddhism improved by making equanimity with regard to one's own joys and sorrows the test of progress on the road which leads to bliss in extermination of pain. Loosen the shackles of worldly existence by constant application to escape from the fatal thraldom imposed by birth and rebirth! Life is continued misery; no salvation from the distress caused by passion and sin is possible except by cessation of self, by merging individual in universal vacancy, mounting the four steps of the Dhyana in contemplative evolution of the Nirvana, refining perception and speculation to total impassibility, extinguishing reason itself in eternal voidness, where we have nothing to fear and nothing to hope for, taking refuge in non-existence, the only conceivable verity.

XXXIX.

THE DAGOB OF THE BORO BUDOOR BEFORE ITS RESTORATION

(C. Nieuwenhuis.)

Heart and head rebel against such a religion, which considers conscious life the great enemy to be destroyed, seeks life's meed in dissolution of energy, man's best part flickering out as the flame of a spent candle. With the gladdening odour of the garden of Java in our nostrils, rational instinct struggles free from the torment of imposed passivity and we rather take a more militant stand concordant with the Buddha's dying words: Work out your salvation with diligence. How is it to be done? Shall we turn for guidance to the creed of the men of power and pelf, who seem to think that their best recommendation to divine favour is the defacement, in their western theological mill, of the gospel they received from the East; whose mouths are filled with promises while their hands sow calamity; whose moral superiority is but a delusion; who mar impiously what they pretend to improve; who boast of investing their moral surplus in political efficiency, as King Siladitiya did, for the benefit of their wards, but whose greedy immorality spoils even the reckoning of their own selfishness! Not so: their deeds giving the lie to their words, their iniquities increasing, their trespasses growing up into the heavens, who can wonder that the glory of the deity they profess to worship, suffers in the estimation of the native? And yet, how might Christianity thrive in a soil prepared by the doctrine of elimination of self, by adherence to the three duties Buddhism laid down as far more important than Brahmanic sacrifice: continence, kindness, reverence for the life of all creatures. Insisting on man's obligations to his fellow-men, the Buddha anticipated by six centuries the precept: Thou shalt love thy neighbour as thyself. If he did not match it with the first and greater commandment of the Christian dispensation, his atheism, to quote Hunter, was a philosophical tenet which, so far from weakening the sanctions of right and wrong, gave them new strength from the doctrine of Karma or the metempsychosis of character. Teaching that sin, sorrow and deliverance, the state of a man in this life, in all previous and all future lives, is the inevitable result of his own acts, the Buddha applied the inexorable law of cause and effect to the soul: What we sow, we must reap. "All spirits are enslaved which serve things evil," as redemption flowers from straight vision, straight thought, straight exertion in truthful endeavour. The lesson might be profitably taken to heart in furtherance of a nation's Karma by statesmen who have no explanation for the unsatisfactory condition of dependencies oversea but evasive oratory backed by a dexterous shuffling of cooked colonial reports and doctored colonial statistics when the sinister farce of the colonial budget is on the boards. And each of us, however limited his sphere, finds his own opportunities for individual transition to a higher state: like Gautama we meet every day the poor and needy, the old and decrepit in want of assistance, the prostrate sufferer in agony of death.

And, like Gautama, each one who strives for

enfranchisement, must have his struggle with Mara, the Prince of Darkness. After the first watch on the Boro Budoor, night thickens and covers the earth as a pall; the wan stars glimmer weakly, shining on the misery of deficient fulfilment of intention. Reflecting on our errors of commission and omission, seeing our deeds laid bare and their why and wherefore, dejection masters hope, though steadfast determination might take an example at the Buddha wrestling with the Enemy, who offered him the kingdom of the four worlds; though we know that the giving or withholding of the fifth, the world of glory, is beyond the Enemy's power. We see the contest re-enacted before us and tremble. Appearing bodily, horrible to behold, Mara, the god of carnal love, passion and sin, Papiyan, the very vicious, besets the incarnate word, surrounded by his demons of ever changing gruesome aspect, barking dogs with enormous fangs and lolling tongues; roaring tigers with sharp, murderous claws and bloodshot eyes; hissing serpents, darting forward to strike and crush their prey. While we fancy the contest raging hottest round valiant patience, personified in the image of the dagob, the maimed statues of the *chaityas* and lower niches join in the dire battle as the headless spirits that rode upon the tempest when Evil assailed the elect's purity. Papiyan cannot prevail and seeing the futility of violence, he has recourse to his daughters, the winsome *apsaras*, who dance and provoke to lascivious commerce by their seductive arts. But they make no more impression than their brutish brothers and, in spite of themselves, they are compelled to praise the fortitude of a virtue which will not succumb even when one of them assumes the shape of a beloved youthful spouse. The baffled *apsaras* dissolve in floating vapour, and Papiyan, in despair, traces flaming characters on the dome of the dagob with his last arrow: My empire is ended. The stars resume their brightness and a sense of coming light pervades the gloom of despondency. It is borne toward us in the flower tendered by Chandra, the deity of the chaste radiance proceeding from the conqueror's crest. Lo, his crown is transferred to the sky and, climbing slowly, the cusped moon invests the moulders of past and future worlds with halos of liquid silver.

This is the time, the stilly hour before dawn, the last watch before morning, the chosen moment of the Buddha's attainment to the summit of the triple science, wherein the supernatural beauty of the Boro Budoor, cleansed and reconsecrated after the white man's profanation, by the burning fire of day and the mellow touch of night, helps us to penetrate the meaning of his promise. He who holds fast to the law and discipline and faints not, he shall cross the ocean of life and make an end of sorrow. The blitheness of spirit which consists, because of that whereby the sun riseth and setteth, and the moon waxeth and waneth, in discarding the ignorance engendered by conceding to this world a reality it does not possess, regarding as constant

THE DAGOB OF THE BORO BUDOOR AFTER ITS RESTORATION

(Archaeological Service.)

that which changes with every wind that blows,—the exaltation born from silent contemplation, loses its vagueness in the manifestation of the godhead in ourselves. For contemplation becomes seeded and blooms in the triad of meditation, the recognition of the entities of time and space, and connecting thought as the unity of universal relationship. The Dhyani Buddhas, wrapped in the shadows from which dawn will deliver them, seek to comprehend, and our mentality expanding with theirs, looking down upon the gray waves of mist that break on the old temple as on a rock of ages in a stormy sea, we feel the dagob rise to meet the moonbeams and soar to unutterable delight. Presently the first smile of day salutes and awakens mother earth; a murmur of contentment thrills the air in harmony of praise: the dimming, quivering stars, the crimson mountain-tops, the purple and azure perspective between, all creation combines in a song of thanksgiving. The mystic planetary music, the singing together of earth and heaven in melody of colour and sound, welcomes the bright morning. Dawn, with blushing face and heart of gold, bewrays the glory of her eternal abode to the world of man, sending her outriders before, the Asvins, the lords of lustre, whose shining armour, forged of the sun's rays, illumines the pearly sky with dazzling splendour. They roll the billowy vapours together and chase them up the hill-side "like wool of divers changing colours carded," that the eye of the life-giver may rest on the plain where the palm-groves rise in the hazy dew as emerald islands in an opalescent lake. The Merbabu and the Soombing are still half in darkness when the Merapi, flecked with orange and violet, blazes in reflection of aërial effulgence, soon to commingle the smoke of its fiery crater with the clouds mounting its slopes. The fire-mountains keep a good watch on the garden of Java, than which Jatawana, the famous pleasance where the Buddha enounced the substance of his teachings preserved in the Sutras, cannot have been more delicious; and the Merapi in particular makes the land pass under the rod when sacred covenants are broken.

The heart too is illuminated as thoughts take their hues from the skies, knowledge clearing up the anarchy of conflicting creeds which exercised and exercise their sway over Java. Brahmanic terrorism and Buddhist despondency, Moslim fanaticism and Christian dissensions vanish before her unsophisticated children's delight in life for its own sake, as the morning dew before the warmth of the sun. Twining memories of the *jaman buda* with current happenings, they take their spiritual nourishment directly from nature and the symbolic form of their natural religion from everywhere. Without troubling about erudite dissertations regarding the legend of the Buddha as the development of an ancient solar myth, or Buddhism as a development of the Sankhya system of Kapila; without going into abstruse speculations anent the evolution of the universe from primordial matter, they are in constant intercourse with the surrounding worlds, seen and unseen. The virile Surya, impregnating air and earth, unfailing source of plenty, enters deep into their metaphysics as the cosmic pivot of faith. When high-born dawn rouses the tillers of the soil to go forth to their work and the eye of day showers benediction, the solar word, spoken from the eternal throne and descending on wings of happiness, the living word, is found emblazoned on the sea of light which floods the Kadu just as the fertilising water of the mountain-rills floods the *sawahs*;[1] is found embodied in that superb temple, the Boro Budoor, whose soul, the soul of humanity in communion with the all-soul, is the soul of Java. Adorned with that priceless jewel of sanctity, the plain lifts its sensuous loveliness to heaven as the bride meets the caresses of her wedded spouse, trembling with love. They obey the divine law which bids them follow nature in drinking the *amrita*, gaining immortality like the gods in creation of life, which may change, yet never dies, aging but reviving, the mystery of the Trimoorti. Clothed with the resplendent atmosphere, touched by the beams of the rising sun, its effulgent dagob a mountain of gold, the Boro Budoor bursts out in the bloom of excellence, not the sepulchre of a discarded religion, of a fallen nation's dreams, but a token of the germinal truth of all religion, a prophetic expression of things to be. The tide of destiny runs not always in the same channel and

[1] *Sawahs* are ricefields, terraced and diked for the purpose of copious irrigation, in contradistinction to *ladangs* (Jav. *gagas*, Soond. *humas*) without artificial water-supply.

there is promise in the joy of day, promise of a slaking of the thirst for freedom, an abatement of the fever engendered by doubt of enfranchisement always deferred. If hope endures in the battle with darkness, patient fortitude will lead to victory. It baulked the power of Mara and blunted the weapons of the demons who assailed the Buddha and turned aside the missiles which did not harm him but changed into flowers before his feet, into garlands suspended over his head. When knowledge shall cover the world at the advent of Vishvapani, deceit and avarice will cease tormenting and glad content will dwell in the *negri jawa* for ever.

So be it!

BIBLIOGRAPHY

IT has been suggested that the practical value of this volume might be enhanced by the addition of a short bibliography indicating the works to which students, who wish to go deeper into the subjects touched upon, could turn for more ample information. *Il y a l'embarras du choix* and, always abreast with latest research, particularly the publications of learned societies as the Royal Institute of the Dutch East Indies, the Royal Geographical Society of the Netherlands, the Batavian Society of Arts and Sciences, are rich depositories of Dutch East Indian lore, many of the most important monographs they contain, being available in book or pamphlet form. Not to speak of the specific knowledge derivable from such sources as the official Reports of the Archaeological Commission for Java and Madura, the Bulletins of the Colonial Museum at Haarlem, etc., from periodicals as *Het Tijdschrift voor Binnenlandsch Bestuur* (organ of the Dutch East Indian Civil Service), *Het Indisch Militair Tijdschrift*, etc., less scientifically or professionally dressed but just as weighty observations on different aspects of Dutch rule in the Malay Archipelago can be found in monthlies like *De Gids*, *De Tijdspiegel* and, of course, *De Indische Gids* in which *Het Tijdschrift voor Nederlandsch Indië*, founded by W. R. Baron van Hoëvell, has been incorporated. The *Encyclopaedie van Nederlandsch Indië* is a very serviceable storehouse of general intelligence, though new discoveries made and old theories exploded since its appearance, emphasise more forcibly with every year, the necessity of its usefulness being sustained if not by occasional new editions, revised and brought up to date, then at least by frequent supplements. The *Daghregisters* of the Castle of Batavia, the *Nederlandsch Indisch Plakaatboek* (1602–1811), the *Realia*, a register of the General Resolutions from 1632 to 1805, offer almost inexhaustible material for the history of Java and the other islands in the days of the Dutch East India Company. J. C. Hooykaas' *Repertorium* (1595–1816), continued by A. Hartmann up to 1893, and by W. J. P. J. Schalker and W. C. Muller up to 1910, furnishes an excellent index to Dutch colonial literature; C. M. Kan's *Proeve eener Geographische Bibliographie van Nederlandsch Oost-Indië* (1865–1880) and Martinus Nijhoff's *Bibliotheca Neerlando-*

Indica, 1893, should also be mentioned The following miscellaneous list is an attempt briefly to enumerate the works, apart from papers accessible only in serial publications, which seem specially adapted (allowing a good deal in not a few of them for mutual admiration and all too courteous, excessive panegyric) to give interested readers further particulars, according to each one's individual line of investigation, with regard to various matters treated of or alluded to in *Monumental Java.*

A. BASTIAN. *Indonesien oder die Insel des malayischen Archipel.* 1884–9.

J. G. A. VAN BERCKEL. *Bijdrage tot de Geschiedenis van het Europeesch Opperbestuur over Nederlandsch Indië* (1780–1806). 1880.

N. P. VAN DEN BERG. *Debet of Credit.* 1885.

N. P. VAN DEN BERG. *The Financial and Economical Progress and Condition of Netherlands India during the last fifteen years and the Effect of the present Currency System.* 1887.

L. W. C. VAN DEN BERG. *De Mohammedaansche Geestelijkheid en de Geestelijke Goederen op Java en Madoera.* 1882.

L. W. C. VAN DEN BERG. *De Inlandsche Rangen en Titels op Java en Madoera.* 1887.

H. BOREL. *De Chineezen in Nederlandsch Indië.* 1900.

J. L. A. BRANDES. *Pararaton* (*Ken Arok*) *of het Boek der Koningen van Toemapèl en van Madjapaït.* 1896.

A. CABATON. *Les Indes Néerlandaises.* 1910.

J. CHAILLEY BERT. *Java et ses habitants.* 1907 (new. ed.).

J. A. VAN DER CHIJS. *De Nederlanders te Jakatra.* 1860.

A. B. COHEN STUART. *De Kawi-Oorkonden.* 1875.

J. CRAWFURD. *History of the Indian Archipelago.* 1820.

CLIVE DAY. *The Policy and Administration of the Dutch in Java.* 1904.

A. J. W. VAN DELDEN. *Blik op het Indisch Staatsbestuur.* 1875.

M. L. VAN DEVENTER. *Het Nederlandsch Gezag over Java en Onderhoorigheden sedert 1811.* 1891 (first vol.).

S. VAN DEVENTER. *Bijdragen tot de Kennis van het Landelijk Stelsel op Java.* 1865.

E. DOUWES DEKKER (MULTATULI). *Max Havelaar of de Koffieveilingen der Nederlandsche Handelmaatschappij.* 1860 (first ed.).

J. FERGUSSON. *History of Indian and Eastern Architecture.* 1910 (new. ed.).

P. W. FILET. *De Verhouding der Vorsten op Java tot de Nederlandsch Indische Regeering.* 1895.

P. H. FROMBERG. *De Chineesche Beweging op Java.* 1911.

J. GRONEMAN. *De Garebegs te Ngajogyakarta.* 1895.

J. GRONEMAN. *Boeddhistische Tempel- en Kloosterbouwvallen in de Parambanan-vlakte.* 1907.

J. Groneman. *Boeddhistische Tempelbouwvallen in de Progo-vallei, de Tjandis Baraboedoer, Mendoet en Pawon.* 1907.

F. de Haan. *Priangan. De Preanger Regentschappen onder het Nederlandsch Bestuur tot 1811.* 1910 (first vol.).

G. A. J. Hazeu. *Bijdrage tot de Kennis van het Javaansche Tooneel.* 1897.

J. E. Heeres. *Bouwstoffen voor de Geschiedenis der Nederlanders in den Maleischen Archipel.* 1895 (third vol.).

W. R. van Hoëvell. *Reis over Java, Madoera en Bali.* 1849–1854.

J. K. J. de Jonge (cont. by M. L. van Deventer and P. A. Tiele). *De Opkomst van het Nederlandsche Gezag in Oost-Indië.* 1857.

F. W. Junghuhn. *Topographische und naturwissenschaftliche Reisen durch Java.* 1845.

F. W. Junghuhn. *Java, zijne Gedaante, zijn Plantengroei en inwendige Bouw.* 1849.

A. G. Keller. *Colonization.* 1906.

J. H. C. Kern. *Eene Indische Sage in Javaansch Gewaad.* 1876.

J. H. C. Kern. *Over de oud-Javaansche Vertaling van het Mahabharata.* 1877.

J. H. C. Kern. *Over de Vermenging van Ciwaïsme en Boeddhisme op Java naar aanleiding van het oud-Javaansche Gedicht Sutasoma.* 1888.

J. H. F. Kohlbrugge. *Blikken in het Zieleleven van den Javaan en Zijner Overheerschers.* 1907.

C. Leemans. *Boro-boedoer op het Eiland Java.* 1873.

H. D. Levyssohn Norman. *Britsche Heerschappij over Java en Onderhoorigheden.* 1857.

P. A. van der Lith. *Nederlandsch Oost-Indië.* 1892 (second ed.).

J. A. Loebèr Jr. *Het Vlechtwerk in den Indischen Archipel.* 1902.

J. A. Loebèr Jr. *Javanische Schattenbilder.* 1908.

J. de Louter. *Handleiding tot de Kennis van het Staats- en Administratief Recht van Nederlandsch Indië.* 1895 (new ed.).

P. J. F. Louw (cont. by E. S. de Klerck). *De Java-Oorlog.* 1909 (sixth vol.).

L. Th. Mayer. *De Javaan als Mensch en als Lid van het Javaansche Huisgezin.* 1894.

L. Th. Mayer. *Een Blik in het Javaansche Volksleven.* 1897.

J. J. Meinsma. *Geschiedenis van de Nederlandsche Oost-Indische Bezittingen.* 1872.

G. Nypels. *Oost-Indische Krijgsgeschiedenis.* 1895.

T. S. Raffles. *History of Java.* 1817.

G. C. K. de Reus. *Geschichtliche Überblick der administrativen, rechtlichen und finanziellen Entwicklung der Niederländisch-Ostindischen Compagnie.* 1894.

C. B. H. von Rosenberg. *Der malayische Archipel.* 1879.

G. P. Rouffaer. *De voornaamste Industrieën der Bevolking van Java en Madoera.* 1904.

L. SERRURIER. *De Wajang Poerwa, eene Ethnologische Studie.* 1896.

C. SNOUCK HURGRONJE. *Nederland en de Islām.* 1911.

F. V. A. DE STUERS. *Mémoire sur la Guerre de l'Ile de Java 1825–1830.* 1833.

F. VALENTIJN. *Oud en Nieuw Oost-Indiën.* 1724–61 (1856–8 and 1862 new but incomplete edns.).

R. D. M. VERBEEK. *Oudheden van Java. Lijst der voornaamste Overblijfselen uit den Hindoe-tijd op Java, met eene Oudheidkundige Kaart van Java.* 1891.

P. J. VETH. *Java. Geographisch, ethnologisch, historisch* (1895, new ed. by J. F. SNELLEMAN and J. F. NIERMEYER).

E. DE WAAL. *Nederlandsch Indië in de Staten Generaal sedert de Grondwet van 1814.* 1860–1.

E. DE WAAL. *De Koloniale Politiek der Grondwet en hare Toepassing tot 1 Februari 1862.* 1863.

E. DE WAAL. *Aanteekeningen over Koloniale Onderwerpen.* 1865–8.

A. R. WALLACE. *The Malay Archipelago.* 1869.

A. W. P. WEITZEL. *De Oorlog op Java.* 1852–3.

G. A. WILKEN. *Handleiding voor de vergelijkende Volkenkunde van Nederlandsch Indië* (ed. by C. M. PLEYTE). 1893.

G. D. WILLINCK. *De Indiën en de nieuwe Grondwet.* 1910.

A. WRIGHT and O. T. BREAKSPEAR. *Twentieth Century Impressions of Netherlands India* (PLEYTE, VAN ERP and VAN RONKEL on Archaeology, etc.). 1909.

GLOSSARY

(Of the words here explained, only the meaning or meanings are given, attached to them in this book.)

agama buda—lit. Buddhist creed; in native parlance, however, the word includes every pre-Muhammadan religion.
aksara—character representing a Javanese consonant.
aloon aloon—square or outer court before the dwelling of a native prince or chief.
ampilan—articles of virtu belonging to a royal family, emblems of royalty.
amrita—immortality, all-light; rejuvenating nectar of the gods.
api—fire.
apsara—heavenly nymph, produced by the churning of the ocean and living in the sky; spouse of a *gandharva*.
arahat—he who has become worthy.
astana—abode of some exalted personage.
avatar—descent of a deity from heaven to assume a visible form on earth; incarnation of a god, especially of Vishnu.

babad—chronicle.
banaspati (*wanaspati*)—conventional lion's (or tiger's) head, a frequently occurring motive in the ornament of Javanese temples.
banjir—freshet.
batik—the art of dyeing woven goods by dipping them in successive baths of the required colour, the parts to be left undyed being protected by applying a mixture of beeswax and resin.
batu (*watu*)—stone.
bedoyo—young female or male dancer of noble birth at the Courts of Surakarta and Jogjakarta.
bikshu—Buddhist mendicant monk.
bolook—squirrel of the *Pteromys nitidus* and *Pteromys elegans* variety.
boreh—preparation of turmeric and coconut-oil used in sacrifice and acts of adoration.
bupati—regent.

chaitya—place deserving worship or reverence.

chakra—disk, wheel.

champaka—tree, *Michelia Champaca L.*, fam. *Magnoliaceae*, with sweet-smelling flowers.

chandi—any monument of Hindu or Buddhist origin.

dagob—structure raised over a relic of the Buddha or a Buddhist saint.

dalam—lit. inside; private apartments of a royal palace or the dwelling of a chief.

dessa—village.

dzikr—lit. remembrance; invocation of God.

gamelan—native orchestra.

gandharva—heavenly singer, whose especial duty it is to guard the *soma*, to regulate the course of the sun's horses, etc.

gardu—guard-house.

garebeg besar—feast of the sacrifice (*id al-qorban*).

garebeg mulood—feast of the Prophet's birth (*maulid*).

garebeg puasa—feast of the breaking of the fast (*id al-fitr*).

garuda—mythical monster-bird, enemy of the serpent-race; bearer of Vishnu.

grobak—cart.

gunoong—mountain.

guru—teacher.

hadat—usage, traditional custom.

haji—one who has made the pilgrimage to Mecca.

hinayanistic—pertaining to the canon of the southern Buddhist church or doctrine of the Lesser Vehicle.

inya—nurse, maid, waiting-woman.

ishta devata—pre-eminent god chosen for particular worship.

jaman (*zaman*) *buda*—lit. the time of the Buddha, pre-Muhammadan days.

jataka—birth, nativity; *jataka*-tales: stories connected with the birth and life of the Buddha in one of his successive existences on earth.

kabayan—chief of a community.

kakèh—old man, grandfather.

kala—time as the destroyer of all things, the bringer of death; destiny.

kali—river.

kamboja—tree, *Plumeria acutifolia Poir.*, fam. *Apocynaceae*, often found in cemeteries, the sweet-smelling flowers of which are much used in funeral rites.

kampong—group of native dwellings.

kananga—tree, *Cananga odorata Hook. f. et Th.*, fam. *Anonaceae*, with sweet-smelling flowers.
kanari—tree, *Canarium commune L.*, fam. *Burseraceae*, frequently met in gardens and planted along roads for its shade.
kanjeng goosti—a high title of honour.
kantil—flower of the *champaka*.
kedaton—that part of a princely residence occupied by its owner, his wives, concubines and children.
kembang telon—flowers of sacrifice, especially *melati*, *kananga* and *kantil*.
ketèq—monkey.
kidool—south.
kinnari—bird-people.
kitab—book.
klenteng—Chinese temple, joss-house.
krakal (*ngrakal*)—hard labour in the chain-gang.
kramat—holy grave.
kraton—residence of a reigning native prince.
kulon—west.
kurang wang—lacking money.

lakon—Javanese drama.
legèn—a liquor prepared by fermentation of the sap drawn from some trees of the palm family.
linga—male organ of generation, emblem of Siva's fructifying power.
lontar—high-growing tree, *Borassus flabelliformis L.*, fam. *Palmae*, with large fan-like leaves.
lor—north.
loro—a title designating a lady of very high birth.

machan—tiger.
mahayanistic—pertaining to the canon of the northern Buddhist church or doctrine of the Greater Vehicle.
makara—a mythical sea-monster.
makuta—head-dress, crown, crest.
mantri—in Malay countries a native official of high rank : minister of state, councillor ; in Java a native official of lower rank.
maryam—cannon.
mās—lit. gold ; title given to native noblemen and also, in courteous address, to commoners.
mboq—title given to women in courteous address.
melati—shrub, *Jasminum Sambac Ait.*, fam. *Oleaceae*, with sweet- and rather strong-smelling flowers.
meliwis—a kind of duck.
mesdjid—mosque.
murid—disciple.

naga—serpent.

narasinha—man-lion.
negri jawa—country of the Javanese, Java.
nirvana—extinction of existence, the highest aim and highest good.

oombool—source, well.
oorna—tuft or bunch of hair between the Buddha's eyebrows.
orang kechil—lit. the little men, the lower classes.
orang slam—Muhammadan.
orang wolanda—Hollander.

padi—rice in the hull.
padmasana—lotus cushion or seat.
padri—one of a sect which, in the manner of the Wahabites, tried to rouse the Muhammadans of the Padang Highlands in Sumatra to more orthodox zeal.
paman—uncle on the father's side; appellation used in respectful address of any senior in years.
panakawan—page, follower, retainer.
panchuran—water-conduit.
pangeran—prince.
pantoon—old and still very popular form of native poetry.
pasangan—character representing a Javanese consonant in the place or (generally modified) form which marks the vowelless sound of the preceding one.
pasangrahan—rest-house for officials on their tours of inspection.
pasar—market.
payoong—sunshade.
pendopo—open audience-hall in the dwellings of the great.
prabha—light, radiance, aureole.
pulu—island.
puri—name of the princely residences in Bali and Lombok.
pusaka—heirloom.

raden—title of nobility.
raksasa—evil spirit, ogre, generally of hideous appearance though the female (*raksasi*) sometimes allures man by her beauty; *raksasas* do service as doorkeepers at the entrances of some Javanese *chandis*.
ratu—title for royal personages; king, queen.
recho (*rejo*)—any sort of statue.

sakti—personification of the energy or active power of a deity as his spouse; a god's female complement.
sangharama—endowed convent.
sanka—conch-shell blown as a horn.
sankara—auspicious; causation of happiness.
saptaratna—the seven treasures.
sasrahan—wedding-present.

satrya—noble knight.
sawah—watered ricefield.
selir—wife of lower degree than the *padmi* or first legitimate spouse.
sembah—v. salute; n. (*persembah'an*) salutation.
slamat (*salamat*)—success, blessing, prosperity.
soma—beverage of the gods.
srimpi—young female dancer of noble birth at the Courts of Surakarta and Jogjakarta.
stupa—mound, tumulus; edifice raised to commemorate some event in the life of a Buddhist saint or to mark a sacred spot.
sugata—pious brother on the road to Buddhist perfection.
suling—native reed-pipe.
sumoor—source, spring.
susah—trouble.

taman—pleasance.
tara—spouse of a Dhyani Buddha.
telaga—lake.
tempo dahulu—olden time.
tengger—pieces of wood or stone posts set up at the head- and foot-end of graves.
tesbeh—string of prayer-beads.
trimoorti—(Hindu) trinity.
trishula—trident.
tumenggoong—regent in an official capacity somewhat different from that of a *bupati*.

upachara—royal heirloom.
upawita—thread or cord worn by high-caste Hindus over the left shoulder and passing under the right arm.

vahana—any vehicle or means of conveyance; animal carrying a deity, representative of his characteristic qualities.
vihara—monastery; Brahma Viharas: sublime conditions of perfection.

wali—governor or administrator of a province; name given to those who introduced the Muhammadan religion in the island.
waringin (*beringin*)—tree of the genus *Ficus* of which the most frequent types in Java are the *F. consociata Bl.*, the *F. stupenda Miq.*, the *F. Benjaminea L.* and the *F. elastica Roxb.*
wayang—lit. shadow; the Javanese national theatre, which seems to have a religious origin: the invocation of the shades of deified ancestors.
wedono—native chief of a district.
wetan—east.

yoni—female organ of generation, emblem of the fecundity of Siva's *sakti* or female complement.

INDEX

Q

R

S

T

U

V

W

Y

Z

THE END